ISBN 978-1-331-88191-9
PIBN 10249298

English
Français
Deutsche
Italiano
Español
Português

www.forgottenbooks.com

Mythology Photography **Fiction**
Fishing Christianity **Art** Cooking
Essays Buddhism Freemasonry
Medicine **Biology** Music **Ancient
Egypt** Evolution Carpentry Physics
Dance Geology **Mathematics** Fitness
Shakespeare **Folklore** Yoga Marketing
Confidence Immortality Biographies
Poetry **Psychology** Witchcraft
Electronics Chemistry History **Law**
Accounting **Philosophy** Anthropology
Alchemy Drama Quantum Mechanics
Atheism Sexual Health **Ancient History**
Entrepreneurship Languages Sport
Paleontology Needlework Islam
Metaphysics Investment Archaeology
Parenting Statistics Criminology
Motivational

ROMANTIC
EDINBURGH

JOHN GEDDIE

WITH EIGHT COLOURED AND FORTY-ONE BLACK-AND-WHITE
ILLUSTRATIONS

SECOND EDITION, REVISED

LONDON: SANDS & CO.
NEW YORK: E. P. DUTTON & CO.
1911

CASTLE FROM THE GRASSMARKET.

From a water-colour after D. L. Leitch.

ROMANTIC EDINBURGH

BY
JOHN GEDDIE

WITH EIGHT COLOURED AND FORTY-ONE BLACK-AND-WHITE
ILLUSTRATIONS

SECOND EDITION, REVISED

LONDON: SANDS & CO.
NEW YORK: E. P. DUTTON & CO.
1911

"Mine own Romantic Town"

INTRODUCTORY

IN bringing out, for the Coronation Year of George V., a new and revised edition of this book, acknowledgment has to be made to Bailie Macfarlane, Convener of the Museum Committee of the Town Council, for permission to reproduce, in colour or in black-and-white, a selection of the views of Old Edinburgh, in which the Municipal Museum is so rich. Thanks have also to be given to Mr T. L. Usher, of the Park Brewery, for leave to reproduce the water-colour drawing of Edinburgh, in the opening year of the reign of Queen Victoria, that is to be found at page 212. The growth of the City and the removal of ancient landmarks in the interval since the first edition appeared, have rendered necessary many additions and alterations. Doubtless there are errors that remain uncorrected. It is hoped, however, that the volume provides—brought up to date—"a *Vade Mecum* which the explorer of Edinburgh can take with him on his walks, or profitably peruse at the fireside."

The author has to thank his friend, Mr Bruce J. Home, for his kindness in reading the proofs, and for many valuable suggestions.

228525

CONTENTS

CHAP.   PAGE

I. THE OLD AND THE NEW 1

II. NOR' LOCH AND NORTH BRIDGE . . . 11

III. THE HIGH STREET AND ST GILES . . 24

IV. OLD HIE-GAIT LIFE 43

V. FROM THE TRON TO THE CASTLE HILL . . 45

VI. THE LAWNMARKET AND THE CASTLE HILL . 60

VII. THE CASTLE 71

VIII. THE NETHERBOW PRECINCTS . . . 85

IX. THE CANONGATE 96

X. HOLYROOD 112

XI. THE KING'S PARK 124

XII. ROUND THE FLODDEN WALL—THE COWGATE . 130

XIII. ROUND THE FLODDEN WALL—THE UNIVERSITY 142

XIV. ROUND THE FLODDEN WALL—THE GREYFRIARS

AND GRASSMARKET 156

XV. NEWINGTON AND GRANGE 172

XVI. FROM MORNINGSIDE TO THE WEST KIRK . 189

XVII. THE NEW TOWN—PRINCES STREET . . 204

vii

Contents

CHAP.		PAGE
XVIII.	THE CALTON .	220
XIX.	GEORGE STREET AND ITS ENVIRONS	229
XX.	THE WEST END	244
XXI.	THE WATER OF LEITH	254
XXII.	LEITH, PORT AND BURGH	268
XXIII.	PORTOBELLO .	279
	INDEX .	283

LIST OF ILLUSTRATIONS

IN COLOUR

The Castle from the Grassmarket (from a water-colour after
W. L. Leitch) . . . . . *Frontispiece*

FACING PAGE

Advocate's Close (from a water-colour by James Heron) . 56

Allan Ramsay's Shop, opposite Niddry's Wynd (from a
water-colour by M. P. Taylor) 90

Trinity College Church before 1848 (from a Lithograph) . 130

The Old Mint (from a water-colour by D. Ritchie) . . 135

Crombie's Land, Wester Portsburgh (from a water-colour
by James Drummond) 166

Plainstanes Close, Grassmarket (from a water-colour by
R. Noble) 169

Princes Street in 1837 (from a water-colour by J. D.
Swarbreck) 212

IN BLACK-AND-WHITE

The Castle from East Princes Street Gardens . . 14

St Giles Church from the East 28

The "Heart of Midlothian" 28

The "Mercat Croce" 36

St Giles Church, Interior 36

Lower High Street and Tron Kirk 44

ix

List of Illustrations

FACING PAGE

Parliament Square 48

The Royal Exchange 54

The Mound from Princes Street Gardens . . . 58

The Bow-head and Lawnmarket (from a water-colour after W. L. Leitch) 60

Somerville's Land, Lawnmarket (from a drawing by B. J. Home) 64

View from the Castle, towards Calton (from a sketch made in 1848) 70

St Margaret's Chapel 72

The Netherbow (from an engraving in the *Scots Magazine*, 1764) 84

John Knox's House 94

White Horse Close 94

Canongate Tolbooth 96

Moray House (from a water-colour after J. Nash) . . 100

Bakehouse Close 102

The Chapel Royal, Holyrood Abbey 112

Arthur Seat from St Leonard's 112

Holyrood and Arthur Seat 114

James V.'s Tower, Holyrood Palace 116

Holyrood Palace, showing "The Regent Murray's Lodging" (after a drawing by E. Blore) 118

Holyrood Palace, Principal Doorway 120

Queen Mary's Bedroom 122

Charles I.'s Bed 122

The University 142

Gosford's Close, on site of George IV. Bridge (from a water-colour by W. Geikie) 148

Old Greyfriars 156

Heriot's Hospital 156

List of Illustrations

FACING PAGE

Swanston	190
Roslin Chapel	190
Craigmillar Castle	192
Merchiston Castle	192
Princes Street, looking Westward	204
The Scott Monument	218
The Calton Hill from the South-west	224
Mons Meg	230
George Street, looking East	230
The Water of Leith Valley, from the Dean Bridge . .	260

ROMANTIC EDINBURGH

CHAPTER I

THE OLD AND THE NEW

ON a plan of Edinburgh of the year 1765 there is traced, at the bottom of that Hollow of the Winds which divided what is now known as the New Town from the Old, the solitary pier of a bridge. It is the footprint of Old Edinburgh setting out for fresh woods and pastures new. The first step is half the journey. This one had been meditated for a century, and it was taken at last timidly and tentatively. The ground below was marshy and unstable; not long had it been reclaimed from the waters of the Nor' Loch. The fields beyond were bare and wind-swept. Like David Hume, the good town was loth to begin its flitting—to come down from its high chambers which, if they were confined and hard of access, looked abroad over wide prospects of land and sea—and go forth from the narrow closes, clarty but cosy, to pitch its tent on those cold slopes fronting the north. For a couple of years after it had laid down, with all due pomp and ceremony, the stepping-stone in the valley, it rested there, balancing and hesitating. Not until 1772 was the work complete, and the way open and passable " between the High Street and the fields to the north."

The Old and the New

As yet the New Town was not. Plans had been drawn, and a few sanguine and adventurous spirits had begun to build. But the population north of the Rubicon consisted chiefly of the dwellers in the "Beggars' Row" of St Ninian's and the Calton—folk at odds with fortune, whose more reputable employments were smuggling, and poaching on the privileges of the Incorporated Crafts within the city bounds; and the villagers of Moultrie Hill and Broughton. The Nor' Loch still slumbered under the shadow of the Castle Rock, although it had much shrunk from its former proportions and become a swamp, offensive to the nostrils of a more fastidious generation. Until the gap was formed for the North Bridge, through the line of the old Cap-and-Feather and Hart's Closes and the Green Market, the great wall of lofty houses that, on the left hand and on the right, hemmed in High Street and the Canongate remained almost intact. From the Castle Hill to the Netherbow, and from the Netherbow to Holyrood, stretched this noble thoroughfare—the wonder and admiration of all comers—pierced only by innumerable closes, and by a few narrow wynds. The close and unbroken ranks of those tall old tenements must have deepened exceedingly the impression they gave of height and strength and stateliness. The visitor might well fancy that he had wandered within the walls of some huge fortification—some rock-cut Eastern city, from which egress was possible only to those who held the clue to its labyrinth of straitened passages.

Fortified and defended the Old Town was on all hands against access and influences from without. Towards the sun, it is true, it had spread a little beyond its walls and ports in a maze of squalid and straggling

" Hampered in a Honeycaim "

streets; although in this direction also it was hemmed in by the Burgh Loch and the Burgh Muir, and the roads leading south and west were ill-made and unsafe. On the north side no egress could be found for wheeled carriages until the low latitudes of Leith Wynd were reached, and only in favourable weather could the sedan chair make the parlous descent into the valley by the short cut of the steep and malodorous Halkerston's Wynd. For the traveller London-wards the nearest route lay through the adjoining burgh of Canongate, and forth into the outer world by the Water Gate, Abbey Hill, and Restalrig, beyond which he must ·brave the terrors of highwaymen and footpads in passing through the Figgate Whins, on the site now occupied by Edinburgh's sea-bathing suburb of Portobello. Returning, he must pass barrier after barrier, ending with the Netherbow, where, as at other ports and exits of the city, stood on guard the toll-keeper and the town watch.

Under these conditions grew up the strangely marked features of the social life and customs, as well as of the architecture, of the Edinburgh of last century. But, by the time when George the Third became King and the Jacobite risings were beginning to fade into a tradition, the old capital was already irking itself of being so isolated and self-contained. It was tired of being chained, like Prometheus, to its rock. Down to the days of the early Jameses, its houses are believed to have been straw-thatched and comparatively low. The nature of the site and the exigencies of defence required that it should build ever higher and closer on its confined and narrow space. Like the structure of some coral reef, the high "lands" rose, storey after storey, till they overtopped the pinnacles of St Giles. The citizens, in

The Old and the New

Dunbar's phrase, were "hampered in a honeycaim" of their own making. To the needs and conditions that had reared the grey old city on the ridge succeeded the problems of modern life. Sanitation, or as it was concretely called in those days, "the disposal of the town's fulzie," grew a crying question. The craving for more air and light and space became irresistible. It manifested itself in the decade before the founding of the North Bridge, and during the years when that structure was in progress, in a somewhat indiscriminate removal of ancient landmarks which were felt to be obstructive. "Claudero" raised his voice in vain in raucous denunciation of the destroyers of the Gothic porch to the courtyard of Holyrood, and of those who had laid impious hands on the Mercat Cross and the Netherbow.

When at length the pent-up forces became too strong for the retaining walls, it was through the North Bridge that the breach was made. The upper strata of Old Edinburgh society, the store of wealth and of new ideas which had been gathering since the Union, began to flow chiefly by this channel towards the north. Lords of Session and city merchants, philosophers and divines, not to speak of the commoner clay, were by and by emptied forth into the New Town. David Hume, the representative of the new era of free thought, was himself, as we have seen, caught in the current and stranded on the bank opposite. Champions of the older philosophy and theology stood for a time on the old ground and in the old ways; fashion lingered long in the Edinburgh closes. But the fiat for change had gone forth, and the opening of the North Bridge was the final signal.

Changed Times, Changed Manners

Contemporaries of that event were vaguely aware of its far-reaching and many-sided significance ; although, at the time, it was spoken of as merely the forming of a new and shorter road of access to the port of Leith. The more orthodox and conservative shook their heads over the symptoms of growing laxity in morals and manners that immediately became visible in their eyes. "Theophrastus," in an appendix to Hugo Arnot's " History," laments the declension in the once strict and exemplary religious habits of the people, apparent to anyone who compared the Edinburgh of 1763 with that of 1783. In the former year—that in which the North Bridge centre pier was laid—" it was fashionable to go to church, and people were interested in religion. Sunday was observed strictly by all ranks as a day of devotion ; it was disgraceful to be seen on the streets during the time of public worship." Twenty years later, " attendance in church is much neglected ; Sunday is made a day of relaxation ; families think it ungenteel to take their domestics to church with them ; the streets are often crowded in the time of worship ; and, in the evenings, they are often loose and riotous. Family worship is almost totally disused ; and it is even wearing out among the clergy." Old things were being swept away with what seemed, even to the unhistorical eye, ruthless and unthrifty haste. Revolutionary ideas poured in through the gap of the North Bridge. Not with impunity did Edinburgh " come out of its shell "— break from its grey chrysalis on the hill, and flutter out into the open.

Most portentous of the signs of the times was that modification of the habits and the point of view of the Scottish clergy concerning which " Theophrastus " raises

The Old and the New

his note of alarm. A minister of the Church—John Home of Athelstaneford—had written a tragedy, which had been acted on the stage of the Old Playhouse in the Canongate; and other clergymen of the Establishment had witnessed and applauded the performance. He had been chased from his kirk by the zealots while the North Bridge was being founded. But scarcely had the arches spanned the valley when the Spirit of Evil, whom the "unco guid" of the time believed they saw embodied in the theatre, took up new and bolder ground, on the further side of the valley. Beside the north-eastern abutment of the Bridge, on the spot now occupied by the General Post Office, rose the first regularly licensed theatre in the Scottish capital. This ground, on the green slope of Moultrie Hill overlooking the Physic Gardens, and facing the range of the Old Town dwellings, had been the site of the house of the Provost of Trinity College Church, and had afterwards been part of the "green" of the Orphan Hospital where the open-air preachings were held, and to which thousands had trooped across the valley to listen to the eloquence of Whitefield. Great, it seems, was the wrath and despair of that evangelist when, returning to the scene of his labours, he found the place "appropriated to the service of Satan," and the preaching green in the course of being transformed into "Shakespeare Square." The rise of the playhouse walls where the Gospel tent had been pitched, he called the "plucking up of God's standard, and the planting of the Devil's instead." Whitefield himself had been banned and excluded from the pulpits of the Secession Presbytery for lax and unsound doctrine. We can imagine the feelings with which these excellent but narrow-minded

From Preaching-Green to Theatre

men watched from the battlements opposite the rise of this fortress of the enemy.

And yet the Old Theatre Royal, afterwards to be so closely associated with the genius and triumphs of the Siddonses and Kembles, with the Murrays and Sir Walter Scott, and with the other names and events that shed lustre on the Edinburgh stage of the end of last and the early part of the present century, did not ill fulfil the aspiration of its first manager and proprietor, David Ross, that it might be the means of promoting " every moral and every virtuous principle." Long before the Bridge was complete, the cream of Edinburgh society, grave and learned divines among the rest, had begun to acquire the habit of resorting to the shrine of the mimic muses across the valley ; and Bozzy's lines, recited at the opening of the Theatre on 9th December 1767, grew of less and less application to the attitude of the Scottish mind towards the stage—

> Mistaken zeal, in times of darkness bred,
> O'er the best minds its gloomy vapours spread ;
> Taste and religion were opposed in strife,
> And 'twas a sin to view this glass of life.

Not without some peril and adventure would the passage be made after dark, even when the North Bridge had stretched its helpful arm across the gap, in those days of linkboys, and sturdy beggars, and unpaved and unlighted streets. The hollow between the Old and New Towns has always been a very Cave of the Winds. It is the chief channel by which the East Wind— Edinburgh's great enemy, since her English invaders come no longer to burn and raid, but as pilgrims of the beautiful—breaks in upon her streets and squares. By

The Old and the New

this way steals in the main body of the fogs and "haars" out of the North Sea, that choke the valley, blot out of sight the towering houses of the Old Town, or spread a grey veil through which their outlines loom vague and gigantic like a city of cloudland. Past the piers and parapets of the North Bridge the gales of the west rush with redoubled fury, bearing wild flurries of snow brought down from the Highland hills, or onsets of rain that have crossed the whole breadth of the country from the Atlantic, to spend their force on what the author of " Picturesque Notes " calls " the high altar of the northern temple of the winds." The sweep of the blast must have been yet stronger before the Earthen Mound— Edinburgh's next great means of exodus to its northern fields—had risen high enough to break the force of the breezes from the west. The Bridge, in its early years, had open balustrades, and we read of public complaints that "passengers continue to be blown from the pavement into the mud" in the middle of the roadway. Those openings also afforded unpleasing glimpses of the "blood and slaughter" in the Fleshmarket below. Plainly, it was high time they were closed.

Then, as now, the passengers by the Bridge had sights worth seeing. We can easily imagine the delight with which the citizens of the years before the outbreak of the American War gazed upon the wonderful spectacle, then possessing all the charm of novelty, afforded from this high vantage-ground. The near surroundings and accessories are strangely altered, but the framework and the main features of the scene remain. The Castle Rock — which Robert Louis Stevenson has called "the most satisfactory crag in nature; a Bass Rock upon dry land "—blocks out a

North Bridge Prospects

great part of the south-western horizon, and casts its "warlike shadow" over the ground which it has dominated throughout the recorded history of the city. The solid mass of the Old Town buildings—"Auld Reekie" itself, ragged with spires and chimney-tops on its skyline; the smoky grey of its ground colour strangely scored and chased by the darker shadings of its closes, and the high relief of its many-storeyed gables —continues the line of the Castle battlements down the long slope towards Holyrood. Rising in a sheer cliff above the roofs of the Canongate, the Salisbury Crags shine ruddily in the sunlight, or hang black and threatening in foul weather, like the crest of a tidal wave about to break and engulf the town below. Behind is the couchant lion of Arthur Seat; and looking eastward past its sides one can descry, from the parapet of the Bridge, the pyramid of the North Berwick Law, the uplifted edge of the Bass, the links and sandhills of Gullane, the woods of Gosford, and the waters of the Firth, across which flashes after nightfall the winking eye of the May.

The "Craig-end of Calton," on the other side of the valley, did not bear in those days its sheaf of prison towers; nor had monuments begun to rear themselves on the Hill behind. The green slopes and precipices, still carrying a fragment of the chapel of St Ninian and the stones of the old Calton burying-ground, may, however, have looked none the less picturesque on that account. The prospect from the North Bridge a hundred and forty years ago was, in many respects, even more spacious and unobstructed than it is to-day. Princes Street had been planned on the line of the old Lang Gait, but the first house only began to rise in

The Old and the New

1769; the stately front of that magnificent thoroughfare did not shut out the glimpses of Fife. The buildings on the west side of the Bridge, at the northern end, did not come into existence till half a century later, and their erection raised a strong protest from Lord Cockburn, from "The Man of Feeling," and from other citizens of taste of the day, who complained that the block closed out the much-admired view of the Castle and the valley from Shakespeare Square and Waterloo Place. On their site a great railway hotel has now climbed the skies from the level of the hollow below, and this structure, too, has encountered æsthetic objection on the ground that it dwarfs by its bulk and height the surrounding buildings, and hampers the free look-out from the North Bridge.

Westward along the hollow, although the Mound and its classic façades break the middle distance, one can see out and away beyond the city spires and the city smoke. If the sea bounds the view to the east, the woods clothing the sides of Corstorphine Hill close the prospect in the other direction. Surely in no spot within the limits of a busy hive of population, or nowhere else except in Edinburgh, can one view so wonderful a mingling of the beauties of nature and of art, of the old and the new, of precipices of the living rock rising out of gardens, and glimpses of green country and wave-beaten islands caught between the white and pillared fronts of Grecian temples and masses of high-piled masonry black with age and reek.

CHAPTER II

NOR' LOCH AND NORTH BRIDGE

HITHERTO we have only looked abroad from the Bridge on the level of the eye or above it. But there is a world below that has seen great changes since the arches first bestrode the valley. That the changes have been wholly improvement would be a bold thing to say. But they seize one with a keen sense of the contrast of the present with the past.

In the depths of the hollow to the eastward many smoky industries have pitched their camp. Foundries and breweries now occupy the site of the gardens and pleasances of the burghers of the Canongate and the lower High Street, whose close-ends used to be " steikit " with stone and lime when the town hermetically sealed itself in time of war. The space once occupied by the ancient Trinity College Church with its adjoining Hospital and College, the princely foundation of the Queen of James II. of Scots, is covered by signal-boxes and platforms and a spider's web of railway lines.

Long ago, too, the tentacles of the Waverley Station seized and swallowed the ground on which, at the making of the North Bridge, stood the first Orphan Hospital, the original Lady Glenorchy's Chapel, and the Old Physic Gardens, among the earliest of the many

Nor' Loch and North Bridge

venerable institutions which have been ejected or destroyed by the tide of change that has swept through the valley. The Gardens, the first planted in Scotland for the promotion of the study of botany, hardly waited to fall under the shadow of the Bridge. The erudite Sir Robert Sibbald and Sir Andrew Balfour, the eminent physician and naturalist, the original projector of the Royal College of Surgeons and of the Royal Infirmary, had been at the founding of the Gardens a hundred years before, when the ground had been in part recovered from the Nor' Loch, which, once on a time, stretched almost to the Craigs of Calton. But the Loch strangely revenged itself in the troubles of the Revolution. The besiegers of the Castle bethought them to drain it as a means of approaching the defences of the citadel, and the escaped flood over-flowed the Gardens, and covered the beds of costly exotic plants with the refuse of the town drains. Botany had ultimately to flit and seek other "lown" quarters for its herbs and flowers under the lee of Holyrood, by Leith Walk, and finally in Inverleith Park.

This same Nor' Loch, the dwindling residue of which was still visible to the earlier passengers over the Bridge, had curious vicissitudes as a feature of Edinburgh landscape, and played an ambiguous part in the city's history. According to most authorities, the whole period of its stay in the valley was not much more than three centuries. Geologists, on the other hand, have held, from the configuration and character of its bed, that there must always have been a lake, or at least a marsh, in this spot. Certain it is that the Loch existed before 1450, the date that has been

A Moat of Defence

assigned for its formation as part of the defences of the town against "skaith" from the "auld enemies" across the Border.

The north side of Edinburgh in those remote days probably presented a precipitous front, a continuation of the Castle cliffs, descending into a wilderness of swamp and brake, in the snuggest corner of which, near St Margaret's spring and the Wellhouse Tower, King David of pious memory is supposed to have laid out a modest garden of trees and herbs. This craggy face has been gradually smoothed over with a mass of "travelled earth," which has been found covering the lower part of the slope to a depth of thirty feet and more. It is the accumulated rubbish of old Edinburgh, a "kitchen-midden," in which have been picked up coins and fragments of armour and other relics of the life of a fighting past, when the "back lands" and narrow slips of pleasure ground of the Auld Reekie closes descended to the very edge of the Loch, whereon the well-to-do citizen might keep a "boat o' his ain" for paddling out on a fine evening among the swans and smaller water-fowl, and, belike, after nightfall, quietly smuggle over "an anker of Hollands" from a friend in Leith.

Thus, while defence was its main purpose—down to the '15, when the magistrates gave orders to the sluice-keepers at the foot of Halkerston's Wynd to raise its level in order to keep Borlum and his Highlanders at a distance—the Loch was made to serve for the sport and recreation of the townsfolk. Bonspiels were played on its frozen surface in hard winters, and the town drew a small revenue from the "eel-arks" of the Loch. Among its pastimes must

Nor' Loch and North Bridge

be reckoned, we fear, the torture and judicial murder of many a poor wretch who had fallen under the ban of the savage laws of the time. Heretics and suspected witches have been drowned in the Nor' Loch, as a thrifty substitute for, or test preliminary to, the major penalty of burning at the stake. There is record of a band of eleven gipsies, men and women, being thus disposed of, in the days when to belong to the wandering race was proof conclusive of capital crimes. For the punishment of the incontinent a special pool was reserved. This fateful water and its margins have been the scene also of private tragedy and of public riot. The "image of Saint Geille," long the palladium of the city, and carried in procession at its high festivals, was dragged hither ignominiously by the zealots of the Reformation, and "droonit" before being given to the flames. There were more reasons than one why the Nor' Loch should have taken an ill savour.

Still, standing on the North Bridge of to-day, one cannot help regretting that Edinburgh should have served its old moat of defence so ungratefully as to turn it first into a receptacle for its cast-out dross and garbage, and then to drain off what was left of it in order that a passage might be made for its railway traffic. What an opportunity was lost with the falling through of the favourite scheme of the Earl of Mar—Mar of the Rebellion—by which a pure stream would have been diverted into the hollow, and a stagnant and evil-smelling pond would have been transformed into a cleanly and ornamental piece of water, stretching from the West Church to beyond the arches of the North Bridge! Of that project, once hopeful and

THE CASTLE FROM EAST PRINCES STREET GARDENS.

"What might have been"

feasible, all that remains—if it does remain—is the name of "Canal Street" clinging to one of the accesses to the Waverley Station.

One's fancy dwells lingeringly and wonderingly on the vision of "what might have been"—on the Castle Rock rearing itself out of deep water and, in place of a trail of engine smoke, a placid lake, reflecting the garden and palaces of the Old and New Towns and their connecting bridges. Edinburgh was otherwise to "dree its weird." The Great and the Little Mound—the latter on the site of what is now the Waverley Bridge—rose and spread athwart the valley. The spaces of low ground between and to the westward became more noisome. Robert Chambers could remember when the ground now forming West Princes Street Gardens still contained pools—remnants of the Nor' Loch—where excellent skating and sliding were to be had in winter, and desert patches, meet scenes for the battles with stones and fists between the Old Town and New Town callants. Lord Cockburn speaks of it in 1816 as still holding a filthy and impassable swamp, "the receptacle of many sewers, and seemingly of all the worried cats, drowned dogs, and blackguardism of the city." So solitary was it that part of the space was utilised by the volunteer companies of the day for ball practice; and until well into the century the damp bed of the old Nor' Loch was the resort of snipe and water-fowl.

It was Walter Scott's friend, Skene of Rubislaw, who set about reclaiming this "pest-bed," and turning it into the beautiful gardens which divide Old from New Edinburgh. The author of "Waverley" records, in January 1826, how, "after a good day's work," he

Nor' Loch and North Bridge

strolled from his house in the neighbouring Castle Street into the new pleasure-grounds laid out by this Good Samaritan, and found all very good. "It is singular," he writes in his Journal, "to walk close beneath the grim old Castle, and think what scenes it must have seen, and how many generations of three-score and ten have risen and passed away."

The coming of the railway has brought the greatest change of all. A "river of human life," swift and strange, has taken a forth-right way through the trough where once lay the "Dead Sea" of the Nor' Loch. Growing steadily stronger with lapse of years, it has scoured for itself a wider channel under the West Kirkyard, past the foot of the Castle Rock, and through the Craigs of Calton. But the focus of its forces is under and around the arches of the North Bridge. Here converging currents from south and north, and from east and west, meet and jostle; and there are times and seasons when travelling and holiday-making humanity swells in an autumn flood that seethes and eddies about the piers and abutments. Under stress of this irresistible movement, older structures are continually being undermined and toppling down. The Waverley Station is the centre of a dissolving view of city alterations. Looking down upon it in this year of grace, you behold a furrowed and spreading "sea of glass," from which escape the smoke and the shriek of the toiling locomotives; and, bounding it, ancient walls that crumble to their ruin, and new walls that climb the sky in their place; while at night, when you can carry your eye away from the brilliant constellation of the New Town lamps and the dimmer but more impressive galaxy that irradiates the dark

A New North Bridge

mass of the Old Town, the gulf below is seen to be filled with many-coloured lights, fixed and moving.

The Bridge itself is not the same structure that Lord Provost Drummond opened with civic state in 1772, and across which migrated the "conscript fathers of the city" on their way to a freer air. It has needed repeated widening and renewal to accommodate the growing stream of traffic between the Old and New Town. A hundred years after its erection it was broadened by the device of throwing out brackets for the support of the footways. More lately it has received entire renovation in arch, pier, and roadway. It became a new North Bridge—lock, stock, and barrel. None the less, but rather the more, does it remain what Lord Rosebery has called it—"the foundation of the city's beauty"; for, while the roadway has been widened, the gradient has been altered, and the level heightened. On the inimitable site has been placed one of the most spacious thoroughfares of the kind in Europe.

Alas that this great and necessary improvement should have disturbed or destroyed so much of the substance and the shadow of the past! The original breach in the walls of the Edinburgh of last century has been widened threefold by the changes that have accompanied the building of the new North Bridge. To right and to left the older dwellings have fallen under the scythe of the city improvers, not singly, but in swathes. The tall and stately frontages of hotels and of bank and newspaper offices have risen in their place. One may look in vain on the eastern side of the Bridge for any trace of Halkerston's Wynd, named after David Halkerston of that ilk, who held it bravely, and to the death, against Hertford's ruthless onslaught. Steep

Nor' Loch and North Bridge

and narrow though it was, this minor outlet of the city, leading down to the dam and sluices of the Nor' Loch, was of historic and even strategic interest in Edinburgh annals. Alongside of it were other closes, with their fore and back "lands," occupied in their time by bishops and feudal lords, and later by Jacobite lairds and magnates of the law. Adjoining the head of the wynd, in the High Street, stood the timber-fronted house to which "Allan Ramsay, periwig-maker," brought his bride, and where, "at the sign of the Mercury, opposite Niddry's Wynd," he wrote plays and lyrics and printed broadsheets before he removed to "Creech's Land," in the Luckenbooths.

All have disappeared; and along with them has, of course, gone the eastern side of the old "Cap-and-Feather Close," a portion of which remained to the last an actual part of the former Bridge Street. In this close—not improbably in one of the humble tenements whose windows continued to look down on the passengers who crossed the North Bridge, possibly on the site afterwards associated with literature as the publishing house of Adam Black and of the "Encyclopædia Britannica"—was born another genuine Scottish poet, who loved dearly the "Edinburgh plainstanes" and the sound of the "Tron Kirk bell"—Robert Fergusson.

On the other, or western, side, all the old buildings that interposed between North Bridge Street and Cockburn Street—itself an earlier "improvement" that cut traversely across a series of famous High Street closes, and thus through a section of city history—have gone "at one fell swoop." In their place, next neighbour to the Bridge, and overlooking it as well as

A Dissolving View of Changes

Market Street and the Railway Station, lying many storeys below, rise the new offices of the *Scotsman* newspaper. Part of the site, on the edge of the valley, appears to have been once occupied as a "town ludging" by the monks of the Abbey of Newbattle; and it has some claim to be the spot on which stood, in the years 1568 and 1569, a house occupied by John Knox.

Better remembered are the associations of the Old Fleshmarket Close with the drinking "howffs" and drinking customs of the Edinburgh of Burns's day, when, as W. E. Henley paints it (laying on his colours over thick), it was "a centre of conviviality—a city of clubs and talk and good-fellowship—a city of harlotry and high jinks—a city, above all, of drink.

> Whare couthie chiels at e'enin' meet,
> Their bizzin' craigs and mou's to weet."

The name of these Old Edinburgh Clubs was legion, and some of the most famous of them met in the Old Fleshmarket Close. Here and in the neighbourhood their traditions lingered longest. Near the head of the close, in the remanent fragment of this famous alley, which still gives a narrow access from High Street to Cockburn Street, is the turnpike stair up which Pitt's friend, Henry Dundas, first Lord Melville, had his chambers while he was a struggling advocate, and the "laigh cellar" where Burns's crony and publisher, William Creech, began business as a bookseller. But the lower section has been finally swept away, and with it have gone visible links with the Burke and Hare murders and Deacon Brodie, and with the tavern gatherings, the Homeric feasts, and the bacchanalian orgies, in which judges of the High Court, of the lost

Nor' Loch and North Bridge

type of Lord Hermand and the "mighty" Newton, did not disdain to play a leading part.

They were a natural, and almost a necessary, outcome of the conditions of the domestic and business life of the time in which they originated, those social meetings in chop-house and oyster-cellar. There was scant room for the sedater hospitalities of home in those days, when even families of title and estate were pigeon-holed in narrow chambers up many flights of stairs in some tall tenement, where they could shake hands with their neighbours on the other side of the close—when, as related in Chambers's "Traditions," a leading Scots lawyer, afterwards raised to the bench, had to accommodate his household in three rooms and a kitchen : the children, with their nurse, having their beds made down nightly in the room of the head of the family, the housemaid sleeping under the kitchen dresser, and the one manservant seeking his night's quarters elsewhere ; and when a thriving goldsmith in Parliament Square "stowed away his *ménage* in a couple of small rooms above his booth, plastered against the walls of St Giles."

Men, and eke women, including women of quality, had, in those Auld Reekie days, to seek social diversion abroad, and, not being hard to please as to fare or surroundings, they found it in the tavern. There were clubs of many kinds, and for all ranks—clubs that kept alive the Jacobite tradition, and clubs that celebrated in deep draughts the "Glorious Revolution" ; societies like the Easy Club, for which "Honest Allan" wrote his first poems, and the Crochallan Fencibles, of which Robert Burns was admitted a member, that gave more than a passing thought between bumpers to letters ; and others that devoted themselves to drinking, pure

Auld Reekie Days

and simple. While the learned judge or the eminent counsel would be firing off broad jests and quaffing jorums of punch and magnums of claret in Clerihugh's Tavern, Writers' Court, or in Paterson's Chop-house, in the Fleshmarket Close, his clerk would be found regaling himself with mutton pies and "twopenny" in "Lucky Wood's, in the Cowgate," or some other howff suited to his degree. Gentle and simple, these eighteenth-century revellers could not, as Councillor Pleydell boasts in "Guy Mannering," be charged with the fault of Sir John Falstaff in wandering from tavern to tavern in Eastcheap. They were conservative even in their excesses in the matter both of their drink and of their drinking quarters. After business hours, boon companions and clients knew where they were to be found.

If jest and conversation were lacking in refinement, they were certainly not wanting in boisterous vigour. Our great-grandfathers, and our great-grandmothers as well, had a fine gift for calling a spade a spade. They knew, also, how to combine thrift and pleasure. They supped sumptuously on rizzered haddies or sheep-head and trotters in lowly quarters, where they could themselves keep an eye on the progress of the cooking.

The names bestowed upon their convivial societies often reflected the rough wit and the manners of the day. The members of the "Spendthrift Club" were debarred from spending more than "a groat and a bawbee" on supper. The "Six-Foot Club" were tall fellows, and mighty men also in potations, as those who have met with a company of them at Hunter's Tryst, in the tale of "St Ives," can testify. The "Marrowbones Club" feasted on marrow bones, in the belief that "a large quantity of drink could be superimposed" on that

Nor' Loch and North Bridge

dish. Their meeting-place was long in Paterson's Chop-house, and the members, each of whom had his silver spoon, bearing his own coat of arms and the club motto, *Nil nisi Bonum*, included a host of the luminaries of the law and of Edinburgh society. The " Cape Club," of which Fergusson was a member, is understood to have taken its name from the difficulty with which one of its founders, who lived in the outlandish region of St Ninian's Row, weathered the " Cape " of Leith Wynd on his way home, with the contents of more than one "lang-craig" as cargo under his belt. They found housing in later years in Bourgois's, made famous by the Frenchman who was its first landlord for " its matchless steaks on the grill and unrivalled porter." Here, too, in the building whose gable-end projected, until the other day, cheek-by-jowl with the North Bridge, the " Poker Club " lingered out its last days, and the " Edinburgh Select Subscription Library " had its beginnings.

The last survivor and perpetuator of some of the traditions and more seemly customs of these old-time Clubs—the " Presbytery "—continued to meet, under the staff of its " Moderator," and in the inspiring presence of its other heirlooms of the past, in Gilchrist's Tavern, up a " common stair," in Mylne's Square, until the demolition of this nook of Old Edinburgh compelled the Presbyters to remove to the neighbouring Cockburn Street, where the Club shortly after expired, from change of air. Mylne's Square, built by and named after one of the " Royal " line of Master Masons, who constructed the first North Bridge, was a confined courtyard, hemmed in by many-storeyed, many-windowed houses, to which access was had from North Bridge Street by a flight of steps, and from High Street by a narrow entry.

" The end of an Auld Sang "

In one of the tenements on the west side of the Square, now laid in the dust, lived Lord Justice-Clerk Alva, who died in the year that the North Bridge was founded. The stairway was often ascended by the old fox Lovat, in his crooked game of hide-and-seek with the law. Afterwards, this house with the narrow windows and quaint gables witnessed the levees of the first Earl of Hopetoun, when, in the early years of last century, after his return from the Peninsular campaigns, the warrior became Lord High Commissioner. Beside the High Street entrance was the "laigh shop" of Mrs Macleuchar, opposite the Tron Kirk, whence the "Antiquary" and his companion started in the Hawes fly for the Queen's Ferry, and the spot where Neil Gow began selling fiddles and reel music; and in what are now the cellars of a bank, the Scottish Commissioners, furtively, and in fear of the raging mob of patriots without, attached their signatures to the Treaty of Union, and so made "an end of an auld sang."

CHAPTER III

THE HIGH STREET AND ST GILES

FROM its first beginnings the heart of Edinburgh has beat in its High Street. Nay, during nearly all the centuries of its history, this famous thoroughfare has contained the body, as well as the soul, of the Scottish capital. It was not only the centre and chief part, it was Old Edinburgh Town itself—that Old Edinburgh which Carlyle in his posthumous " Historical Sketches " describes as " a sloping high street and many steep side-lanes, covering like some wrought tissue of stone and mortar, like some rhinoceros skin, with many a gnarled embossment, church steeple, chimney head, Tolbooth and other ornament or indispensability, back and ribs of the slope," on which stands the " City on the Rock."

Earlier writers have found this figure of a backbone and the connected ribs appropriate to " the King's Hie Street " and its wynds and closes, using that title as descriptive, not merely of the " place " between the Church of St Giles and the Netherbow, to which it was once restricted, but of the broad highway that extends, under different names, from the Castle Esplanade to Holyrood. Other quaint similes were employed to express the singular aspect and structure of Edinburgh's

The Genesis of the High Street

main street, as it presented itself to the eyes of visitors well accustomed to the appearance of mediæval towns and town life; one of them likens it to "an ivory comb, whose teeth on both sides are very foul, although the space between 'em is clean and sightly." Two or three centuries ago, much as now, the height of its buildings, the spaciousness of its roadway, and the contrasting narrowness and darkness of the diverging closes, chiefly impressed the newcomer. Fynes Moryson praised, in 1598, the "fair and broad streete," which was "sole ornament" of the town; and, a few years later, Taylor, the Water Poet, breaks out, after his wont, into a rhapsody over its beauty, noting shrewdly enough, however, that while merchants and tradesmen lived on the High Street, the houses of the gentlefolks were "obscured in bye-lanes and closes."

The thoughtful visitor may still, as in the days of our Scottish Solomon, "reason out the genesis, the manner of growth, and the shape taken by the ancient city," as turning into the High Street by the North Bridge he passes up it towards the Castle, or down towards the Palace, and glances as he goes into the depths of the steep and dingy closes that plunge down, to right and left, into the bounding valleys. Great, indeed, have been the changes of three centuries; and every year removes a landmark, or defaces some venerable feature of this historic street. With the widening of the North Bridge, as we have seen, an interesting part of the Old Town has been swept into the dust-bin. And other "improvements," destructive of memorials of the city's past, are in progress or in contemplation. The extended Council Chambers have swallowed up Clerihugh's Tavern; the close-heads on

The High Street and St Giles

the north side of the Lawnmarket, and on the south side of High Street between Parliament Square and the Tron, lead to open spaces instead of closely ranked files of historic houses ; " New Street" itself is a thing of the memory. An ancient building in Campbell's Close, sorely stricken with decay, is going the way of its fellows.

Yet the imprint of its history remains, and will long remain, on Edinburgh High Street. In its plan and architecture one can still recognise the natural product of the site, and of the conditions under which the town first took root and grew. It was a city of refuge and defence, the joint offspring of the Castle and the Abbey, which guarded and enclosed it to the west and east, as did its marshes on the north and south. The old citizens had perforce to build "close and high" when their rock left them so little space to build upon. "On one side was the Border, and on the other the Highlands. The houses huddled together on the confined and comparatively safe foothold of the ridge, like refugees from a flood."

To this day the ground on which the High Street stands carries more houses and population, and perhaps more history and romance, than any corresponding area in Europe. Many of its famous houses and picturesque closes have been weeded out, but many are left. The old "fifteen- and sixteen-decker" buildings have been purged away by fire; but the High Street can still reckon nine and ten storeys in its "backlands," and faces the thoroughfare with a bold front, five, six, and seven storeys in height. Aloft, from its many windows, it flaunts its washings, to the wonder of the visitors below ; a few forestairs project into the pavement; a few "laigh shops" dive down below the level of the

The Cockpit of Scotland

plainstanes, and a few timber-fronted gables overhang them. To those who know where to go in search of them, moulded doorways with armorial bearings, dates, and texts; carved finials and dormers; locks and door-handles; "tirling-pins," "stands" for sedan-chairs, link-extinguishers and other memorials of the Edinburgh of the sixteenth, seventeenth, and eighteenth centuries are not difficult to find.

For one feature of the old High Street, those who know their Edinburgh only from the pages of the historian and the romancist will look in vain. While huge lateral breaches have been made in its walls, the main channel of Old Edinburgh life has been swept almost clean of obstructions—if we except the Town Wells, memorials of the city's first water supply. We have seen that the Netherbow and the Mercat Croce disappeared in the middle of last century. Sometime later the City Guard House at the Tron, the headquarters of the "Town Rats," went the way of all the earth. The Luckenbooths and the Tolbooth lingered in their places until nearly the end of the second decade of the present century.

These and other buildings, dropped down in the fairway of traffic, were of strategic as well as social importance in the city's annals. Like the closes, they were rallying points and places of refuge in the times when the High Street was the cockpit of Scotland— the ground whereon, as has been said, private and party feuds, the jealousies of the nobles and the burghers, and the quarrels between the Crown, the Plebs, and the Kirk, were for centuries settled at the sword's point. The bruilzie, long known as "Cleanse the Causey," in which Cardinal Beaton nearly lost his

The High Street and St Giles

life in 1515, was but one of many street frays in which the same cry was raised.

Between the time when young Roland Graeme rode down the street towards Lord Setoun's lodging in the Canongate, and the time when Dandie Dinmont shouldered his way to Writers' Court, much blood was spilt in Edinburgh High Street; and it was well for a hot-tempered Borderer or Highlander, with family and personal feuds on his hands, if he knew of some friendly port, in an adjoining booth or wynd, where he could take shelter in case of his getting the worst of it in attempting to "keep the crown of the causey." Young King Jamie himself, as we know, found such a place of refuge handy, when, coming down the High Street from the Tolbooth in 1591, he got mixed unwittingly in a fray, and, fleeing into a close-head, stood "shaking for fear in a skinner's booth." Worse still was his plight, five or six years later, when he was besieged in the Tolbooth itself by an enraged populace, and, escaping, vowed that he would "raze to the ground" the accursed and tumultuous town.

Occasionally the Netherbow would divide a hostile army or parliament encamped in the Canongate from a rival faction whose headquarters were in the Edinburgh Tolbooth; or cannon shot from High Street and St Giles would reply to the fire of the Castle, when city and citadel stood out, as they often did, for opposing sovereigns and religions. One can understand the need of the order given in 1552 by the Burgh Council to the occupiers of booths and chambers in the High Street, "heich and laigh," that, because of the "great slauchters and tulzies" that had taken place, they should take care to have "lang weapons at hand,

ST GILES CHURCH FROM THE EAST.

THE "HEART OF MIDLOTHIAN."

[*To face page* 28.

The Crown of St Giles

and sally forth incontinent when the common bell rang."

The Crown of St Giles, which has a recorded history almost coeval with that of the High Street itself, has always been the chief ornament of Old Edinburgh. The Cathedral or Collegiate Church, dedicated to Edinburgh's patron saint, holds a more prominent place than ever in the ancient thoroughfare, out of the midst of which it rises like some massive grey rock, crusted with Gothic ornament. It is believed that a Christian place of worship has stood on the spot ever since the time when, as is supposed, Northumbrian King Edwin founded the town and named it as his "burgh." But of the parish church of the straw-thatched Anglian hamlet there is no trace; and, since the removal more than a hundred years ago of the north doorway, with its grotesque early Norman carvings, there are few vestiges left of the twelfth-century St Giles which was burned, along with the town, during an English raid in 1385.

The bases of the tower and the adjoining arches of choir and nave may belong to the earlier structure; and marks of fire have been detected on some of the pillars. But the church arose in more stately form and spacious dimensions on its restoration by Robert III., who bestowed it on his Abbey of Scone to meet the expenses of royal coronations. Succeeding kings showed it favour, although it long remained a simple vicarage under the Perthshire religious house. Fresh sanctity came to it along with the "armbone of St Giles," which was brought thither by Preston of Gorton, "with the aid of the King of France," in 1454, and which continued to be carried along with the image of

The High Street and St Giles

the patron saint in the Saint's day procession, and on
other high and solemn public occasions, to the sound of
"talbron, trumpet, shalm, and clarioun," until it disappeared in the tempest of Knox's Reformation. Not
long after its coming, a Papal Bull erected the church
into a collegiate charge; the building was lengthened
and heightened as it grew in fame and in wealth; and,
in its palmy days, the forty altars of St Giles were
served by seventy officiating priests.

It was probably under the first "Provost of the
College Kirk," William Forbes, who bestowed his
garden, lying between the church and the Cowgate, to
be used as a burial-ground by the parishioners, that the
beautiful mural crown of St Giles arose in its present
form. But, under the Old Religion, the Metropolitan
Church never rose to the dignity of the seat of an
episcopal see. Its status of Cathedral came late, and
was short-lived; St Giles knew the jurisdiction of
Bishops only during the sixty years between the fling-
ing of Jenny Geddes's stool and the Revolution, and
even then but intermittently.

Within and without, the fabric of St Giles bears the
scars, honourable or otherwise, of the tumults, invasions,
civil wars, and conflagrations of the past. Legend and
history cling to its walls. It has been put to base as
well as noble uses. Councils of barons and of prelates
have met in it in time of national danger; it has given
shelter to the Estates of the Realm and to the High
Court of Justice; it is the traditional scene of the weird
"High Mass" celebrated on the eve of Flodden. Knox
thundered in the "Hie Kirk" against the idolatries of
Rome and the "monstrous regimen of women." When
his voice grew too weak to be heard in the Choir he

Scars of Time and War

"dang the pulpit to blads" in the adjoining and more restricted space of the Tolbooth Church, forming the southern side of St Giles. These were but two out of the four places of worship into which St Giles was divided after the Reformation, the others being the West Kirk, which occupied the nave, and the Old Kirk, which found dark housing in the portion of the transept lying under the tower. Parts of St Giles have been turned to use as an Exchange, as Police Office, and as Town Clerk's quarters; "Haddo's Hole," over the north porch, has been crowded with Covenanting prisoners awaiting execution or shipment to the Plantations; the tower has been used as a lock-up for suspected witches and as a weaving shop; there, too, cannon have been mounted and have exchanged shots with the guns of the Castle. Misfortune of another kind fell on the Choir of St Giles, in 1829, under the name of the "renovation" of the High or East Kirk by the hands of Burn, who so cleared and smoothed the old fabric, without and within, in accordance with the deplorable architectural taste of the day, that the citizens congratulated themselves on it having been made "as fresh as if it were new." Fragments of carved masonry removed during this despoilment have found refuge in rock-gardens and walls in the city and suburbs.

The latest addition to St Giles is an important and interesting one—the new Chapel Royal of the Knights of the Order of the Thistle, which forms an adjunct to the Choir on the south side. Under the will of the late Earl of Leven and Melville, a sum of £40,000 was set aside for the restoration of the Chapel Royal at Holyrood—the nave of the Abbey Church—as a Thistle Chapel; but it was found that the terms of the bequest

31

could not be fulfilled. Through the liberality of Lord Leven and the other heirs, effect has in part been given to the testator's wishes in the form of this richly ornate Gothic structure, one feature of which is its wealth of heraldic embellishments.

The old Church has fallen on kindly days and into appreciative hands. Within it, as around it, obstructions have been cleansed away—all except the three-pence charged to its week-day visitors at the entrance. It is again a noble Church, impressive in the grey austerity of strong and clustered pillars, and the dim rich light that shines through its storied windows. It has become something of a National Valhalla for the great in Church and State—a Temple of Reconciliation preserving the ashes or the memory of men of opposed creeds and parties.

In the Albany Aisle we are asked to recognise evidence of the remorse and penitence of Robert, Duke of Albany—who certainly was a benefactor of St Giles —for the ruthless murder of his nephew David, Duke of Rothesay and heir to the Scottish throne. The Earl of Moray—the "Good Regent" of some, the "Traitor Bastard" of others—sleeps in the Moray Chapel, where sculpture, stained glass, and inscription tell the tale of his virtues and of his assassination at the hands of Bothwellhaugh. In the Chepman Aisle—built by the "Scottish Caxton" in honour of James IV. and his Queen, Margaret Tudor—is a recumbent statue of "the Great Marquis of Montrose." On the other side of the Church, in the Chapel of St Eloi, built by the Craft of Hammermen, a similar honour has been paid to the name of his rival and enemy, "the Great Marquis of Argyle." The sepulchral monument of the family of the

Memorials of War and Peace

Napiers of Merchiston—of whom one was the Inventor of Logarithms—has been removed from the interior to the exterior of the Choir. Tablets have been placed in remembrance of Dean Hanna, who read, for the first and last time, the new service book in St Giles, and of the humble kail-wife who, according to "constant oral tradition," interrupted the reading with the flight of her three-legged stool and the stinging words, "Deil colic the wame o' ye; would ye say mass i' my lug?"

Other memorials there are to the champions who, on one side or the other, fought out with tongue, pen, or sword the long struggle between Prelacy and Presbytery in or around St Giles; and the liturgies and service books over which their quarrels so often raged are laid out for the inspection of the curious. From the walls and pillars hang the tattered flags of old Scottish regiments; and brass, marble, or granite commemorate later and distant battles in which "good Scots blood" has been freely shed, not in civil or religious strife, but for the needs of the Empire. St Giles may still lay claim to be the centre of the nation's religious life; and within it the General Assembly of the Church is opened annually, with the Queen's representative, the Lord High Commissioner, seated in state in the royal pew under the groined roof of the Preston Aisle. But its walls and atmosphere now breathe lessons of unity and forbearance, rather than of the strife and division of old.

CHAPTER IV

OLD HIE-GAIT LIFE

A BROAD and busy highway now runs past the northern
flank of St Giles, while to the south Parliament Square,
its space lately restricted by the projection into it of
the new Thistle Chapel, enjoys—at least when the
Courts are not sitting—something of cloistral seclusion.
Far different were the surroundings of the High Church
in that Edinburgh of the past in which the imagination
loves to dwell. The High Street traffic drained slowly
and with difficulty past the Great Kirk, through a series
of narrow lanes and crooked passages—the " Krames,"
the " Purses," the " Kirk Stile," the " Parliament Close."
Tall buildings were jammed into the middle of the
main street, and raising high their peaked gables, "held
the licht frae the Parish Kirk," as Dunbar complained
four centuries ago. These were the " Luckenbooths,"
which dipped their height—where the " Stinking Stile "
gave access through the block, opposite the head of
Warriston's Close, to the north porch of St Giles—in
order that street passengers might catch a glimpse of
the clock on the tower.

Adjoining to the west was the Old Tolbooth—the
" Heart of Midlothian "—the Prætorium of the town.
By turns it had been the meeting-place of Scottish
Parliaments, of the College of Justice, and of stormy

The Heart of Midlothian

Kirk Assemblies; but latterly it degenerated into a Prison, the character in which it will live in perpetual memory, as the place of durance of Jock Porteous and of Effie Deans. The western end of this grim edifice is believed to have been old in Mary Stewart's time. On a platform looking towards the Lawnmarket was the place of public execution after 1785; and over the northern gable were affixed the heads of "traitors"— among others those of Morton, Montrose, and the Marquis of Argyle. The lock of the Old Tolbooth and other relics of Edinburgh's Bastille have found shelter at Abbotsford.

More to the south, and also ranging close up to the western gable of St Giles, stood the New Tolbooth, or Laigh Council House, built, in Queen Mary's reign, with the stones of the old Chapel of the Holy Rood in the Cowgate. Like its older companion, it was the scene of historic events—of State trials, meetings of the Estates, and ecclesiastical gatherings—before it was given up to the business of the City Fathers, who deliberated here, in a long, low, dimly-lighted room, until better quarters were provided for them in the Royal Exchange. Partly on its site, and on the ground which, until after Knox's time, sloped down towards the Cowgate as the Churchyard of St Giles, have risen the Signet Library and the rest of the classic pile where the High Court of Session is now accommodated; while at the eastern entrance to Parliament Square, the Police Offices of the burgh rise beside the spot where towered, until swept away by fire, the loftiest and, to the taste of our ancestors, the finest of those Towers of Babel which were the roosting-places of Old Edinburgh society.

So precious was space around the High Kirk, that,

Old Hie-Gait Life

as Sir Walter Scott tells us, the little booths of the merchants were "plastered against the Gothic projections and abutments," for all the world like swallows' nests; and the goldsmith's shop of George Heriot—"Jingling Geordie"—where his master and gossip, King James, came often to chat and bargain with the founder of the Hospital, was a tiny "krame" sheltering under the western gable of St Giles. Not less famous in its own way was the shop at the eastern end of the Lucken-booths in which Allan Ramsay set up his wig-blocks when he removed from the sign of the Mercury. Here, in an upper room commanding a magnificent view of the Firth through the vista of the High Street, the poet-barber established his circulating library, and received as visitors Gay and Smollett; here afterwards "Creech's Land" gathered a fresh and rich crop of literary associations as the bookseller's shop of William Creech, the place of publication of the "Mirror" and the "Lounger," and the resort of all the wits and pundits of letters of the Edinburgh of the end of last century.

> Nae mair we see his levee door,
> Philosophers and poets pour,
> And toothy Critics by the score,
> In bloody raw.

Pageant and tragedy were alike familiar to the High Street and the precincts of old St Giles, in the times before the changes of a more peaceful age had swept away the screen of obscuring buildings which had so long veiled "the irregular and grim visage of the Cathedral." Of State ceremonials there remains but a ghost, seen on the days when the heralds and pursuivants of the Lyon Office mount the Cross—the ancient shaft

THE "MERCAT CROCE"

ST GILES CHURCH, INTERIOR.

[*To face page* 36.

The Mercat Croce

of which has been drawn a little aside from its old position and raised on a new pedestal by the liberal act of Mr Gladstone—to make a royal proclamation to the lieges, or when the Lord High Commissioner "walks" in procession from Holyrood to open the General Assembly in St Giles.

Perfunctory and sadly shorn of their former splendour are the modern High Street ceremonials, compared, for instance, with those that attended the visit of Charles I. to his Scottish Capital in 1633, when he opened the first Parliament held in the New Parliament House, and the last in the ancient kingdom ever graced by a kingly presence. "The Old Tolbooth and all St Giles Cathedral," says Thomas Carlyle, "never looked so brave. In the bowels of the High Cross fountain there circulates, impatiently demanding egress, a lake of Claret. Judge if this decoration is a popular one! And a little further on, at the public Weigh-house—what the Scots call a Tron—see the blunt edifice, by plaster, planks, draperies, and upholsteries, is changed to an Olympus, on which hover—the Nine Muses of Antiquity, and much else!"—among the rest, the figure of Fergus the First, the mythical ancestor of the royal line, "in ane convenient habit," to promise his successor, already with the shadow of doom over him, all manner of good fortune.

Rivers of red wine used to flow at the Cross on King's birthdays and other high festivals; and it is recorded that at the Restoration—the occasion when the "kail-wives of the Tron" made a bonfire of their stools, Jenny Geddes's, it is said, among the rest—as many as "thirteen hundred dozen of glasses" were broken on the spot by loyal citizens. But red blood—

Old Hie-Gait Life

the blood of the best as well as of the basest of the land has flowed still more freely. Who can count the harrowing, weird, or quaint spectacles of which Cross, Tron, and Tolbooth have been the centres? From the Cross at midnight sounded the mysterious summons that was the presage of Flodden; and the citizens gathered round it and looked on with feelings unutterable when the "Solemn League and Covenant" was burned here in 1682. It was the spot appointed for major punishments; while its neighbour, the Tron, was the witness of penalties inflicted on minor offenders of the law. Aloft on the scaffold the heads of traitors, patriots, and martyrs fell under the knife of the "Maiden," and thieves and outlaws of distinction had their pre-eminence in birth and crime marked in the manner of their death, as when, in 1603, Alastair Maegregor of Glenstrae was hanged his own height higher than his clansmen, partners with him in "the slaughter of Glenfruin." Not far off was the pillory where "dyvours" or bankrupts were exposed in yellow bonnets and piebald suits, and the "tree mare," ridden on by the drunkard and the scold.

Attached to the Weigh-house, or Salt Tron, was the City Guard House, "a long, low, ugly building, a black snail crawling up the middle of the High Street"; and here was the headquarters of the town sweeps and of those famous protectors of the peace of the burgh, the Town Guards. The beginnings of this body of armed police are lost in antiquity; but for more than a hundred years after their reorganisation, in 1696, the Lochaber axes—of which specimens are preserved in the Municipal Museum—the black uniform and the cocked hats, bound with white tape, of the "Town Rats" were conspicuous

38

"Town Rats" and "Town Callants"

in the High Street, except, as their many foes and critics sneered, when they were wanted. They were part of the humours as well as of the machinery of order of Old Edinburgh; and the ghost of the Black Squad continued to hang about King Charles's statue in Parliament Square, in the shape of two or three time-battered and red-nosed veterans, down to the days of the Waverley Novels. They were recruited chiefly from the Highlands, and to these hot-tempered Celts, many of them discharged soldiers, the dialect of the High Street was an alien tongue. Small wonder if a perpetual war was waged between them and the "town callants," and especially the "baxter lads," who were lodged in the vicinity of the Mealmarket and the Tron.

Of these historic feuds, and of the life and humours of the High Street generally, we get the most vivid pictures in the poems of Robert Fergusson. The unfortunate bard of the "Plainstanes and the Causey" had himself many a brush with the "black banditti," whose exploits he has sung. He paints for us the old "Fourth of June" celebrations, when, in honour of the King's birthday,

> Our bells screed aff a loyal tune,
> Our ancient Castle shoots at noon,
>   Wi' flagstaff buskit;

and how "the blue-coat bodies" march up from the Canongate to cast their scarecrow duds and draw their yearly alms; but chiefly how the "City Guard"

> In military art weel lear'd,
> Wi' powdered pow and shaven beard,
>   Gang through their functions;
> By hostile rabble seldom spared
>   O' clarty unctions.

39

Old Hie-Gait Life

To Hallowfair, and to Leith Races also, those heroes
repair, the "stumps erst used to filabegs, now dight in
splatterdashes"; and after the exploits and hard knocks
of the day are over, they console themselves in some
favourite howff, where they meet their kin, the chairmen
and caddies, over their native usquebaugh—"whisky for
porters, chairmen, and City Guard."

In Fergusson's verse we see a whole panorama of
Old Edinburgh street life, in the days when the
"cumbersome and stinking bigging" that sheltered the
Guard still "rode the rigging" of its main thoroughfare,
and before "the crown of the causey" had been levelled
away, under the direction of the portly city magnates,
in three-cornered hats and kneebreeches, made so
familiar to us in "Kay's Portraits." As soon as

> Morn wi' bonny purple smiles,
> Kisses the air-cock o' St Giles,

the "barefoot housemaids" are abroad, scrubbing the
turnpike stairs, and exchanging amenities with other
early risers. The "stair-head critics" gather in the
Luckenbooths,

> Wi' glowering eye
> Their neighbours' sma'est faults to descry.

Lawyers, merchants, and their clerks repair to business,
to issue forth anon to meet their clients at the Cross, or
to forgather in some favourite coffee-house or oyster-
shop, when the bell gives the signal for the locking of
places of business at two o'clock. This old-fashioned
dinner hour was a busy time during the "Sitting of the
Session," at "Rob Gibb's" and "Indian Peter's";

> Barkeepers now at open door
> Tak' tent as folks gae back and fore;

40

Old High Street Fashions

and there is much replenishing of snuff mulls and sampling of Hollands gin. Business is resumed in the afternoon, until, at the "five-hours bell," the lawyers' clerks begin to "show their faces and rax their een"; or when

> Auld St Giles at aught o'clock
> Gars merchant loons their shoppies lock.

It is now the leisure hour, when fashion comes forth from its closes and throngs the plainstanes; ladies in hoops and pattens, with the "modest bongrace" over the face, parade the pavement, exchanging courtesies with the bucks and "macaronis," or enduring brushes from "mealy bakers," or the "dunts" of the Highland chairmen who jostle in the roadway; while the "daunderin' cit" delights to stray to the Castle Hill or elsewhere, to exhibit his "new kaimed wig and silken hose." Then, with the failing light, the caddie comes forth with his lanthron;

> Through ilka gait the torches blaze,
> And globes send out their blinkin' rays.

The sedan chair and its link-bearers on the way to rout or assembly are in evidence—hackney coaches only came in, a little ahead of umbrellas, between 1760 and 1780—the place of fashionable resort, perhaps, some "laigh" oyster-cellar. The noisy ten-hours drum "gars a' the trades gang daunderin' hame." But the night is only beginning in the Clubs, whose members, "jocose and free, gie a' to merriment and glee," whether they quaff claret and punch in the company of judges of Session and reverend divines in Daunie Douglas's,

41

Old Hie-Gait Life

or Stewart's Oyster-Shop, or more lowly in their tastes,

> To Lucky Middlemass loup in
>   And sit fu' snug,
> Owre oysters and a dram o' gin,
>   Or haddock lug.

Old Edinburgh, it must be confessed, was a dirty as well as a picturesque place. The visitors who praised most the stately aspect of its High Street had something to say in censure of the "sluttish" ways and usages of its inhabitants—usages, it may be said, which were almost imposed on them by the conditions under which they lived. The reproaches which William Dunbar addressed to the "merchants of renown" in the first years of the sixteenth century were not inapplicable in the last half of the eighteenth. "Nane may pass your principal gaits," complained the poet, "for stink of haddocks and of skates." The streets, before Flodden, swarmed with "common minstrels" and beggars, and were cumbered with "vile crafts."

> At your Hie Cross, where gold and silk
> Suld be, there are but curds and milk ;
> And at your Tron but cockle and wilk,
> Panshes, puddings for Jock and Jame.

And, after Culloden, Edinburgh still bore the reproach of being "the dirtiest town in Europe." The customs of the closes are preserved in the experiences of Humphrey Clinker and Winnifred Jenkins, and in the famous law plea concerning the "waterdrap" in Mary King's Close. Pigs rooted in the dunghills of the High Street; fish offal and cabbage leaves were strewn in front of the Tron; the oyster-criers had their stances

Clarty, but Cosy

at the head of the Fishmarket Close, near the chief rendezvous of the literati and people of fashion; stalls and booths invaded the roadway; by the Cross Well stood a long queue of "water caddies"; the streets were "infested" with ballad singers. A petition from the "nobility, gentry, and magistrates" inhabiting the steep and strait passage of Burnet's Close throws a curious light upon the town and its customs in 1714. They complain that, by widening and improving their close, they had only made it "a convenient short-cut to the slaughter-house," so that they are "masterfully and cruelly opprest by the pudding-wives, nausious servants carrying beast's blood, their graith, tripes, and other nastiness," and by "the rustick servants and mastive dogs of the fleshers, driving up the Wind their great fedd cattle, Highland cowes, sheep, and lambs."

Truly the beggar's toe galled the noble's kibes in Auld Reekie Hie Street. Poverty and riches elbowed each other on the pavement, and entered and issued from the same close-head. Long after the court had forsaken the city, and after the clash of arms had ceased to be heard on the causeway, saint and sinner, gentle and simple, dwelt amicably together; and a section of one of the High Street tenements would last century have shown a section of society from top to bottom, arranged in regular strata, touching each other, yet never mixing. The humble tradesman lived on the ground floor or in the cellar, while the lord of Session or the dame of quality mounted to the fourth or fifth storey.

It was this strange conjunction of squalor and fashion which gave its peculiar charm to the old High Street. The modern street may be airier and better

43

swept; but neither street nor street life can compare in picturesqueness with the Edinburgh known to Queen Mary and John Knox, to Montrose and the Covenanters, or to Dr Johnson and Dr Adam Smith. The change by which the dregs of the population rose to the top of the High Street houses, and filled the place once occupied by the best and most gifted of the land, was already noted and commented on before the close of last century. "The Lord Justice Clerk Tinwald's house," says a writer of 1783, "was lately possessed by a French teacher; Lord President Craigie's is possessed by a Rouping-wife or Saleswoman; Lord Drummore's house was lately left by a Chairman for want of accommodation." The mansion of the great Marquis of Argyle, in the Castle Hill, had already fallen to the estate of a hosier's shop; and the house that belonged to the Duke of Douglas at the Union was in the occupation of a wheelwright.

There can be no doubt that the improvement of Edinburgh meant for long the degradation of the High Street. A crowd in that quarter of the city is apt to this day to be a gathering of the "great unwashed"; vice and penury are found housed in panelled rooms that are reached by staircases of carved oak. But the tide has turned from ebb; and with more air and light, prosperity and even gentility may flow back again into the High Street.

LOWER HIGH STREET AND TRON KIRK.

[*To face page* 44.

CHAPTER V

FROM THE TRON TO THE CASTLE HILL

To this day the "Tron Corner" is the great trysting-place of the Old Town; and glass is still abundantly broken at it with the ringing-in of the New Year. We may take it as the starting-point of a rapid survey of the High Street closes and houses as far as the Castle, returning hither later to continue the tour down towards Holyrood.

The formation of the South Bridge, in 1785, was the next great breach made in the continuity of the High Street, after the building of the North Bridge, which the new thoroughfare prolonged southward in a series of arches bestriding the Cowgate valley in the direction of the University. It was part of a grand scheme of improvements carried out under Provost Sir William Hunter Blair, who has left his name stamped on Hunter Square and on Blair Street. It removed old Merlioun's, or "Merlin's Wynd," called after the Frenchman—

> Merlin, who laid Auld Reekie's causey,
> And made her o' his wark richt saucy;

and the scheme included the levelling of the High Street, by which the "causey's crown" finally disappeared. Kennedy's Close, on the site of Hunter

From the Tron to the Castle Hill

Square, was also swept away, and with it the house in which George Buchanan died, "without means to defray his funeral expense." The Tron Kirk, a dingy building dating from Charles I.'s reign, with a Dutch-looking tower, which was replaced by a spire after the great fire of 1824, was left, where it still is, an island at the intersection of traffic.

By a new plan of city improvements, a whole series of old closes from the Tron to the neighbourhood of Parliament Square, on the south side of the High Street, have been weeded out, and replaced by open spaces, and by blocks of "model tenements." The sanitary advantages of this change are manifest; but alas for the landmarks of Edinburgh history that have been carted into oblivion with the old houses of Bell's Wynd, and of Stevenlaw's, Burnet's, Borthwick's, the Old Assembly, the Old Fishmarket, and the Covenant Closes!

It would take a book to recount their story; and, indeed, Mr John Reid has devoted a volume to the purpose. Stevenlaw's Close was once the home of the "merchant princes" of the town; near its head was the "Black Turnpike"—according to one tradition, the place of refuge of Mary Stewart after Carberry. The not less celebrated "Clamshell Turnpike," the episcopal residence of that "magnificent housekeeper" but poor priest, George Crichton, Bishop of Dunkeld and Abbot of Holyrood in the days of James V., stood at the High Street entrance to the adjoining Bell's Wynd. Here, in "my Lord Hume's lodging," Mary and Darnley are said to have sought shelter after the "slaughter of Davie"; here harboured later the blue-gowned "Bedesmen of St Thomas" and the remnant of the City Guard. In a

Departed Landmarks

third storey in Bell's Wynd lived quietly the father of the "Admirable Crichton," while his son was pursuing his meteor-like course through the universities of the Continent; from it issued the first numbers of the *Edinburgh Gazette*; and Burns often entered it bringing songs for the "Museum" of his friend James Johnson, engraver and music-seller. It was sacred not only to music and letters, but to the "art of periwig-making," which had an "academy" and a professor, and kept "live bears on the premises" in Bell's Wynd. "St Mary's Chapel" flitted hither from Niddry's Wynd. It was also the headquarters of Masonry, and the building, now removed, in which the Grand Lodge met, became successively a Trades' Hall, where assembled the Incorporations of Wrights and of Weavers (the former for a time with Deacon Brodie as convener), a Congregational Church, and a Children's Shelter.

In Burnet's Close lived Dr Hugh Blair and Lord Auchinleck; and here, it seems probable, Bozzy was born. An old sixteenth-century house, with turreted staircase projecting into the close, a window lighting the kitchen fireplace, and an oak-panelled oratory within, seems to have had no particular history; it has disappeared with the "eighteen hundreds." On the other hand, the "long room," entered by a secret door off the kitchen of an ancient edifice in the branch alley of Covenant Close, has always been identified with the signing of the Solemn League and Covenant, when that national pledge was renewed in 1649. It was, in the popular belief, miraculously preserved during the great conflagration of 1700, when the tall lands built by the persecuting Bailie Robertson were relentlessly consumed by fire; but its semi-sacred fame did not prevent it from

From the Tron to the Castle Hill

being turned into a tavern and oyster-shop. In Covenant Close, too, a host of law lords, including Macqueen of Braxfield, the "Hanging Judge," had residences convenient to the Court; and in it Nanty Ewart studied crabbed divinity.

The associations of the other closes nearer St Giles have a more convivial and literary flavour. The Old Assembly Close recalls memories of the eighteenth-century dancing assemblies, at which Miss Nicky Murray was presiding genius, and whose stiff formality has been described by no less a guest than Oliver Goldsmith. For nearly half a century, down to 1766, the assemblies abode here, after removal from the West Bow, and they only halted a little time in Bell's Wynd before departing, with fashion, to the New Town. In Old Assembly Close dwelt that Lord Durie, President of the Court, who was spirited away from the Figgate Whins to the Borders by moss-trooping "Christie's Will"; from the adjoining Borthwick's Close would emerge Lady St Clair, wife of the builder of Rosslyn Chapel, in almost princely state, attended by "eighty torch-bearers"; and in the Old Fleshmarket Close, still further west, George Heriot began married life.

Some of the most favoured and famous of the last-century taverns and coffee-houses were in this quarter. Stewart's Oyster-House, where the jovial members of the Mirror Club regaled themselves, and whence they issued to post poems and articles in Creech's contributors' box, was down the Old Fleshmarket entry, which gave access also to the office of the old *Courant*— frequented, a hundred years after Daniel Defoe's editorship, by Walter Scott and his literary and political cronies—and to the first Edinburgh Post Office.

PARLIAMENT SQUARE.

[*To face page* 48.

The "Great Fire"

Strangely altered since Sir Walter's time is the neighbourhood of this eastern access to Parliament Square or Close to which we have now come. Scott himself was a looker-on at the fire which failed to destroy "Salamander Land" but consumed the other sky-raking tenements, "the pride of Edinburgh," that occupied the site of the present Police Offices and part of the entrance to the Square; while Nasmyth, of the steam-hammer, surveyed the scene from the Crown of St Giles. John's Coffee-House stood near the spot to which the Mercat Croce, raised once again on its "turreted octagon of stone," has been removed. The narrow passage into the Parliament Close was Edinburgh's Paternoster Row; and in it was the little shop in which Kay sold prints and took note of the town worthies and characters who reappear in his "Portraits."

The "Great Fire" entirely altered the aspect of the Parliament Square. The "President's Stairs," descending into the Cowgate, disappeared with the fifteen-storey houses that once rose beside them in a sheer wall of masonry, 130 feet in height. The quaint façade of the Courts of Parliament and of Justice, built in 1632, was replaced, or rather masked, by the present heavy piazzaed frontage, surmounted by sphinxes that not inappropriately guard the portals of the law. The stone figures of "Justice" and "Mercy" that ornamented the chief doorway have lately been recovered from a backgarden in Drummond Place, and occupy a place in the Parliament Hall. The Square is still on most days a quiet haven to which one can retire from the stir of the High Street, and call up the visions of the past. For three centuries and a half the great and the learned of the land have paced the stones; counsellors of state, nobles, and bishops have stood here in high and hot debate; the spot has witnessed feasts over which Royalty presided, and scenes of riot and bloodshed; many a poor wretch has taken his last look of the free sky over the pinnacles of St Giles from the plainstones of Parliament Square. If spirits walk, it should be thronged with the ghosts of the eccentric old judges and the famous advocates who passed in and out so many hundred times in their lives; and those "maggots of the law," Peter Peebles and Saddletree, should still be furtively haunting the place that once held them, soul and body.

But for many hours of the day almost the only visible figure in the close may be the leaden, bandy-legged, and begarlanded Charles II., "bestriding a tun-bellied charger," and seeming, as R. L. Stevenson says, to be strolling clumsily away from his dangerous neighbour, John Knox, whose grave, marked simply by the initials and the date 1572, is a few yards behind. Opposite is the door of the Court of Justiciary, and in the south-west corner, under the arcade, the entrance to the Great Hall of Parliament, now familiarly known as the "Parliament Lobby." Where the three Scottish Estates once met under one roof, counsel in black gowns and powdered wigs walk up and down, if the Court be sitting, in earnest discourse with agents or clients, or tourists drop in and stare around upon the effigies of the mighty men of law ranged round the walls.

A noble and lofty chamber, 120 feet in length, and with a fine old oak roof as its chief ornament, is this "hall of lost footsteps" of the Scottish Bar; and it holds mementoes of the forms and faces—or, at the least, of the heraldic bearings—of nearly the whole line

The Hall of Lost Footsteps

of illustrious lawyers and statesmen who have graced the Court of Session since its institution in 1532 by James V.—the scene depicted on the stained glass of the great southern window, below which once stood the royal throne. The great legal and judicial dynasties of the Dundases of Arniston and the Dalrymples of Stair are represented by picture, statue, and bust in this Gallery of Justice; here, too, are brilliant and familiar ornaments of the bench and bar, like Henry Erskine, Henry Cockburn, and Francis Jeffrey; men who left a deep mark, sinister or otherwise, on the national history and on the statute book, such as the "Bluidy Mackenzie" and Lord President Duncan Forbes; judges of the old hard-drinking school—the Newtons, the Eskgroves, and their compeers—whose judgments from the bench were flavoured by broad Scots and sometimes by broad jokes; and other eminent lawyers, Mansfield and Brougham among them, who cast only a reflected or a meteor-like light on the Scottish Courts. One misses, in the ranks of faces that look down from its walls, that of Walter Scott. Yet the "Shirra" is the true genius of the place; his favourite seat by the fire is pointed out; his burly form, crowned by the white "peak" at which Lord "Peter" Robertson once threw a jest that was returned with usury, still seems to hobble back and forth among the other shadows of the Parliament Hall. It is still, says rumour, a mart and exchange for gossip; and the brotherhood of the briefless, with whom Stevenson served his apprenticeship, are said to devote themselves, in the dearth of other work, to the manufacture of "good stories."

But grave business is also done here; and the Macer mounts his box in the Lobby, to call the cases

that come before the Lords Ordinary of the Outer
House, no longer compelled to deal out justice at
"side-bars" within the Great Hall, but relegated to the
seclusion of four small court-rooms at its southern end;
or to summon witnesses and litigants before the judges
of the Inner House, who sit in two Divisions, in groups
of four, to hear appeals in civil causes.

Three Libraries, attached to three important legal
bodies, find housing in the precincts of the Parliament
House. One is that of the Solicitors before the
Supreme Courts, whose quarters are in a handsome and
ornate new building of red stone dominating the
Cowgate. The Signet Library, peculiarly rich in works
of Scottish antiquity and topography, is accommodated
in two spacious halls—the upper one remarkable for its
beauty of design and ornament—in the north-western
wing of the Parliament buildings, adjoining St Giles
and the High Street. Older and more famous is the
Advocates' Library, of which Sir George Mackenzie
was founder in the seventeenth century, and David
Hume librarian in the eighteenth.

Since it was burned out of its original quarters by
the fire of 1700, the Advocates' Library has been
lodged chiefly in the "Laigh Parliament House,"
underneath the Great Hall. In the descent to this
somewhat dim and musty world of books, one is
reminded of the free field of acted history, by the Earl
Marshal's pennon, carried at Flodden by "Black John
Skirving." The long, low chamber, with its many-
arched recesses crammed from floor to ceiling with
books, is alleged, by unauthenticated tradition, to have
been the place of question and torture of the prisoners
brought before the Privy Council in the "Killing

The Advocates' Library

Time." Some half a million volumes of books and manuscripts, some of them of a rarity and value beyond price, are collected here and in the neighbouring apartments; and among the relics laid open to the eyes of the visitor are the "King's Confession," Scotland's renunciation of the Papacy; the "Solemn League," by which, two generations later, the nation abjured Prelacy; holograph letters of Mary Stewart and of her great-grandsons, Charles II. and James VII.; illuminated missals and breviaries; old black-letter editions of the classics; and last, not least, the original MS. of "Waverley," all fitly presided over by a seated figure of Sir Walter.

The closes on the north side of High Street are as much crammed with history and haunted by legend as their neighbours opposite. Time has, if possible, laid his hand on them more heavily. In one respect, at least, they have an immense advantage over the alleys across the way. These dive down, by paths often foul as well as narrow and slippery, into the murky and unlovely depths of the Cowgate. The north side closes are still steeper. Winds from the sea and from the hills blow freely through some of them; peeping down the entries as you walk westward you get an occasional glimpse, charming as it is surprising, of the sky and the trees, of the busy crowd and stately frontage of Princes Street, and beyond these of the Firth and the Fife hills, when you only looked for an obscure vista of smoke-grimed dwellings.

Some of these closes have been so swept and garnished as to lose almost all trace of their former identity. From the Old Stamp Office Close has been entirely cleared away Fortune's Tavern, where Assembly

From the Tron to the Castle Hill

levees have been held; where once lived the Countess of Eglinton, to whom Allan Ramsay dedicated his "Gentle Shepherd," and possessor, along with her seven beautiful daughters, of the "Eglinton air" admired even by the bearish author of "Rasselas." The Anchor Close and Craig's Close long gave access to the premises of the *Scotsman* newspaper; Dr John Hill Burton, Professor Blackie, and Alexander Russel have been among the host of later notabilities, in letters and journalism, who have been familiar with the Anchor stairs and the legends preserved above its door-ways. But the literary history of the close began long before. Putting aside the tradition of "Queen Mary's Council Chamber," it was here, under Daunie Douglas's roof-tree, that the "Crochallan Fencibles" met, with "blythe Willie Smellie" as presiding genius, and Burns as a guest. As tavern, or as printing-house, the "howff" in the Anchor Close has known the faces of a host of the Scottish literati of the last century and a half, from the time of Hume and Blair, and Beattie and Henry Mackenzie downward. Nor can less be said of the brilliant past of dingy Craig's Close. Here was the "heigh booth" of old Andro Hart, the printer; here, two centuries later, Provost Creech held his morning levees; here also was the headquarters of Constable, and of the "Edinburgh Reviewers"; and in the "Isle of Man Tavern" Robert Fergusson, David Herd, Raeburn, and other heroes of the Cape Club spent their evenings in "mirth, music, and porter deepest-dyed."

The Royal Exchange buildings, in which the Municipality made its home after abandoning its gloomy quarters in the Laigh Council House, took the place of a cluster of ancient houses and closes, of which only a

THE ROYAL EXCHANGE

The Municipal Museum

faint memory remains. With Mary King's Close disappeared a host of gruesome ghosts and traditions. By the entrance to the Exchange quadrangle stood the "ludging" of the Lord Provost of the day, Sir Simon Preston of Craigmillar, to which Mary, Queen of Scots, was conducted by the Edinburgh rabble after her surrender to the Lords of the Congregation, and where she slept for the last time in her capital. Clerihugh's Tavern, in Writers' Court, the scene of the "high jinks" described in "Guy Mannering," has, as already noted, been incorporated in the addition recently made to the Council Chambers.

At the back, these Municipal Buildings rise to a height of nine or ten storeys, and seem to overhang, like a sheer cliff, the winding Cockburn Street below. Within they accommodate, along with the offices of the burgh officials, a little Municipal Museum, where one can examine a collection of curious and interesting mementoes of the old burghal life—carved and inscribed door lintels, weights and measures, bells and water-pipes; the veritable muskets and Lochaber axes in use during the Porteous Riots, and other "auld nick-nackets"—and perhaps even more interesting still, a fine series of pictures in oil and of water-colour drawings and engravings of the Edinburgh of the past, and, in a separate room, a valuable collection of Burns's MSS. and other relics of the National Bard. To the west they now extend to Warriston Close, steepest of the steep Edinburgh alleys, whose "steps," plunging down to the level of Waverley Bridge, have been climbed by many generations of "town's bairns." It is named after that dour champion of the Covenant, Johnston of Warriston, who suffered ignominious death not many yards from the close-head.

From the Tron to the Castle Hill

His house had belonged at an earlier date to his maternal grandfather, the great feudal lawyer, Sir Thomas Craig, and Cromwell and his officers are believed to have been entertained here. But the researches of Mr Robert Miller appear to have established the fact that Warriston Close had a more illustrious "indweller"—that where the extension to the Council Chambers has been built stood the real "John Knox's House," where the leader of the Scottish Reformation lived during five or six of the most memorable years of his own and of the nation's life; that it was the house to which he brought home his young bride; where he supped and held counsel with ambassadors and nobles; and whither he returned, weary enough no doubt, from fiery preachings in St Giles, or not less fiery interviews with the Queen at Holyrood.

The east side of Warriston Close has long been occupied by the printing-house founded by the two brothers, William and Robert Chambers—one, the restorer of St Giles, and the other the writer of the "Traditions of Edinburgh." Further on come Roxburgh Close, once the town residence of the Kerrs of Cessford, Earls and afterwards Dukes of Roxburgh; and then Advocates' Close, named after the astute Revolution lawyer and King's Advocate, Stewart of Goodtrees, known to his contemporaries as "Jamie Wylie." We may imagine Colonel Mannering and Dandie Dinmont stumbling down the narrow passage, for in it lived Andrew Crosbie, the original of Councillor Pleydell. Byres' Close has been nigh-hand squeezed out of existence. Yet here is a fragment of the stately ancient mansion, with gables and finialed dormer windows commanding a grand prospect to the north, in which

ADVOCATE'S CLOSE.

From a water colour by James Heron.

Historic Closes

of old abode that time-serving prelate, Adam Bothwell, Bishop of Orkney and Commendator of Holyrood, who, after officiating at the ill-starred marriage of Mary Stewart to the Earl of Bothwell, afterwards placed the crown on the head of Mary's son. The Queen herself has feasted in this house; and so too has James VI., in the time of the Bishop's successor, Lord Holyroodhouse, who accompanied his royal master to England; and it was the home of the unhappy Lady Anne Bothwell, of the ballad.

St Giles Street has broken through the ranks of the High Street houses, whose back lands and gardens descended, over ground now covered by the Bank of Scotland and Market Street, to the Town Wall and the Nor' Loch. The stump of Dunbar's Close is left, but nearly all trace is lost of the " Rose and Thistle," where Cromwell's troopers are said to have been quartered; while, through the changes in the thoroughfare, the sites of Beth's Wynd, Adamson's Close, and Fullarton Wynd, on the opposite side of the way, have become somewhat conjectural. These ancient alleys, often mentioned in old Edinburgh annals, occupied ground on or beside which now stand the statue of the fifth Duke of Buccleuch and the Midlothian County Buildings. Until a few years ago, the County business was transacted in a structure which presented handsome façades of fluted Ionic columns towards St Giles and the High Street, and its " seamy side " to George IV. Bridge, where the passenger, by looking over a low wall, could get a peep of a narrow passage marking the line of a more cele-brated High Street close. This was Libberton's Wynd, memorable for having at its head the scaffold on which Burke, the murderer, and many other criminals suffered the law's last sentence; and in its lower recesses, "Johnie Dowie's"—the "Mermaid Tavern" of the Edinburgh of a hundred years ago—a convivial haunt of Robert Burns and of his cronies, William Nichol and Allan Masterton.

The Midlothian authorities have lately replaced the former County Buildings by a structure, appropriate to the fine site, that affords more ample accommodation and present a more seemly frontage to George IV. Bridge. The name of that wide and handsome street, which here branches south from the High Street in the direction of Bristo Port, is a memorial of the visit to Edinburgh of the "First Gentleman in Europe," whose presence in his Scottish capital filled its citizens, with Sir Walter Scott at their head, with loyal enthusiasm. It was one of the Old Town improvements begun before the close of George IV.'s reign. Its formation entailed the destruction of a number of ancient tenements, besides those of Libberton's Wynd, none of them, however, so well worthy of preservation as Robert Gourlay's House, in the Old Bank Close, on whose site now rises the Tudor frontage of Melbourne Place. "Gourlay's House," lying conveniently near the Tolbooth, and the property of a wealthy servitor of James VI., was a frequent scene of "ward" and refuge in the troublous years at the latter end of the sixteenth century. The Regent Morton ranged restlessly up and down the floor of one of its chambers, "clanking on his finger and his thowmbe," on the night before his head was set up "on a prick on the highest gable of the Tolbooth." The King himself took shelter in it from the lawless attempts of Francis, Earl of Bothwell. The Earl of Huntly and Kirkaldy of Grange were among those held in ward in the Old

THE MOUND FROM PRINCES STREET GARDENS.

[*To face page* 58.

Old Bank Close

Bank Close, where also occurred, in the year of the Revolution, the deliberate slaughter, at his own door, of Sir George Lockhart, President of the Court of Session, by Chiesley of Dalry.

At the foot of this historic close, which drew its designation from the fact that the first Bank of Scotland was housed up its dark entry before removal to the breezy front of the Mound, was the dwelling in which the great lawyer, Sir Thomas Hope, founder of the House of Hopetoun, lived at the time when he helped to frame the Solemn League and Covenant. The site is now covered by the Free Library—the gift to the town of Mr Andrew Carnegie—which rises from the "dark profound" of the Cowgate, and contributes, with the Sheriff-Court Buildings and other public structures, to the architectural effect of George IV. Bridge.

Bank Street, which continues that thoroughfare at right angles with the High Street, is an outlet of much older date from the contracted heart of the Old Town. Down its winding track, and over the Earthen Mound, has flowed northward for a century, and still flows, the stream of Edinburgh's notables, when the hour comes for their release from the Courts and the Council Chambers in the High Street. Walter Scott and Lockhart have often sauntered by this airy road towards Castle Street, admiring the grandeur of the view, or discussing the next Waverley novel as they went; and Christopher North and Aytoun, with perhaps the "Shepherd" in tow, have strolled by the Mound to the New Town, purposing a halfway halt at "Maga's."

CHAPTER VI

THE LAWNMARKET AND THE CASTLE HILL

AS is now usually reckoned, the Lawnmarket begins where the line of High Street is intersected at Bank Street. No longer are its causeys occupied by the canvas booths of the merchants in lawn and other woven stuffs from whom it took its name. It is many a day since the Weigh-house, or "Butter Tron," at the head of the West Bow, intercepted the prospect Castlewards. Dealers in butter and other farm produce, as well as the sellers of cloth, held their fair in this spacious "place," almost under the guns of the citadel. It was the old city's "West End," in which ambassadors and other visitors of consideration had what was then thought princely lodging.

At the gateway at the Bow Head, receptions were given to guests whom Edinburgh delighted to honour. Thus, at the first coming from France of the fair young Queen of Scots, welcome was given to her, by a quaint and ingenious allegory, at the Butter Tron. From a cloud emerged a "Bonny Bairn," who presented her with a Bible and a Psalm Book, before "the cloud steikit," and the bright vision disappeared from sight— a more significant emblem of Mary's fortunes than devisers or onlookers imagined. In later as well as

THE BOW-HEAD AND LAWNMARKET.

(From a water-colour after W. L. Leitch.)

[*To face page* 60.

The Lawnmarket

earlier times, the Lawnmarket Weigh-house was used as a redoubt or blockhouse in defence or attack of the Castle. Cromwell employed it for both purposes in 1650, finally clearing away the original building, which, to judge by old prints, had a spire and other picturesque features. It was "re-edified," in a mean style, at the Restoration; and was turned to account, during his blockade of the Castle, by Prince Charles Edward, whose officers had their quarters in the adjoining Milne's Court; finally, it was cleared away in 1822 to make room for the public entry of George the Fourth.

Till quite recently, two or three of its once characteristic timber-fronted lands beetled over the Lawnmarket; one in particular, at the head of West Bow—in which the founder of the publishing firm of Nelson began business in a humble way—will be long remembered and regretted. There were forestairs and "low-browed shops," in which the imagination could, without difficulty, place the "Nag's Head," kept by Mrs Saddletree, in the Lawnmarket, with Effie Deans as "servant lass." Most of its genuinely archaic features have now gone. But there are still few street vistas in Europe that excel in bold pictorial effect the view of the Lawnmarket and the Castle Hill, whether one gazes back upon it from the Castle and the Esplanade, or looks up the winding and narrowing defile towards the battlements of the citadel. The pavements are raised several steps above the level of the roadway; the lofty houses have still, in gables and windows, some reminiscences of their former picturesqueness; while the Assembly Hall spire is a graceful object in the middle distance.

In the Lawnmarket closes improvements of new and old date have made a complete transmogrification. To

The Lawnmarket and the Castle Hill

the south, where the gardens of the town house of the Dukes of Buccleuch once sloped all the way down to the Cowgate, the descent of the remanent alleys is arrested halfway by the piazzaed terrace of Victoria Street, overhanging the winding thoroughfare which is now the chief access to the Grassmarket; while the "sanctified bends of the Bow," the quarters of Knights Templar and Hospitallers, and afterwards of elect saints of the Covenant and turbulent workers in leather and hardware, are represented mainly by steep flights of stairs. To the north, the tall walls of the back lands that domineer over Bank Street and the Mound are already of an age and standing that entitle them to be counted among the city antiquities.

There has been of late a gutting-out of historic Lawnmarket closes, and an open space now extends from James's Court on the west to Paterson's and Baxter's Closes on the east. Entering the latter by an archway wide enough for an Old Edinburgh street, you can glance from the black-letter inscription on the lintel let into the wall on the right to the tenement on the left, within which, one stair up, Burns found humble lodgings, at 1s. 6d. per week, with his early friend, Richmond, when he made his first acquaintance with Edinburgh society. Lady Stair's Close—before Bank Street the chief access from the High Street to the Mound—is immediately adjoining, and Lord Rosebery has made a gift to the town, after restoration, of the fine old mansion, built by Sir William Gray of Pittendrum in 1622. It takes its name from a Countess-Dowager of Stair who occupied it in the first half of the eighteenth century, the mother-in-law of the more celebrated Lady Stair, who "led Edinburgh fashion in the second flat of

David Hume at Home

a common stair in a narrow Old Town close," and who saw, in the time of her first marriage, with Viscount Primrose, the vision of her peccant husband's bridal in the Low Countries, as told us in the tale of "My Aunt Margaret's Mirror."

The Lawnmarket front of this close has been known since the early part of the seventeenth century as Gladstone's Land, so named after a worthy burgher belonging to the same vigorous Border family as the famous Prime Minister of the name. Its face has altered of late. But, continuing the exploration of the linked series of closes behind, one can view in James's Court the front of a solid and lofty "land," which the years have altered only by making more weather-beaten and soot-begrimed since David Hume moved into it, when George the Third had been two years on the throne. David— "a fine, guid-natured cratur, but waik-minded," as his mother described him—had been a tenant of Riddle's Close, on the opposite side of the Lawnmarket, and had plunged down into the jaws of the Canongate as far as Jack's Close before he came to reside in James's Court.

Hume had been content in his home over the way with "a maid and a cat, cleanliness, warmth, light, and plenty." And he was happy also here, where his house-keeping was on a rather more ambitious scale. His "History" now off his hands, he had more time to entertain his friends—Adam Smith, Drs Robertson and Blair, Lord Kames, and the rest—who looked with him from his windows in the third storey of James's Court (twice that height above the Mound behind) over the Nor' Loch and the beginnings of the New Town, to the Forth and the Fife hills. So much in his element did the cheerful philosopher feel in his Lawnmarket refuge, that when he returned to it from his short experience of diplomacy and Paris high life, he wrote that he was settled in James's Court, "body and soul." Yet a few years later he is found in the first flight of fashion across the Valley. Boswell afterwards tenanted these historic chambers, and played the host in them to Paoli and to Dr Johnson, who, while gambolling clumsily among the Edinburgh wits, and earning from the wife of his biographer the title of "Ursa Major," little dreamed that he had been "entrapped into the arch-sceptic's very mansion."

Riddle's Close, on the south side of the Lawnmarket, of which mention has just been made as connected with Hume and his "History," is one of the best preserved and most interesting of the Old Edinburgh alleys. Here, as across the highway, are apparent the taste and enterprise of Professor Geddes and his associates, who, in their restorations of Old High Street buildings, have had in view not merely the preservation of their picturesque features, but high social and educational purposes. The close forms a double courtyard, and the inner sanctuary especially has an air of seclusion and distinction rarely met with in these days as an element of the picturesque in the former haunts of Auld Reekie fashion and letters. Nearly all these closes have changed their designations more than once in their time, and this one was long named after Bailie MacMorran, a worthy magistrate slain in a riot of the High School boys more than three centuries since. His house appears to have been occasionally used for civic entertainments. It is at present occupied as a Mission and Lecture Hall by the United Free High Church. King James and his Queen, Anne of Denmark, are said

SOMERVILLE'S LAND, LAWNMARKET

(From a drawing by B. J. Home.)

[To face page 64.

Deacon Brodie

to have been feasted, at a banquet given in honour of the Duke of Holstein, in the principal chamber, which continues, like the rest of this typical example of the sixteenth-century town mansion of the better class, to possess features that are reminiscent of its period and history. A neighbouring portal invites one to explore it, not so much by its aspect as by the label it bears of "Brodie's Close." Within it was the house of the "Jekyll and Hyde" of Edinburgh domestic annals and traditions—of that "Deacon - Convener of the Wrights" whose twofold life of villainy and industry— of reputable citizenship and of midnight gambling and burglary—has made a mark in the memory of the town and of the world. It is the world's way that earlier and worthier possessors and name-fathers of this Lawnmarket block—the learned and generous Littles of Craigmillar, who were founders of the University and its library—should be forgotten, and the infamous William Brodie held in perpetual remembrance.

At its head, beyond the West Bow and the site of the Weigh-house, the Lawnmarket tapers into the Castle Hill, which widens suddenly into the spacious and airy promenade and exercise-ground of the Esplanade, lying directly under the guns of the Half-Moon Battery, and overlooking Princes Street and its gardens, on the north and on the south the crowded gables and chimney-pots of the Grassmarket and the West Port. To the left deviates the comparatively modern thoroughfare of Johnston Terrace, winding towards St Cuthbert's Church round the southern front of the Castle Rock, whose cliffs, tufted with wild flowers and crowned by the walls and battlements of the citadel, rise sheer above the roadway, while the ground on the other side slopes

The Lawnmarket and the Castle Hill

rapidly down to the Grassmarket and the King's Stables Road.

Scott's "Kittle Nine Steps" have been blasted away in the interest of public safety. But, straining the eyes, one can discern, above the trees and shrubs that screen the western and more accessible side of the Rock, the postern, with an inscription over it, to which "Bonnie Dundee" climbed to hold parley with the Duke of Gordon, the Governor of the Castle, before riding away to raise the standard of King James in the North. Continuing the route by the West Princes Street garden walks and the ruins of the Wellhouse Tower, under the overhanging crag surmounted by the Argyle Battery, one can complete the circuit of the Rock, returning by the Castle Braes back to the Castle Hill.

This access from the city to the citadel makes a great figure in local history. It is the neck which unites the trunk of Old Edinburgh—the High Street—with its head, the Castle. Before the ground was levelled and "made up," about the middle of last century, with earth and rubbish from the foundations of the New City Chambers, the narrow ridge on which the Castle Hill houses are built continued in an uneven line to the portal and drawbridge of the Castle. On this scrimp space of "debateable land" once stood stake, gallows, and heading block. Witches and warlocks have been "worried" on the Castle Hill; "heretics" have been burned, and traitors—real or suspected—done to death with tortures, king, nobles, and people looking on. Here was the scene of the cruel execution of the beautiful Lady Glamis, suspected of practising sorcery against the life of James V., her imprisoned husband

Castle Hill Scenes

and son spectators of her death from the Castle walls above. The first smoke of the martyrs of the Reformation went up from this high place.

The Castle Hill has been an avenue of State processions in days when Edinburgh Castle was a royal residence and Parliament met on the summit of the Rock; and the site of the Esplanade was constituted, by royal mandate, part of the soil of Nova Scotia, in order that money might be coined by the investiture in batches of Charles I.'s "baronets of Nova Scotia." Naturally, this single way of approach to the Castle has witnessed struggles that decided for a time the fate of city and kingdom; and tradition has it that a cannon ball lodged in the wall of an old building, the most westerly of the Castle Hill houses, facing the "King's Bastion," and bearing the date 1630, was the last shot fired from the guns of Edinburgh Castle in the Scottish civil wars. This was, of course, in the '45, since when the "Hill of Strife and Sorrow" has had time to gather associations of a more pacific and cheerful kind. The slopes of the Castle Hill were favourite resorts of the sweethearting couples of last century; the "cits" poured hither from the closes to take the air and to display their finery; "wagering" on the green and open promenade was a form of Sunday desecration denounced by our stricter forefathers. Crowds still come to this high place of the city to listen to military music, and to watch the martial exercises of the garrison, or to look abroad over the roofs of the Old Town and the New.

On both sides of the Castle Hill there formerly congregated a number of ancient and stately houses, some of which had in their day official relations with their

The Lawnmarket and the Castle Hill

neighbour, the Castle. The "Palace" of Mary of Guise was one of the buildings which had to make way for the Free Church College and Assembly Hall. Outside and inside it had many curious architectural features, in moulded doorways, carved panels, and secret oratories; but in its best days it must have been an inconvenient royal residence. All the more easy was it to connect this grim lodging with the troublous experiences of the Queen Regent, brought up in the gay Court of France, when she attempted to guide the fortunes of the rough Northern Kingdom. It stood conveniently near the Castle; and the same could be said yet more emphatically of the "Gordon House," in which a Duchess of Gordon lived while her husband held the citadel for King James at the Revolution of 1689.

A Board School has now partly usurped the site; and the remains of the other "seats of the mighty" on the Castle Hill—the town houses of great nobles and country magnates—are few and dwindling. The names of half-demolished closes recall the fact that the Semples of Castle Semple—a house whose branches produced more than one writer of vigorous vernacular verse—dwelt on the Castle Hill, and that opposite was the house in which that impetuous rider and fighter, Sir David Baird of Seringapatam, spent his boyhood. Ramsay Lane is supposed to be consecrate to the memory, not of Allan of the "Gentle Shepherd," but to an early "Laird of Cockpen." But with the cheery little poet who, with a fine eye to situation, built his "goose-pie" villa on the edge of the Castle Braes, when he had made a little competency by his barbering, his song-writing and other literary ventures, the locality

The Head-streams of Presbytery

will always be associated. Ramsay Lodge, in these days, forms the core of a group of buildings imposingly and picturesquely disposed on the northern slope and crest of the Hill, in which the enterprise of Professor Patrick Geddes has housed one of his "University Halls," and where the traditions of the spot are duly reverenced and perpetuated. The adjoining "Outlook Tower"—of which only the lower storeys have a claim to antiquity—is another centre of culture, and is identified with the various schemes, geographical and sociological, which owe their origin to Professor Geddes.

Since the days when it was found necessary to supplement the town wells with a supply drawn in pipes from the Comiston springs, under the brow of Pentland, Edinburgh has looked up to the Water House on the Castle Hill, and to the rock-founded Reservoir which has succeeded it, for the indispensable boon of water. To the same high quarter, not the capital alone, but Presbyterian Scotland, has long been accustomed, during one season of the year at least, to turn expectant eyes in search of guidance and refreshment in the ecclesiastical questions which fill so considerable a place in the national consciousness. Since the Disruption of 1843 a double stream has flowed from this source. The General Assembly of the Church of Scotland meets and deliberates in the graceful building (occupied also as the Tolbooth Church) crowned by Gillespie Graham's far-seen spire, placed at the junction of the Castle Hill with Johnston Terrace. "Over the way" is the United Free Church headquarters, already referred to, which front the Mound with two square towers, and with Divinity College, Church, and Assembly Hall enclose a quadrangle in

69

The Lawnmarket and the Castle Hill

which stands a recently erected statue of John Knox, the *genius loci*. These possessions have been restored, under an Act of Parliament, to the Church which represents the Union, in 1900, of the United Presbyterian Church (itself an earlier combination of the Relief and Secession Churches) with the main body of the Church of the Disruption, after the momentous House of Lords decision of August 1904, which decreed that the property of the Free Church belonged to the "faithful remnant" who refused to enter into alliance with Voluntaryism. This residue, the Free Church of to-day—familiarly known as the "Wee Frees"—meet close by in Johnston Terrace, and their offices, from which the larger body have been ejected, face the Mound. So that the "double stream" of Presbyterian Church life has now become threefold. Black-coated ministers and elders, with their womankind, cluster like bees in the precincts of these ecclesiastical parliaments during the May meetings; and within the walls are occasionally heard the sounds of heated controversy as well as those of grave and earnest debate.

VIEW FROM THE CASTLE, TOWARDS CALTON.

(From a sketch made in 1848.)

UNIV. OF
CALIFORNIA

CHAPTER VII

THE CASTLE

THE beginnings of the history of Edinburgh Castle are, as the phrase runs, "lost in the mist of antiquity." Much ink, as well as blood, has been spilt over the site of this "Maiden Castle," overhanging the "Vale Dolorous." Historians, philologists, archæologists have disputed concerning its names and traditions and their origin and meaning, and have succeeded mainly in darkening counsel with their multitude of words. Dim glimpses of the Rock of Dunedin are caught in Saxon annals; vague echoes of the name are heard in Arthurian legend. The Romans built roads and formed camps in the neighbourhood; the military genius of that great people could not have overlooked the advantages of the wonderful natural stronghold, which rose like an island out of its protecting marshes, and dominated the fertile low country between the Forth and the hills, afterwards known as Lothian. Edwin, the Northumbrian King who is supposed to have founded the.burgh on the adjoining ridge and to have called it by his name, could not have failed to occupy and fortify the Rock which commanded the town. But the authentic records of Edinburgh Castle begin long after his time; and we reach solid ground of history only when we

The Castle

come down to the days of Malcolm Canmore and Saint Margaret.

There can be no doubt that Malcolm with the Big Head—the Malcolm of Shakespeare's "Macbeth"—and his beautiful and pious Queen made the "Castrum Puellarum" a place of refuge and of residence, and that they have left a memorial of their presence in the little church they built upon its highest platform. The capital was still at Dunfermline, almost visible beyond the Firth from the door of St Margaret's Chapel, and more than three centuries were to elapse before the Scottish Court and seat of Government were finally to settle in Edinburgh. The pleasures of the hunt may have drawn them, for the wild country that surrounded the Castle was, in those days, full of beasts of the chase. But no doubt, also, they came hither for the purpose of overawing and controlling the Southern and Anglian part of the Kingdom, which was already leavening the Celtic North with a new culture and speech; it was a first step towards the union of the two ends of the island.

However this may be, the saintly Queen Margaret was living here in the lowering days of November 1093, in a fortress and royal lodging all trace of which has disappeared, but whose form may be traditionally handed down in the three towers of the city's arms. With her were her younger children, three of whom were to be kings, while a third became the Queen of Henry Beauclerc. She was awaiting news of her husband and her eldest son, who were fighting in Northumbria, and when the tidings came of their death, the frail thread was cut of her own life, worn by sickness and the long vigils in her oratory, of which Bishop

ST MARGARET'S CHAPEL.

St Margaret and St David

Turgot tells us. The Castle was immediately invested by the usurping Donald Bane, and the orphan children were smuggled away by the western Sally Port, where long years afterwards Claverhouse held parley with the Governor. By the same precipitous pathway Margaret's body was lowered, and, hidden from the enemy's eyes by a miraculous mist, was borne to its resting-place across the " Queen's Ferry."

The next to leave his mark upon the Rock was Margaret's son David, the " Sair Sanct." While hunting in the neighbouring forest of Drumsheugh on Rood Day, 1128, he was assailed, in a lonely valley with precipitous crags on either hand, by a wonderful white hart with a cross between its antlers. In memory of the vision and his escape he vowed to found a monastery on the spot, where accordingly arose the famous Abbey of Holyrood, planted with Augustinian canons. But, for long, the monks of Holyrood had to house in the Castle, and even that airy lodging was not particularly safe and conducive to quiet religious meditation. It fell for the first time into the hands of the English as a pledge for the surrender of William the Lion, captured at Alnwick, and was given up as part of the dowry of his Queen, Ermengard.

Another royal lady from the south, Margaret, daughter of Henry III. of England, found the Rock "a sad and solitary place " until she and her young husband, Alexander III., found means to escape from the clutches of the Scots nobles who kept them apart. Edinburgh Castle seems to have had its full share of the "gamyn and glee " of this reign—the Golden Age of Scotland. But days of peril and disaster were near. Edward Longshanks captured it in 1291, and

The Castle

again in 1296; Wallace recovered it, but for the third
time in a few years it was besieged and taken by the
English, and it was still in their hands in 1311 when
Randolph made his daring and successful midnight
escalade of the rocks behind the Wellhouse Tower.
That ancient structure, by the way, with the Wellhouse
or " Wallace " Cradle—the fragment of masonry on the
cliff above—formed the means by which the garrison
obtained and protected their water supply from St
Margaret's Spring, and by a natural but mistaken
association of sounds the names have become identified
with the exploits of the Scottish Liberator.

For many years the Castle Rock lay dismantled and
desolate; and the next native monarch who has stamped
his name on its history was David II., the last male
descendant of the Bruce, who, after it had been once
again cleverly captured from the English by Sir
William Douglas, built the lofty keep on the highest
summit of the Rock, known as " David's Tower,"
destroyed long afterwards, along with the fragment
left of " Queen Margaret's Tower," in the siege of 1573.
Here the second David died; here the early Stewart
Kings entertained ambassadors from France and legates
of the Pope; from hence the unfortunate young Duke of
Rothesay sent a message to Henry IV. of England,
then vainly besieging the Castle, to meet him in knightly
combat; on its battlements the Duke of Albany, seeing
a bright meteor flash over Fife, a little before the
miserable death of his nephew in Falkland, pointed to
it as presaging the fall of some great prince—thus
" prophesying the thing that he did know." Then came
Queen Jane Beaufort fleeing hither for shelter after the
murder of her husband, the poet-king James I., in the

The Flodden Wall

Blackfriars at Perth, and carrying with her the young James II., whom she had to rescue later from the hands of the ambitious Chancellor Crichton, by smuggling him outside the walls in an "ark" or clothes-chest. A year or two afterwards the seed of the "Douglas Wars" was sown in this spot, when, as a signal for their treacherous slaughter, the "black bull's head" was set on the board at the feast to which the two young heirs of the House of Douglas were invited in the new Banqueting Hall—

> Edinburgh Castle, town and tower,
> God grant thou sink for sin ;
> And that even for the black dinour
> Earl Douglas gat therein.

About the middle of the fifteenth century measures were taken to surround the town and the outer defences of the Castle with walls, perhaps in addition to, or in substitution for, earlier and weaker defences. They were afterwards strengthened and extended by the building of the "Flodden Wall," and they embraced within their limits the whole of the Old Town from the Canongate to the Castle, and from the Greyfriars to the Nor' Loch. This latter, which is said to have been formed, but which more probably was only enlarged and deepened, in 1450, made a sufficient defence on the north; and on other sides there were "ports" or gates of entrance and egress—among them the West Port, the Bristo Port, the Potterow Port, the Cowgate Port, and, chief of all, the Netherbow Port—protected by strong towers. Fragments of these old defences are still to be seen at the Wellhouse Tower, where they touched the waters of the Loch beside the spot where Saint David is said to have cultivated his

The Castle

"garden of herbs"; and also, as we shall see, in the
narrow lane of the Vennel ascending from the Grassmarket and bounding Heriot's Hospital grounds, and in
the Pleasance. The place where the "Flodden Wall"
met the base of the Castle Rock is marked by an
inscription on the Married Soldiers' Quarters lying
immediately below Queen Mary's Apartments.

These walls bound the fortunes of town and Castle
more closely together, and served, at least, their purpose
of preserving for more than a century the heart of
Scotland against sudden invasion. Even Hertford,
after he had stormed his way through the "ports,"
battered in vain against the defences of the Rock. The
Castle took the commanding part natural to it in all the
civil broils of those years of violence and unrest, when
the unhappy Kingdom suffered from long minorities,
and was the prey of faction and feud. But royalty was
gradually withdrawing from it the light of its counten-
ance, and making for itself a home of more amenity at
the other end of the city. Mary of Guise spent in the
Castle the last anxious and calamitous months of her
life, and died here in 1560, with the sound in her ears of
the guns of the Lords of the Congregation and their
English allies besieging the French garrison of Leith.
A year later the young Queen of Scots, a vision of
beauty, landed in her native Kingdom, and ascended
to this high place to take possession. Brighter days, it
seemed, were in store for Scotland; but the fair prospect
was soon overcast. Some of Mary Stewart's best days,
however, were spent in the Palace on the Castle Rock,
which was refurnished and partly rebuilt for her use.
What are now called the Royal Apartments bear above
the doorway the monogram of Mary and of Henry,

Lights and Shadows

Lord Darnley, with the date 1566; and within, on the 19th of June of that year, was born their son, James VI., destined to unite the warring kingdoms.

Yet, for nearly two hundred years to come, light and shadow continued to chase each other in the fortunes of Edinburgh Castle. For three years Kirkaldy of Grange, as the "Queen's man," defended it against the party of the Kirk and of the King, and yielded only when the older buildings were beaten down about his ears by the batteries sent by Elizabeth. Charles I., surrounded by the nobility of Scotland, held his Coronation Banquet in the Great Hall, in 1633; but a few years later, Alexander Leslie, the "little old crooked soldier," and his Covenant men had blown up the gate with a petard, and carried the fortress by assault, surrendering it to the faithless King, only to be at the trouble of afterwards reducing it by blockade. Cromwell was feasted here on his first visit to Edinburgh, but when he returned with fire and sword, he had to march and to counter-march, to fight the battle of Dunbar, and to batter the walls from the Castle Hill and Heriot's Hospital before he could again taste of the hospitality of Edinburgh Castle.

Ill-omened, it was thought, was the bursting of "Mons Meg" in firing a salute at the coming of James, Duke of York, to be Scotland's Governor. And the presage was fulfilled, for in the dark days that followed, the Castle vaults were filled with prisoners for conscience' sake. The Earl of Argyle became one of the tenants of the State Prison—the "Argyle Tower"—whence his father had been led to death; and he shared his father's fate, notwithstanding that his daughter-in-law, Sophia Lindsay of Balcarres, once succeeded, by her

The Castle

courage and presence of mind, in carrying him safely through all the Castle guards, disguised as her lackey. When the last of the Stewart kings fled, their ancient capital seemed, for a time, to go mad with the new wine of liberty. But although the populace might wreck the Palace and Chapel Royal, and the "Lords of Convention" proclaim William and Mary in the Parliament House, there was Dundee to be reckoned with outside; and the Duke of Gordon stood guard over the Castle and the Scottish Regalia, and yielded to the powers of the Revolution only after a gallant and stubborn defence.

The later annals of Edinburgh Castle have been peaceful, except for the fiasco of a Jacobite attempt at surprise in the '15; and the rather tame exchange of challenges, in the shape of blockade and cannonade, when the youthful Prince Charlie held court in his father's place in Holyrood, and the citadel was defended by two octogenarian warriors, Generals Guest and Preston, for King George. The fortune of war declared itself for Age, but Romance and the "Scottish Muses" have made themselves the partisans of Youth and the Lost Cause. The Castle witnessed some of the last episodes in the last struggle for the Stewarts; for in its vaults Jacobite prisoners, both men and women, were detained, among them that Lady Ogilvy who made her escape in the garb of a washerwoman, and James Mohr Macgregor, son of Rob Roy, and father of "Catriona." In the same dismal quarters were confined the French prisoners of the Great War, not, however, so strictly that they were without opportunity of looking about them, of planning escape, and even (if we may trust the story of "the Vicomte Anne de

78

The " Honours of Scotland "

St Ives") of making love in the free air of the Castle ramparts.

Last among the romantic incidents in the annals of the Rock may be mentioned the recovery, in the dark and cobwebbed vault, where they had lain hidden and almost forgotten for over one hundred years, of the Regalia, or " Honours of Scotland." Once before in their strange history, the " Honours" had been lost, when they were carried away from Edinburgh to Dunottar, to be safe from the hands of Cromwell, and were thence secretly conveyed, by woman's wit, to the Kirk of Kinneff, and buried at midnight under the floor. They reappeared at the Restoration, but at the Union they were committed to the depths of a huge oaken chest and sealed up in their vaulted chamber, lest the sight of the insignia of former independence might stimulate too strongly the sentiment of Scottish patriotism. They were raised once more out of their grave in 1817—Sir Walter Scott a keenly interested onlooker. And now the Regalia—the Crown, traditionally assigned to Bruce, but re-formed and embellished by later monarchs ; the Sword of State, presented by Pope Julius II. to James IV. ; the Sceptre, made for James V., and the Royal Jewels, including Charles I.'s coronation ring, bequeathed to George IV. by Cardinal York, the last heir of the old line of Scotland—are laid out for all eyes to see in the " Crown Room."

Thus it may be said that nearly all that is really venerable among the relics of its history is gathered on the summit of the Castle Rock ; and you ascend to these "fossils of the past" through more recent and less precious formations. The ascent is easier than of yore, but is still something of a trial to the short of breath.

The Castle

The Moat, now a dry ditch, is supposed to be cut down to the level of the natural " Spur " of land from whence, before the Esplanade was formed, it was necessary to scale the Castle; and drawbridge, gateway, and guard-house occupy the place of the Outer Port, against which so often the enemy has hammered in vain. Up the steep causeway winds the road, lined on the right by garrison buildings, while rising precipitately on the left is the living rock, eked out by masonry, and patched in the crevices by grass and a clinging tree or two. It dives under the Portcullis Gate, and comes out upon the Argyle Battery, while overhead is the Argyle or Constable's Tower, once the State Prison. A steep flight of steps leads past the door of this fateful building, the upper part of which has been restored through the liberal act of the late Mr William Nelson. So that, with the help of a little imagination, the visitor is able to call up the conditions and surroundings in captivity of " Gillespie Grumach "—the " gleyed Argyle "—and of Principal Carstaires.

By the stairs, or by an inclined way through Foog's Gate, one reaches the King's Bastion, where, on the highest pinnacle of the rock, commanding a surpassingly fine view of the town and country below, the battered form of Mons Meg mounts guard over the still more time-worn fabric of St Margaret's Chapel. Something of the history of these two ancient neighbours has already been told. The Chapel, which has been much patched in the course of the eight centuries it has stood here, is one of the tiniest as well as oldest of places of Christian worship in Scotland still covered by a roof; and its apse has features that make it of

" Roaring Meg "

peculiar interest to the student of architecture and ecclesiology.

"Roaring Meg," now chained so immovably to her rock, has been a traveller in her day. Name and origin are matters of controversy; and Gallovidians dispute the statement that the great piece of ordnance was forged at Mons towards the end of the fifteenth century, contending that "Brawny Kim" of Mollance was the artificer two generations earlier, and helped to place the monster in position at the siege of Threave Castle. The Exchequer Accounts appear to prove that this "great iron murderer" was dragged, with vast toil and trouble, to old wars and sieges in the West Country and on the Borders; and long after being crippled from active service by the mischance of 1682, this great gun, of which our forefathers had been so proud, was ignominiously carried off to the Tower as part of the spoils of Scotland in the '45 Rebellion, and was only restored through the good offices of the author of "Waverley" in 1829.

"Other times, other fashions"; and from the adjoining Half-Moon Battery, on the site of "David's Tower," and beside the draw-well which in extremity of siege was the one source of water supply of the garrison, the Time-gun utters its peaceful daily message in place of "Meg's" angry roar. Behind is the entrance to the quadrangle known as the Palace Square.

The northern side of this square is said to have been occupied by the Castle Church, described as a long and large Gothic building of which all trace, beyond a few fragments of carved stones, has disappeared. Barracks have taken its place and

The Castle

appropriate also the western part of the quadrangle. The buildings of historic interest are ranged on the eastern and southern sides, and form the Royal Lodging and the Parliament or Banqueting Hall. Part of the former structure was rebuilt after the Union of the Crowns, as indicated by the style and decoration and the date, 1615. The portion actually associated with royal residence looks down sheerly from the south-eastern angle of the rock on the houses of the Grassmarket. There are separate entrances from the Square to the Crown Room and Queen Mary's Apartments.

Into both we have already peeped. The bare outer chamber retains none of the sumptuous furnishing bestowed on it in preparation for the residence and accouchement of the Queen of Scots—the tapestries of green brocaded velvet and cloth of gold bearing the arms of famous princes and the stories of classic, scriptural, and mediæval champions; the chairs of gilded leather and damask; and the books, hangings, and pictures. The Bedroom—little more than a closet—retains the faded decorations of its panelling and a scrap or two of furniture of dubious authenticity Out of its window Mary must often have looked with strangely mingled feelings of hope and fear on the grim, grey city below, which held more foes than friends, and on Arthur Seat, "a couchant lion, watchful over Scotland's honour and Scotland's religion." Here, a few hours after the birth, took place that famous interview with Darnley in which she "spoke daggers" to the weakling, as she showed him the heir of three realms, brought to life in the midst of "battle, murder, and sudden death." Some have seen

A Hall of Arms

the clue to yet another and secret tragedy of the
Stewart dynasty in the discovery in 1830, in a recess
of the outer Palace Wall, close to the entrance of the
Royal Apartments, of the remains of a male infant
wrapped in decayed cloth of gold bearing the letter
"I"; the mystery, whatever it may be, has been
reburied with the bones in the place where they
were found.

The "Great Hall" of the Castle, the scene of so
many State ceremonials, festivities, and debates,
suffered much from defacement and neglect. It
was divided into floors, and long served as a garrison
hospital and dispensary. The restoration and decoration of this Banqueting or Parliament Hall, as it has
been alternately called, is another of the public-spirited
works of the late Mr Nelson. The spacious room, in
which kings, princes, and ambassadors have feasted,
is now displayed in its full proportions—80 feet in
length by 30 feet in breadth and 40 feet to the fine
open-timbered roof; the range of windows overlooking
the King's Stables and the West Port are filled in
with the armorial bearings of distinguished figures in
Scottish history; and the old shields and embellishments, dating from the time when James IV. rebuilt
or refurbished the hall for the home-coming of his
bride, Margaret Tudor, have been carefully preserved
and others added in the same style and taste. In
another sense it has become a "Hall of Arms," for
around the walls are ranged the colours of old regiments
and a collection of arms and armour brought hither
from the Castle Armoury and from the Tower of
London.

A "luggie" or concealed staircase led from the

The Castle

Banqueting Hall to the Royal Lodging; and another flight descends to the Prison Vaults below. With these, the list of the Castle antiquities may be said to close. For the other buildings on the Rock, in the occupation of the garrison, are of comparatively recent date, and of unromantic aspect. The encircling walls and other fortifications on the western part of the Rock belong chiefly to the closing years of the seventeenth and early part of the eighteenth centuries. The buildings they enclose are of the reigns of Queen Anne and the early Georges—an unpicturesque and uninspiring period of architecture—and cannot be called worthy of the site. There is, however, a certain quaintness of aspect about the old "Governor's House," now part of the Officers' Quarters. The former Armoury and Magazine, which occupied the north-western angle of the Rock, has been demolished, and its place has been taken by a block of buildings, containing the Garrison Hospital, which imitate the gabled and crow-stepped Scottish baronial style of architecture, and from some points of view—and from some only—combine well with their surroundings. For purposes of modern warfare, the defences of Edinburgh Castle are almost as obsolete and harmless as "Mons Meg"; it is great as a monument of history, and as a Mount of Vision.

THE NETHERBOW

(From an engraving in the *Scots Magazine*, 1764.)

[To

CHAPTER VIII

THE NETHERBOW PRECINCTS

AT the lower as well as at the upper end of the old " Hie Street of Edinburgh " there was a fighting Border or Debatable Land. If the Castle guns dominated it from the west, to eastward it marched with the alien and often hostile territory of the Canongate—the burgh of the canons of the Abbey of Holyrood, and in the days when kings lived in the Palace, the "Court" quarter of the capital of Scotland. Sometimes in its history the city came under a cross-fire from these opposite directions—from the Rock, and from the town's chief and most accessible "port of entry," the Netherbow. The spot where once stood this famous "Temple Bar" of Old Edinburgh is easily discovered by the constriction of the thoroughfare, which here, on its long way from the Castle to the Abbey, narrows to half its width. The Canongate continues the line of the High Street, and, except that it is more contracted, dilapidated, and dingy, preserves something of its general aspect and atmosphere.

At and around the Netherbow are gathered, as at the bottom of a bag net, a wonderful collection of the famous scenes, passages, and traditions of Edinburgh history. Twice, in successive years, the English stormed

The Netherbow Precincts

their way into the city through its chief Port, in prosecution of their "rough wooing" of Mary Stewart for young Edward of England; and a century later another "Lord Protector" had repeatedly to preach, with similar forcible arguments, from the mouths of guns mounted at the head of the Canongate and on the "Dow Craig," or Calton Hill, before the stubborn Scots would open to him their city gates. Between these dates the Netherbow was the favourite scene of struggle and skirmish between the Lords of the Congregation and the party of Mary of Guise, and later between the "King's" and the "Queen's" factions in the troublous early years of the reign of James VI. The militant Reformers would often issue through the Netherbow to make a sally against the French garrison of Leith, and be chased home again by St Ninian's Row and Leith Wynd; and the Regent Mar's forces and the faithful adherents of the imprisoned Queen of Scots pounded each other, the one from a battery in the Pleasance, and the other from a platform on Bailie Fullerton's house, in Fountain Close.

Soon after the Union of the Crowns the old war-battered structure gave place to a new Netherbow Port. This was the building with the low vaulted archway and narrow wicket for passenger traffic, and the central spire and flanking round towers and turrets, surmounted by spikes on which were affixed the heads and other grim remains of traitors and malefactors, so familiar to the eyes of many generations of Edinburgh citizens. Cromwell forced his way through it with the strong hand, and Lochiel's Highlanders surprised its guard early in a September morning in the '45. But the city authorities of the latter half of the eighteenth century

Netherbow Port

set little store by historic associations or by picturesque aspect; and it has already been told that the Netherbow disappeared about the time of the founding of the North Bridge. On a new building beside its site there is a carved effigy of this main gate and defence of the Flodden Wall. Quite recently some of the architectural ornaments of the Netherbow have been recovered for the town from a Leith builder's yard, and have been placed within the railings of the adjoining John Knox's United Free Church.

Melancholy changes have overtaken not only the Netherbow itself, but the whole cluster of wynds and alleys, front lands and secluded mansion-houses, once the homes of nobles and church dignitaries, that intervened between the Port and the Tron. With one notable and outstanding exception, all have suffered either demolition or pitiful degradation. There was a time when scarcely one of these narrow and filthy closes did not contain the town house of some powerful baron, or the official residence of some bishop or abbot.

When these took flight, with the Court and the Parliament, the lower end of the High Street and the precincts of the Netherbow continued to be a haunt of fashion and literature; and towards the end of the eighteenth century law lords, men of affairs, academic dons, and ladies of rank were still dwelling in content and comfort in Hyndford Close and other lanes running down to the Cowgate. Walter Scott, as a school-boy, used to find his way from the adjoining High School Yards to the rooms of his maternal uncle, Dr Daniel Rutherford, professor of botany, who lived in what had been the family mansion successively of the Earls of Stirling,

The Netherbow Precincts

Hyndford, and Selkirk. He was a visitor, also, at the tea-parties next door of the old Countess of Balcarres, where he became acquainted with her daughter, Lady Anne Lindsay, the authoress of "Auld Robin Gray," to whom he wrote long afterwards of the degradation that had befallen a spot "once too clean to soil the hem of your ladyship's garment." "I cannot help thinking," he adds, "on the simple and rosy retreats, where worth and talent and elegance to boot were often nestled, and which now are the resort of misery, filth, poverty, and vice." "So wears the world away!"

Among the other legends of the Netherbow is one that figures to us the beautiful Jane, afterwards Duchess of Gordon and hostess of Robert Burns, as a girl, riding in the vicinity of the Fountain Close on the back of one of the vagrant swine that in those free-mannered and insanitary days grubbed in the rubbish heaps of the High Street; while her sister, who later became Lady Wallace of Craigie, whacked the animal with a stick; their mother, Lady Maxwell of Monreith, was also a resident in Hyndford Close.

At the head of the adjoining South Gray's or Mint Close lived the Earl of Buchan, and there, as a tablet over the street entrance tells, were born Lord Chancellor Erskine and his brother Harry, the witty Dean of Faculty. Close by, in Elphinstone Court, lived, in his advocate days, another Scotsman who rose to be head of the English bench, Lord Chancellor Loughborough; and Henry Dundas, Lord Melville, was born in Bishop's Close, on the opposite side of the High Street. The house of Sir George Mackenzie of Rosehaugh—a scholar and wit, as well as the hated King's Advocate —was in Strichen's Close, adjacent to the old-town dwelling of the Abbots of Melrose, the last of whom, Andrew Durie, died of "grief and horror" at the sacking of St Giles Church by the Reforming mob. Tweeddale Court, where a shelter for the accommodation of sedan chairs still keeps its place, was for well-nigh two hundred years the mansion of the noble family of the Tweeddale Hays; its gardens and lime walks extended down to the Cowgate. The house, now the premises of Oliver & Boyd, publishers, afterwards became the head premises of the British Linen Company's Bank, and close to the mouth of the court was perpetrated in 1806 the robbery and murder of Begbie, the bank porter, stabbed to the heart by an unknown assassin, while passing in with £5000 in gold and notes in his possession.

An earlier mystery of the region lying above the Netherbow was the abduction, from her house in Niddry's Wynd, of Lady Grange, daughter of that violent Chiesley of Dalry who killed Lord President Lockhart in a Lawnmarket close. The plot by which this wretched woman was spirited away from the High Street of Edinburgh to a Hebridean rock is supposed to have been concocted between her husband, Erskine of Grange—a judge of Session, a brother of Mar of the '15 Rebellion, and the friend of Pope and Lady Mary Montagu—and the notorious Simon Fraser of Lovat, whose widow, by the way, lived long in the neighbouring Dickson's Close.

Still darker stories of the locality belong to a darker age. The aspect of Blackfriars Street has changed entirely since it was known as the "Frers' Wynd," and was the access from the town to the foundation granted by Alexander II. to the Dominican or Preaching Friars on the site afterwards occupied by the Old Infirmary.

The Netherbow Precincts

In it is the house traditionally assigned to the Regent Morton; in their mansion in Blackfriars Wynd the "lordly line" of St Clair of the Isles held almost royal state; and at the foot, near the Cowgate, stood the "palace" occupied successively by Archbishop James Beaton and by his nephew, the Cardinal. James V. occasionally lodged, and his daughter Mary supped, in this historic dwelling, all trace of which has been removed. It was the rallying-place of Arran and the Hamiltons in the famous street fray of "Cleanse the Causey," their enemies, the Douglases, gathering at the Netherbow; and it was in it, on the same occasion, that the Archbishop's iron "conscience clattered" under his priest's robe of peace. Francis Stewart, Earl of Bothwell, ran Sir William Stewart through the body in the Friars' Wynd, where also Mitchell, a fanatic Covenanter, fired a shot in the "Killing Time" at Archbishop Sharpe that wounded dangerously Honeyman, Bishop of Orkney. But the most dramatic and sinister scene in the history of this narrow and picturesque alley—which has been improved into a commonplace modern street—was when, late one evening in February 1567, Mary Stewart passed through it with blazing torches and archer guard after visiting her sick husband at Kirk of Field, while Hepburn, Earl of Bothwell, and his emissaries, carrying gunpowder for the tragedy, slipped past by the next alley of Todrick's Close.

We have not nearly exhausted the literary and artistic memories that cling to this corner of the Old Town. For, not to repeat the mention already made of Allan Ramsay's house, wig-maker's shop, and printing-office, "at the Sign of the Mercury," opposite Niddry's Wynd, and his playhouse in Carrubber's Close—both of

ALLAN RAMSAY'S SHOP, OPPOSITE NIDDRY'S WYND.

From a water-colour by M. P. Taylor.

Moubray House

them now memories only—was not Falconer, the author of the "Shipwreck," born in another, and lowlier, barber's premises, in World's End Close? Did not David Allan, the "Scottish Hogarth," live and give drawing lessons in Dickson's Close? Was not the residence of Walter Chepman, the first Scottish Printer, in Lovat's Land? Did not Bassendine's great folio Bible, and his edition of Sir David Lyndsay's poems, issue from the Fountain Close? And at the head of Trunk's Close, opposite, and cheek-by-jowl with "John Knox's house," fronting the High Street with forestair and timbered gable, have we not still with us Moubray House, recently rescued from demolition by the intervention of the Cockburn Association? It has a history that goes back to the last quarter of the fifteenth century, to which period may well belong the heavy corbelling of the blind side which the house presents to Trunk's or Turing's Close; and after ceasing to be the residence of the gentle families who dined under the figured and painted seventeenth-century ceiling in the principal room, it descended to be carriers' quarters, a tavern, and finally a lodging-house. Down an adjoining close, and now forming a mission hall attached to the church fronting Jeffrey Street, which inherits the old name, is the rebuilt chancel of Trinity College Church, the stones of which lay long on the slopes of Calton opposite. Some of the carved fragments of this fine fifteenth-century structure are scattered and lost. A few are heaped together in the West Princes Street Gardens. The massive grey fabric, in Chalmers Close, with its projecting gargoyles and heraldic ornaments, is one of the few surviving examples of our pre-Reformation Church architecture.

The purlieus and approaches of the Netherbow

The Netherbow Precincts

are associated, perhaps above all else, with men who have taken leading parts in the religious life and history of Scotland. Other dignitaries of the pre-Reformation Church had their town houses grouped near that of the Primate in the Blackfriars Wynd; and, after the great changes of the sixteenth century, the ecclesiastical traditions of the spot seem to have been perpetuated. "Bishop's Close" took its name chiefly from Archbishop Spottiswoode, the historian; the house of Archbishop Sharpe — "Sharpe of that Ilk" — was at the Netherbow; Thomas Chalmers once lived in Hyndford Close; and Edward Irving has been among the eloquent evangelists who have raised their voices in Carrubber's Close. Here, in a little non-juring meeting-house, the Jacobites of last century had their ecclesiastical head-quarters; while the branch of Scottish Episcopacy that conformed to the law and accepted the Hanoverian Succession had its first chapel in Blackfriars Wynd, near by the earliest places of worship in which the Roman Catholics and the Cameronians of the city ventured to assemble in days of growing toleration. Religious as well as social classes were strangely assorted around the Netherbow.

The hands of time, and of the modern builder, have effaced, or are effacing, the antiquities of the lower High Street and the Netherbow. Hardly one is left of the timber-fronted house, with forestairs and many-paned windows almost flush with the walls, which were once characteristic of the locality. The "Heave Awa" house is the successor to one of the loftiest and most rickety of these "lands," which suddenly collapsed one winter midnight in 1861, burying its thirty-five inmates in the ruins; and its name perpetuates the

John Knox's House

words used to encourage his rescuers, by a boy who was at once pinioned and protected by one of the fallen oaken beams. In the closes there are still a few half-erased texts, and fragments of mouldings and armorial bearings of the proud families that once possessed these now despised dwellings; for example, a shield in fine preservation, with the date 1600, will be found sculptured over the door of a house on the traditional site of the Abbot of Melrose's lodging, in Strichen's Close. But the one memorial of the domestic life and ecclesiastical struggles of the past, which continues to preserve much of the aspect it possessed two or even three centuries ago, is the picturesque and striking building that projects into the highway, just above the Netherbow, and has long been known as "John Knox's House."

It has recently been contended, and evidence, both positive and negative, has been produced in support of the case, that this venerable dwelling has no direct association with the life and work of the Scottish Reformer, whose residence, during at least the greater part of his stay in Edinburgh, was situated, as we have found, much nearer to the scene of his ministrations in the Church of St Giles. It has been shown by Mr Robert Miller, ex-Dean of Guild, and by other patient investigators of the town records, that the so-called "John Knox's House" was in these years in the possession and, for a period at all events, in the occupation of a goldsmith named James Mossman, a zealous Catholic and "Queen's man," who afterwards suffered on the scaffold, along with Kirkaldy of Grange, for his attachment to the cause of Mary Stewart. The error of housing here the "John Knox Legend" is no older, it is held by these critics, than the beginning of

The Netherbow Precincts

the present century, when it made its first appearance in print in the pages of an Edinburgh Guide-book, by Stark, who is supposed to have confused the Reformer with another John Knox, who had a "Close" and local fame near the Netherbow of still earlier date. On this showing, the location—gravely accepted in some points by biographers and historians—of the window from which Knox preached to the populace; of the corner of his "warm study of daills," where he was sitting when an assassin's bullet struck the candlestick and lodged in the ceiling; and the pictures that have been drawn of his holding deep counsel in these dim chambers with nobles and ecclesiastics, supping with ambassadors, and bringing home hither his youthful and gentle-born second wife, or returning, with tottering steps and attended by a weeping crowd, to his own door at the Netherbow, after preaching his last sermon in St Giles —all this must, we fear, be set down as fond and vain imaginings.

But even if mistake has been made in the christening of "Knox's Corner," it must be pronounced a fortunate one in many lights. It has had the happy result of preserving for us, wonderfully intact, both inside and outside, a remarkably fine and interesting example of the domestic architecture of the Edinburgh of the middle of the sixteenth century—the most romantic as well as the most stormy period in the annals of the ancient town. Probably no less potent charm than the belief that it was the veritable "manse" of the strong-willed and undaunted man who was the real hero of the Scottish Reformation could have preserved this picturesque old dwelling, with its projecting gables and outer stairs, its ornamental carvings and

JOHN KNOX'S HOUSE.

WHITE HORSE CLOSE

[*To face page* 94.

A Peep into the Past

pious mottoes, its panelled rooms, with their small and quaintly-placed windows and dusky corners, and its many irregularities, without and within, from the common fate of its class, of being condemned and removed as out of date and an obstruction to the thoroughfare. A debt of gratitude is due, by Edinburgh residenters and visitors alike, to the Free Church of Scotland, and its successor the United Free Church, for the careful guardianship and tendance which enable us, at this late time of day, to take a peep back, if not into the actual home, into the times of John Knox.

CHAPTER IX

˙ THE CANONGATE

IN these days there is little to remind the visitor, as he passes the now invisible barrier of the Netherbow, that he has entered new territory. The main street has become narrower; the diverging closes are, if possible, filthier and more squalid than they are above the Port —that is all. Yet the ground from here down to the Abbey had, for many centuries, a history and fortunes and a municipal organisation distinct from Edinburgh. The burgh of Canongate could trace its origin to a clearer, if not older, source than its neighbour, the city. It has been told how King David, of pious memory, had, in the fourth year of his reign and on the Feast of the Exaltation of the Cross, an encounter in the vale between the crags with a miraculous hart, which, in the graphic relation of old Boece, assailed him with its " awful and braid tindis," and " dang baith the King and hes hors to the grund," afterwards " evanishing in the same place quhare now springis the Rude Well," leaving in the hands of the astonished monarch the cross or rood which, by some accounts, it bore between its horns.

In part fulfilment of the vow then made, David, four years later—in 1128—conferred on the Canons of the new Abbey of Holy Rood the right of establishing a

96

CANONGATE TOLBOOTH.

[*To face page* 96.

The Canons' Burgh

burgh on the land wherewith he had endowed them, lying between their church and the King's burgh of Edinburgh, with market and other privileges. Notwithstanding that it lay open to the brunt of war, the "Canons' burgh" throve under the dominion of the Abbey, which possessed many rich benefices, with mills on the Water of Leith and authority over the adjoining burgh of Broughton. The main street became known as the Canon-gait, or way, and this name was gradually applied to the whole community, which had its Common Muir where Leith Walk now is, and its place of execution on the Gallowlee; its own Tolbooth and Courts; its own Bailies, High Constables, and other officials, including "Doomster," Piper, and Drummer.

Through the Canongate and out by the Water Gate and the Easter Road lay the highway to the east and the south, and by Leith Wynd ran the road to Leith and the Firth; so that down to the beginning of the present century the Canongate was the customary landfall and point of departure for travellers from and to London, whether by land or sea. Thus Dr Samuel Johnson and Boswell, on their memorable tour in 1773, passed through it, and sojourned in the White Horse Close, off St Mary's Wynd, just outside the city walls. It was favourably situated for commerce; but from the time, at the beginning of the fourteenth century, when the Scottish Kings began to make the Abbey a favourite residence, and especially after they built their Palace at the foot of the Canongate, the locality became closely associated with the doings of Court and with the private and public affairs of the Royal Family.

The Canongate

The right of sanctuary also drew thither a mixed multitude, and the Canongate swarmed with courtiers and cut-throats, nobles and beggars. The removal of the Court to London was a blow from which the Palace and the burgh never recovered. But maps of later date still show the Canongate a comparatively open and airy, as well as well-built, place, not stifled by "back lands," but having gardens and lawns running down on either side from the houses fronting its main street; while on St John's Hill, Dumbiedykes, and the Pleasance were promenades, where the dwellers of the burgh could enjoy the magnificent views of the adjoining crags and hill.

As with other places and people, the greater its former fortunes, the deeper has been the fall of the Canongate. Its declension preceded that of the High Street, and is an old story. Allan Ramsay bewailed the low estate of " Canongate, puir eldritch hole," and the losses and crosses that had come upon it with the Union.

> London and Death gars thee look droll
> And hang thy heid.

But, as we shall see, gentility had by no means entirely deserted it even a hundred years later than Honest Allan's lament. Breweries and other industries have monopolised the former open spaces and amenities of the Canongate, and it is now famous for the making of beer rather than of history. There are said to be more than twenty breweries within the limits of the ward, so placed as to tap the seam whose water, from time immemorial, has lent virtue and reputation to Edinburgh ale.

Chronicles of the Canongate

The constitution of the quarter has changed with its fortunes and its means of livelihood. When the control of the burgh was transferred from the Abbots and Canons it came into the hands of the Commendators of the Abbey; and the Lords Holyroodhouse, Bellenden, and Roxburgh, and the Governors of George Heriot's Hospital, were successively Superiors of the Canongate and nominators of its Baron Bailie. Finally, the town of Edinburgh acquired the rights; but the form at least of separate local government—of Canongate Home Rule—was not abolished until 1856, when it had enjoyed a corporate existence for seven hundred years.

More considerate than its superior, the city, of the memorials of its municipal past, the Canongate retains its prætorium, the Tolbooth, which stands, nearly half-way down towards the Palace, with the Parish Church as its next neighbour, on the left-hand side of the street. Before reaching it, one passes several spots worthy of note. On the same side as the Tolbooth, just below Rae's Close, once on a time the only access to the north between Leith Wynd and the Water Gate, is the "Morocco Land," distinguished by the turbaned bust of a Moor above the door, concerning which there is a "chronicle of the Canongate" to the effect that it was built by a local Whittington who, driven from the place through the part he took in a brawl, returned after many years spent in Barbary to wed a Provost's daughter, but, in fulfilment of a vow not to enter the city again except "sword in hand," never passed within the Netherbow. New Street, an early "town improvement," in which once lived, among other pillars of eighteenth century law and literature, Sir David Dalrymple, Lord Hailes, and

The Canongate

Henry Home, Lord Kames, has itself been nearly wiped out, although Lord Kames's house still survives. Jack's Land, a little further down, is associated with a yet more illustrious name—that of David Hume, who worked here on his "History" in the interval between leaving Riddle's Court in the Lawnmarket and taking up house in James's Court. The residence of Dalyell of Binns, that grim hunter of the Covenanters, who vowed that an enemy of the King should fall for every hair in his beard, was in Big Jack's Close adjoining.

Looking to the north side of the street, the spacious Chessel's Court is remembered as the scene of Deacon Brodie's last exploit of robbing the Excise Office. The Old Playhouse Close, conspicuous by the double row of dormer windows, crowned by finials, on the front tenement, was for a time the home of the drama in the northern capital—after its removal from Allan Ramsay's theatre in Carrubber's Close—in days when the play was introduced surreptitiously as an item in a concert programme. John Home's tragedy of "Douglas," on its appearance on this humble stage, cost its author his kirk.

St John's Street, entered through a "pend" opposite the site of St John's Cross, was, like the neighbouring New Street, still a place of fashionable residence when last century was young. James Ballantyne—"Rigdum-funnidos"—held "high jinks" in No. 10, on the eve of the appearance of a new Waverley novel from his print-ing-office on the other side of the Canongate, none of the guests enjoying the mystery more than the "Great Unknown" himself. Two or three doors off are houses that were once occupied by the famous physician and friend of Burns, Dr John Gregory, and by the eccentric

MORAY HOUSE.

(From a water-colour after J. Nash.)

Scottish Judge, Lord Monboddo, whose daughter, Miss
Burnett, was one of the "toasts" of the Edinburgh
society of her day, and had her wit and charms celebrated by the poet. "Lodge Canongate Kilwinning" is
on the opposite side of St John's Street; the Lodge
room retains something of the appearance it had when
Robert Burns was admitted to the "mystic tie"; and his
name, as its Poet Laureate, figures on the Lodge records,
some pages after that from which the name of Secretary
Murray of Broughton has been ignominiously erased.
Tobias Smollett lived with his sister, Mrs Telfer, in the
first floor of the house entered by the roundel tower
near the mouth of the pend, and here collected the
materials for his graphic pictures of old Edinburgh life
and customs in " Humphry Clinker."

If poetry and letters haunted this siding in the
Canongate, history, of a grim sort, has repeatedly taken
up quarters in the remarkable building, with the gateway
flanked by slender pyramids and the stone balcony
overhanging the pavement, in the front of the main
street a few yards farther down. Moray House was
built in 1618 by the widow of the Earl of Home. A
generation later it came into the possession of her
sister, the Countess of Moray, and remained for two
hundred years in that family. Cromwell occupied it in
1648, and again in 1650, after the battle of Dunbar.
Here the Protector held levees, and issued orders and
proclamations to the perverted, unruly Scots nation; here
the resolution is said to have been formed that issued
in the execution of Charles I. It was, it is said, on the
balcony of "Lady Home's Lodging" that the wedding
guests at the marriage of Lord Lorn, eldest son of the
Marquis of Argyle, to a daughter of the Earl of Moray,

assembled in May 1650, when Montrose was led past, bound on a cart, on his way to execution at the Cross of Edinburgh. One of the guests is said to have spat down upon the noble prisoner, who replied with a look of lofty disdain. Within twelve years, Montrose's head was taken down to make room for that of the bridegroom's father. Three of the onlookers—so says Sir Daniel Wilson in his " Memorials "—including the gay and happy bridegroom himself, perished on the same fatal spot to which Montrose was passing. Truly the whirligig of time brings in its revenges!

Moray House was the residence of Lord Chancellor Seafield at the time of the Treaty of Union; and the signatories of that deed, hunted by a mob of patriots from a summer-house in the garden, sought the refuge of a High Street cellar to complete their work. The building, which contains some fine hand-wrought ceilings, is in these days being incorporated in the new structure of the Provincial Committee's Training College for Teachers, the main block of which occupies the former garden of Moray House, and fronts the South Back of Canongate. On or near this site assembled the King's Parliament in 1571, while that which acknowledged the authority of the exiled Queen of Scots was holding sittings in the Edinburgh Tolbooth; and in the street opposite James VI. was received in state by the Canongate Authorities when, "like a salmon," he returned to his native capital and the Palace of his ancestors.

The owner of another Canongate dwelling, a little lower down the street and over against the Tolbooth, met the fate, so common among the Scottish nobles of that day, of execution at Edinburgh Cross, in the year

BAKEHOUSE CLOSE.

[*To face page* 102.

Canongate Tolbooth

before the death of Montrose. This was George, second Marquis of Huntly, head of the great family of the "Gordons of the North," whose annals are nearly as full of tragedy and romance as that of the Stewarts themselves. His father, though deeply concerned in the affair of the "Spanish Blanks" and other plots, managed to die in his bed; his grandfather, the fourth Earl, was slain at Corrichie in 1562, and the corpse was afterwards exhumed and was made the object of a ghastly trial and condemnation in the Parliament Hall. The Huntly House is a large, timber-fronted building, bearing on its picturesque front, along with a number of moral mottoes in Latin, the date of its erection, 1570. It is a specimen of Old Edinburgh domestic architecture that stands much in need of rescue, repair, and preservation. Beside it, in Bakehouse Close, is an interesting example of a dwelling of a later genera-tion in the residence of Sir Archibald Acheson, one of Charles I.'s Secretaries of State and ancestor of the Irish Earls of Gosford, recognisable by the heraldic crest of the "cock and trumpet," the initials, and the date, 1633, graven over the doorway in the courtyard behind.

Canongate Tolbooth, time-worn and turned to commonplace purposes, is still a picturesque feature of the main "gait" of the ancient burgh. It is in the ornate "Scoto-French" style of the period of its erection, indicated by the date, 1591, which, with insignia and dedicatory inscriptions, is imprinted on its front. It has a bell tower bearing a clock projecting over the pavement, and a heavy outside stair up which, in the course of the centuries, many prisoners, mean and noble, have climbed to judgment. The local tradition that the " Great Montrose " was confined in a dark cell in the Tolbooth is, however, not borne out by authentic history. Now that the last semblance of municipal autonomy has been taken from the Canongate, the old Council Chamber has been turned to account as a Literary Institute.

On the Tolbooth, and also on the reconstructed Burgh Cross and the Parish Church beside it, the Canongate arms—the stag's head with the " Cross crosslet" between the antlers—is much in evidence. The Church was built in 1688, after James II. had appropriated as a Roman Catholic Chapel Royal the nave of Holyrood Abbey, which from the Reformation had served the purposes of the parish place of worship. The old " Canongate Kirk," as having the Palace within its charge, and housing for a time under the same roof as royalty, was closely associated with the fortunes of the Stewarts. The Rev. John Brand made proclamation in it on 21st July 1565 of the marriage of " Harry, Duk of Albayne" to "Marie, be ye grace of God, Queene of Scottis," and a little further on in the same Parish Register occur the entries :—" Mon^r· Signior Dauid wes slane in Halyruidhous, ye ix daye o' Merche, 1565," and " Ye King's Grace blaun up wi pud^r· in ye Kirk o' Field, ye x o' Februar, 1566." In explanation of the dates of these quaint and tragic memoranda, it has to be remembered that up to 1600 the year was reckoned to begin with the 25th March, Old Style.

Canongate Churchyard is a competitor with the West Kirk ¡God's acre for second place after the Greyfriars in the interest of its monuments and the riches of its soil in the dust of men of note. A long list

Canongate Churchyard

of the eminent persons buried within its walls may be read at the entrance gate. Adam Smith's tomb is immediately behind the Tolbooth; the last twelve years of the well-spent life of the father of the science of political economy were passed in the mansion in Panmure Close formerly belonging to the Earls of Panmure, a few doors down the Canongate. Dugald Stewart rests not far off. He shared with Lord Bannatyne, the last survivor of the Mirror Club, the substantial dwelling of Whitefoord House, still extant, on the site whereon stood "my Lord Setoun's Lodging," in which, as readers of "The Abbot" will remember, Roland Graeme found shelter after his brawl on the causey. The benevolent professor of moral philosophy had trained private pupils for the University—of whom one was Lord Palmerston—in the "Lothian Hut" in Horse Wynd, which has given place to "Younger's Brewery." In Canongate burying-ground, also, a "narrow house" has been found for artists like David Allan and "Grecian" Williams, the Runcimans, and Watson Gordon; for historians like Bishop Keith; divines and physicians like the Bonars and Dr James Gregory; town worthies like Provost George Drummond, builder of the North Bridge and author of the New Town Scheme; and the founders of Fettes College and Chalmers' Hospital. There is space allotted to "the soldiers who have died in Edinburgh Castle"; and a memorial carved "for the Society of Coach-drivers" reminds us that from the inns and courts of the Canongate the stage-coaches used to set out for London, and that there the citizens of old awaited news from the South. But no other monument has so strong and pathetic a claim to notice as the plain tombstone which

The Canongate

Robert Burns, by petition to "the Honourable Bailies of Canongate," obtained leave to erect, at his own charge, over the grave of Robert Fergusson, who had lain until then "among the ignoble dead, unnoticed and unknown." The lines engraved on it are from the hand of the greater poet, who freely owned the debt of his song to that of his unhappy predecessor.

> No sculptured marble here, nor pompous lay,
>   No "storied urn, nor animated bust";
> This simple stone directs pale Scotia's way
>   To pour her sorrows o'er her poet's dust.

Two old-time Canongate mansions, once standing on spacious grounds of their own on the right or southern side of the street, have met with a full share of the vicissitudes that have overtaken their neighbours. One of them, Milton House, stood on the site of the residence of the Superiors of the burgh—the Bellendens and the Kerrs—and took its name from an eminent Whig judge of the period of the '45 Rebellion—Fletcher of Milton—who fled with the rest of the Court to the country when the Young Pretender occupied Holyrood, and the Jacobite officers and Highland chiefs made the "White Horse Close" their headquarters. A public school has risen in its place. Queensberry Lodge is still extant, but is in sorry case. The big, plain, dingy building was the town dwelling of the Dukes of Douglas and of Queensberry; "Prior's Kitty, ever fair," the wife of the third of the Queensberry Dukes, entertained company in it in her eccentric style, and sheltered here her *protégé*, the poet Gay, who made excursions from it to Allan Ramsay's circulating library in the Luckenbooths, or to the changehouse of Jenny Ha' on the opposite side

The White Horse Close

of the Canongate. That "degenerate Douglas," known as "Old Q."—the last of his line—sold it in the first year of last century to the Government, who converted it for a time into barracks; it now serves the purpose of a House of Refuge for the Destitute.

Other Canongate houses and closes that have witnessed history are but wrecks of their former selves. But the White Horse Close, at the bottom of this long thoroughfare, retains much of the aspect of the courtyard of an inn and its surrounding buildings in the palmy days of this patrician quarter. There is a sixteenth-century date on one of the gables, and tradition associates the name with a white palfrey of Mary, Queen of Scots. But no part of the existing buildings, which have recently been furbished up and converted into artisans' dwellings is supposed to be older than the date 1623, which appears on a dormer window. The tale of "Waverley" takes a cue from history by lodging Fergus M'Ivor and his tartaned comrades in the White Horse Close. A century earlier it had been the scene of the "Stoppit Stravaig," when a vigilant Presbyterian mob headed back a company of the Scottish nobles and their followers when setting forth in response to Charles I.'s summons to confer with him at Berwick where, it was suspected, their zeal for the Covenant would cool in proportion as their loyalty to the monarch was stimulated. Montrose alone slipped through, and thenceforth became the man of the King instead of the man of the Kirk.

The ancient hostelry, over which "Lucky Wood" presided in Allan Ramsay's time, was admirably placed for the intercepting and entertaining of guests; for it was planted just within the "Water Yett," the former

The Canongate

entry into the burgh, which stood close to the Palace grounds at the junction of the "North Back" of Canongate and Abbeyhill. Travellers by the old Easter or London Road must needs come this way; and much of the glory of Canongate departed when the new and more spacious approach to Edinburgh was formed along the southern skirts of the Calton Hill.

Tragic scenes have been witnessed in the vicinity of the Water Port. The Abbot of Kilwinning was slain here in 1571 in the "Black Saturday" skirmish. Thirty years later, the adherents of Francis, Earl of Bothwell, were seized while making their attempt on the Palace and the King's person, and nine of them were hanged "incontinent" at the neighbouring Girth Cross. George, third Marquis of Huntly, was allowed to ride with his head covered when he was led through the Water Yett on his way to prison and death. But the same privilege was not accorded to a more illustrious captive, Montrose, who, not long after, by the same road, went on the same errand.

A quaint building, covering a clear spring of water and known as "Queen Mary's Bath," almost abuts on the site of the gateway; in it, legend asserts, the beautiful Queen was in the habit of "bathing in milk." Over the Palace bounds near this point clambered some of Rizzio's assassins after committing the deed of blood; and a richly-chased dagger found in a recess in the wall has been conjectured to be a relic of the deed. Outside the Gate stood once the hospital of St Thomas; the home of Bishop Crichton's blue-gowned bedesmen was afterwards occupied by the hired sedan-chairs and hackney coaches of eighteenth-century Edinburgh. Further east, and also on the skirts of the

The Sanctuary

Abbey grounds, is the mansion-house of Croft-an-Righ —the "King's Croft"—or, familiarly, "Croftangry," a name well remembered in "The Chronicles of the Canongate." It is probably not so old as the time of the Regent Moray, who is said to have lived in it; and "Queen Mary's Tree" in the garden is, like others of the kind, of doubtful lineage. But, even if its authentic history go no further back than the period when it was the family mansion of the Earls of Airth, it has been next neighbour to the Palace in days when Scottish Kings still made their home in Holyrood.

All this time we have not overpassed the threshold of the "Sanctuary of the Canongate." Its frontier is marked by the "strand," or line of stones in the causeway, near which, at the foot of the Canongate, stood the "Girth Cross." The boundary of the "Sanctuary Girth" ran northward from this point along the Water Gate, and southward through the Horse Wynd, and enclosed the Palace and the whole of the Royal Park behind. The privilege, which at one time extended to criminals, was confined after the Reformation to impecunious debtors. It may have originated in the sanctuary rights accorded to Saint David's Abbey, but was latterly recognised as associated with the royal residence. In the last two hundred years of its existence, it has been calculated that between 7000 and 8000 persons sought protection from their creditors within the Liberty of Holyrood. In 1816 there were as many as 118 of these refugees from the law in residence within the bounds; and as the accommodation was limited, it may be imagined that the little Alsatia at the foot of the Canongate was often inconveniently crowded with ambiguous company. The handful of rickety

The Canongate

dwellings and ancient inns at the Palace gates have witnessed curious scenes, and could tell strange tales of their guests. The "Abbey Lairds," as these lodgers were called, had the privilege of crossing the bounds of the Sanctuary between midnight on Saturday and midnight on Sunday; and there are legends of captures by the stratagem of putting back the hands of the clock, and of a belated fugitive who, after being chased hot-foot down the Canongate by the myrmidons of the law, managed to fling himself prostrate across the boundary mark just as they seized upon him from behind, and was adjudged free, since his "nobler parts were in sanctuary."

The duty of keeping order and administering justice within the Sanctuary was committed to the "Bailie of the Abbey," who was appointed by the Hereditary Keeper of the Palace, and who had in charge to summon the inhabitants to appear on guard at the Abbey gates on the occasion of an election of Scottish Representative Peers in Holyrood. The father of Lord Jeffrey once held the office of Sanctuary Bailie, which came to an end, along with the privilege of sanctuary, with the abolition of imprisonment for debt in 1880. The Courts were held in the "Abbey Strand," on the right-hand side of the entrance to the Palace esplanade, where may still be seen along with an interesting specimen of a moulded doorway of sixteenth century date, some traces of the beautiful Gothic porch of the religious house. A scheme is afoot for restoring this Abbey Porch destroyed in 1751, along with the adjacent Girth Cross, as a memorial of King Edward VII. On or near the same spot, now occupied in part by the Guard House, must have stood the Tennis Court in which the Scottish

The Abbey Porch

monarchs and their courtiers were wont to play at "caiche-pell," and wherein, it is believed, took place under King Jamie's patronage in 1599 and 1601, those stage performances by strolling English companies, of whom, some have conjectured, William Shakespeare may have been a member.

CHAPTER X

HOLYROOD

A FEW steps across the threshold of the Abbey Porch, and one is in the full presence of the " House of Kings," grey old Holyrood. The very name of this Palace of the Stewarts has magic in it, and speaks volumes of history and of romance. Nor, heavily as time and change have laid their hands upon " Holyrood House" and its surroundings, does its site or its aspect belie its strange and romantic story. On two sides of it the squalor and the noisy industries of a poor quarter of the city press close up against the walls of this venerable seat of royal state and sanctity. But on the other sides are the free air of heaven and the everlasting hills. The approaches from the Canongate may have lost their former stateliness; the monuments and terraces of the New Town may look down from the crown and slopes of Calton on the grim and time-battered relic of the past, stranded in the valley below; but the outlines of the red crags and shadowed clefts of its great and quiet neighbour, Arthur Seat, remain unchanged and unchangeable by the hand of man, and half the domain of Holyrood looks much as it did when David selected the spot as the site of his Monastery.

Of the once magnificent and wealthy religious house, of which the Palace became heir and successor, only a fragment is left. Holyrood is by no means a solitary example of a conventual building being taken possession of as a residence of the King and Court. The Black-friars Monastery at Perth, in which James I. of Scots

THE CHAPEL ROYAL, HOLYROOD ABBEY.

ARTHUR SEAT FROM ST LEONARD'S.

[To face page 112.

The Abbey Church

met his death, is another familiar instance in Scottish history. Holyrood was no exception to the rule that the royal guests, having obtained a footing, soon played the cuckoo with the original monkish owners. The Palace occupies part of the ground once covered by the monastic buildings. The north-west wing—the oldest and most historic part of the existing structure—partly screens the view of the fine western front of the Abbey Church; the Palace walls behind, built in the Merry Monarch's time, have usurped the place of one of the square towers of this front, and have actually impinged on the beautiful Gothic doorway and on the ground plan of the nave. The ruined and mutilated nave—afterwards the Chapel Royal—is all that is left of the Church of the Holy Rude; but it is sufficient to give an idea of its former extent and grandeur.

It was cruciform in plan, and had, besides the western towers, a great central tower rising above the intersection of the nave and choir with the transepts. All but a few fragments of these portions of the building have disappeared; although by the recent operations conducted by the Board of Works, the foundations outlining the complete form and extent of the Church have been laid bare. The cloisters were on the eastern side of the present Palace, and some remains of the cloister walk are to be found under the flying buttresses on the southern side of the Chapel Royal. Here, too, may be discovered traces, in round-headed windows and dog-tooth ornament, of the original Norman structure, which may possibly have arisen under the eye of the saintly and royal founder himself, and have sheltered his war-like rival, Fergus, Lord of Galloway, who sought peace in his latter days within the walls of Holyrood.

Holyrood

It is probable, however, that no part of the surviving Abbey buildings go back quite so far as the reign of David I. From the beginning, the monks held this exposed and perilous ground by a somewhat insecure tenure, and were liable to be driven out by fire and invasion; it has been seen that for a considerable period they had to content themselves with housing on the Castle Rock. Many times, in the fighting centuries that followed the War of Independence, the Church and Abbey were burned. Edward II. and Richard II. did their best to destroy them; but they rose again after the invaders had withdrawn. The great restorer and renovator of Holyrood is believed to have been Abbot Crawford, and his handiwork, of the latter end of the fifteenth century, is manifest in the arches and buttresses of the north and south aisles of the nave, and in the richly ornate doorway. But nearly all styles of Gothic are represented in the beautiful wreck of Holyrood Church, including the nondescript additions that bear the mark of Charles I. and James VII.

For the vicissitudes in the Abbey fortunes did not end with the rough handling given to it during the Hertford Invasion and the subsequent Reformation struggles. It was at a later period that the " Queir and Croce Kirk "—the original choir and transepts—fell into irretrievable ruin, and the materials were disposed of to " faithful men," in order to provide funds " for converting the nave into the Parish Kirk of Canongate." The " Royal Martyr " took some pains to preserve and decorate the church which had witnessed the wedding and funeral rites of his ancestors, and in which he was crowned King of Scots; and he designated it the Chapel Royal. His son James fitted it up for the

HOLYROOD AND ARTHUR SEAT.

[*To face page* 114.

The Chapel Royal

Roman ritual, and installed here the first Knights of the Order of the Thistle. But before the Restoration was complete the rage of the Revolution mob broke in upon the building; the very tombs of the Scottish Kings and Queens were desecrated and the bare walls alone were left. A last stroke fell on the Chapel Royal after the middle of last century, when, orders having been given to repair the ruinous roof, the work was entrusted to a bungling architect, who burdened the old arches with a mass of masonry heavier than they could support, with the result that, in a great storm in December 1768, the roof collapsed, leaving only the skeleton of the walls, the vaulting over part of the south aisle, and a portion of the west front. It has already been mentioned that an idea, to which expression was given in the will of the late Lord Leven and Melville, to restore the nave as a Thistle Chapel, has failed to take form. A report furnished by Mr Lethaby, the London architect, indicated that the ancient piers and arches are too much decayed to support the proposed superstructure.

The floor of the Chapel Royal is paved with monumental slabs, covering the burial-places of members of some of the noblest Scottish families—Douglases Hamiltons, Gordons, Sinclairs, Sutherlands, Campbells, Kerrs. Intermixed is the commoner clay of burghers of the Canongate; although the parish churchyard was outside the walls, where the only remaining monument is one to the memory of a " worthy man and ingenious mason " of the famous race of the Mylnes, for many generations Master Masons to the King. Time and the feet of visitors are obliterating the inscriptions, some of them old and quaint, on the pavement of the Chapel; other slabs and epitaphs are ranged round the walls, and commemorate dead bishops and nobles. Within the north-west tower is an imposing monument, in the form of a marble altar-tomb, to Lord Belhaven, "Counsellor to King Charles and Master of the Horse to Henry, Prince of Wales." Inserted in a pillar of the south aisle is a tablet extolling in Latin the most dubious virtues of Adam Bothwell, Bishop of Orkney, and Commendator of Holyrood, who celebrated, not many paces off, the marriage of Mary and Bothwell in the Abbey Church, and soon afterwards deserted her cause. Of greater antiquity are a few stone coffins and incised slabs that have been recovered from the area of the Church; and in the passage leading from the Palace to the Chapel is pointed out the last resting-place of Rizzio. Recent operations have exposed the moulded doorway and oaken door, and cleared the passage beyond, through which, it is believed, the conspirators found access, on the night of his murder, to the royal apartments above.

But the spot where one is tempted most to linger and moralise, in the vein of the monuments around, over the evanescence of earthly state, is the corner of the south aisle, where is placed the sombre and inconspicuous Royal Vault. As an inscription tells, it was put in decent repair by order of the late Queen Victoria. Here, until the tomb was rifled and the bones scattered in 1688, lay the embalmed bodies of King David Bruce, of James II. of Scots, of James V., and of his first Queen, Magdalen, the fair and much-loved "Lily of France" who faded so early in our northern air. Darnley is believed to have been buried in the Holyrood Vault, to which also in the middle of last century the supposed remains of Mary of Gueldres, wife of "James of the Fiery Face," were removed from

JAMES V.'S TOWER, HOLYROOD PALACE.

[To face page 116.

The Royal Vault

the Trinity College Church. The royal place of sepul-
ture is supposed to have been originally close to the
high altar of the Abbey Church, and in the protecting
neighbourhood of that " Black Rude "—a relic of the
True Cross—bequeathed by Saint Margaret to her
children, which may reasonably be regarded as the real
source of the name and sanctity of Holyrood, rather
than the çomparatively late and mythical story of the
"White Hart." When it was carried away by Edward I.
and bestowed .upon the great Church of Durham, part
of the glory of the Abbey and of the liberties of Scotland
seemed to go with it. The Royal Vault, and indeed the
whole interior and exterior of the Church, have lately
received the careful attention of the Commissioners of
Works, as Conservators of Holyrood, under the direction
of Mr Oldrieve ; and while the remarkable structure has
been strengthened and protected as far as possible
against the inroads of time and weather, the bases of
the pillars have been uncovered, and several interesting
archæological discoveries made.

Other notable incidents of the long centuries of war
with England were witnessed within the " Monastery of
the Crag of Holyrood." Parliaments and councils met
there, whereat were provided the funds for buying back
Scotland's independence from Richard Lion-heart ; the
ransom of David Bruce, after the English army, fighting
under the Black Rood, had captured him at Nevill's
Cross ; and the crusading tax imposed under Bagimont's
Roll. Edward Baliol rendered homage to Edward III.
at Holyrood ; John of Gaunt was hospitably entertained
in the Abbey, and out of gratitude his son, Henry IV.,
spared the fane when he came hither afterwards with
hostile intent. The Abbey became an occasional

Holyrood

residence of the Scottish Kings from the days of Robert the Bruce. His son David, we have seen, was buried beside its high altar. James I., the Poet King, lived much in it. He was here in 1429 when the Lord of the Isles humbly implored pardon, dressed only in his "shirt and drawers," and holding a naked sword by the point, for his crime of burning the town of Inverness. In the following year Queen Jane Beaufort bore twin sons in the Abbey, the survivor of whom, James II., was wedded and buried within the walls where he was born. The unhappy Third James also spent much of his time at Holyrood with his fiddling and other favourites; and was married in the Abbey Church to Margaret of Denmark, who thus brought the Northern Isles to the Scottish throne.

But Holyrood never witnessed before such splendour and gaiety as attended the nuptials of James IV. with Margaret Tudor—the union of the "Thistle and the Rose" which after a hundred years more of strife was to bring about the Union of the Crowns. The monastic house seems to have been converted into a "palace of pleasant delights," with Banqueting Hall and Great Chamber, hung with tapestries and provided with "glassin windows" blazoned with the royal arms, and with supping and dancing rooms, where Dunbar footed the "dirry-danton" with Mistress Musgrave; and there was no room for shaven crowns and conventual peace in the round of feasting, games, tilting matches, and plays with which the chivalric and accomplished King welcomed his young English bride—not dreaming that Flodden was only ten years ahead of him.

The father of Mary, Queen of Scots, Pitscottie tells us, founded, in the spring of 1525, "a fair palace in

HOLYROOD PALACE, SHOWING "THE REGENT MURRAY'S LODGING."
(After a drawing by E. Blore.)

The Palace

the Abbey of Holyrood House, and three fair towers till rest into, when he was pleased to come," and hither he brought his beautiful "Queen of Forty Days." But this oldest part of the existing Palace was actually begun by James IV., and the oaken piles driven into the sandy soil to support the edifice have been come upon in the course of recent excavations. The north-western tower is probably all that survives of this work, for in 1544 and in 1547, during the troublous minority of Mary, English armies "brent the Pallais"; and although it rose again, and witnessed some of the gayest, and some of the saddest, scenes in the life of the Queen of Scots, and of her son and grandson, it again fell victim to a fire which broke out while Cromwell's soldiers were in possession. After the Restoration, the Protector's uncouth repairs were removed, the quadrangle completed in the prevailing French style of the time, and the present entrance gateway built in 1671 by Robert Mylne, King's Mason, from designs by Sir William Bruce of Kinross. James VII., as Duke of York and Albany, held Court here ; Prince Charles Edward took up his quarters at the Palace, and slept in the bed (afterwards tenanted by the Duke of Cumberland) where his unfortunate ancestor Charles I. had lain ; and it was twice a place of retreat for Charles X. of France. Occasionally since it has been a residence of royalty ; and annually, at the opening of the General Assembly, the State Apartments are occupied by the King's representative, the Lord High Commissioner, while the elections of Scottish Peers still take place in the Portrait Gallery. Once again, in the Coronation Year of George Fifth, it is restored to its old state and uses.

Having now glanced rapidly through the history of

Holyrood

this "grey romance in stone," one may better appreciate the venerable aspect of Holyrood Abbey and the spirit of the past that broods around and within. The spacious "place," through which the carriage-drive passes to enter the Park, is the old West Court of the Palace, and has witnessed many scenes of pomp and strife. In the centre is a beautiful carved Gothic fountain, erected by the Prince Consort, in the style of an ancient specimen at Linlithgow. Opposite to the Guard House is the grand entrance, columned and pedimented, and surmounted by the Royal arms and crown, and connected by a screen, considerably lower than the rest of the façade, with the two great flanking towers, turreted at the corners, that complete the Palace front. The two towers are uniform, but it needs only a glance to perceive that the north-western one is of the greater age, and that the other has been added to give symmetry to the design. Among the accretions, or supplementary buildings, of the Palace that have long ago disappeared is the structure known as "Regent Moray's Lodging," attached to the north side of this tower, and shown in a view dated 1826.

The gateway gives access to the Quadrangle or Inner Court, which has a colonnade around the four sides. In front and to the right are the Royal Apartments, still intermittently occupied during the sittings of Assembly, and now again opened to receive the descendant and representative of the old race of the Scottish Kings. Their history is comparatively modern and tame. They embrace, however, some noble rooms with handsome furniture and rich tapestries, and the elaborate and beautiful carved and painted ceilings are specially worthy of note. To nine people out of ten, the romance of the spot—the very soul of Holyrood—is concentrated

HOLYROOD PALACE, PRINCIPAL DOORWAY.

The Rizzio Tragedy

in the suite of apartments in the old wing of the Palace, and reached by a staircase on the left, wherein were enacted some of the strangest and darkest passages in the strange and dark drama of the life of Mary Stewart.

It is impossible to feel hard-hearted towards the unhappy Queen of Scots while within the walls where she suffered so many sorrows and humiliations. What weighs upon our thoughts as we visit the scene of Chastelard's frenzy, of the murder of Rizzio, of the folly and guilt of Darnley and Bothwell, is not the weakness of one beautiful and friendless woman who was the centre of the vast maze of plot and crime, but the treacherous savagery of the times and of the men by whom she was surrounded. Here still is not only the stage, but part of the stage-setting of that never-to-be-forgotten story of Old Holyrood. True, not much of royal state is suggested by the moderately-sized Audience Chamber, with its mouldering hangings, and time-worn furniture and decorations. More sombre and faded still is the Bedroom adjoining ; while the small Dressing-room and still tinier Supping-room opening from it give one a vivid impression of the narrow space to which even the great ones of the earth had to accommodate themselves in the indoors life of the Scotland of the sixteenth century. But the blurred mirror may have reflected the stern form of Knox, as he poured his harsh admonitions into the ears of his weeping and angry sovereign ; Queen Mary's bed, a frayed and tattered wreck, must have known many a sad vigil ; the private staircase has echoed to the feet of Darnley and of Bothwell ; the faded tapestries may have swayed at the passing of the conspirators hurrying to the " slauchter of Davie."

Holyrood

The incidents of that tragedy, in some sense the fatal turning-point in Mary's career, are familiar to all. But only in the little supper-room that witnessed it can one fully realise the scene so often pictured and described—the overturned table, the panic-stricken favourite crouching behind his mistress, the guileful and jealous husband with his arms thrown about her in feigned protection, the gaunt, armed figure of Ruthven at the door, the cruel and relentless faces and drawn swords around, and in the midst the outraged and terrified Queen, not long a wife and soon to become a mother, tasting the very bitterest drop in the bitter cup of her life. On the landing of the great staircase outside there used to be pointed out the "irremovable" stain of Rizzio's blood, on the spot to which the body, pierced with more than fifty wounds, was dragged by the murderers. That dark night's work was never wiped out of Mary's memory; and her words, as she dried her eyes and murmured, "I will study revenge," have the ring of fate. If ghosts walk anywhere, it must be in those darkling and deserted chambers of Holyrood.

More than one later romance of history is interwoven with that of Mary Stewart. It has already been noted that in the State bed in the audience chamber Charles I. slept after his coronation as King of Scots, the Young Chevalier before Prestonpans, and the "Butcher Cumberland" after Culloden. Below, on the first floor of the Palace, are "Darnley's apartments," also crowded with relics and associations of the past; and on the same level is the long Picture Gallery, part of the addition made by Charles II., from the walls of which look down the portraits of a hundred kings of Scotland, painted by a contract by a Flemish artist—

QUEEN MARY'S BEDROOM.

CHARLES I.'S BED.

[*To face page* 122.

The Picture Gallery

De Witt—in the last year of the reign of the Merry Monarch.

Needless to say, the very names, to say nothing of the faces, of the bulk of these crowned effigies are mythical. You can begin the series with Fergus the First and the year 330 B.C., and long before reaching King Duncan and Macbeth you will be constrained to cry out, with Banquo, " What! will their line stretch to the crack of doom? " Paintings of much greater historic and artistic interest are the curious diptychs dating from the last quarter of the fifteenth century, and removed from Hampton Palace in 1857. They are believed to represent, on the obverse, James III. of Scotland and his Queen, and to have formed the altar-piece of the old Trinity College Church. In the Picture Gallery were held the receptions and levees of Prince Charles Edward, while he kept brief state in the Palace of his ill-starred race. Flora M'Ivor, and Edward Waverley, and the Chief of Glennaquoich are among the many ghosts that haunt it.

The Palace Gardens, although like the rest of Holyrood, they have of late had the benefit of taste-ful restorative touches, are remarkable neither for extent nor for beauty—beyond the beauty of green-sward and of venerable walls and associations. The sundial, named as Queen Mary's, is but one of the many objects in and around Holyrood annexed by unsupported tradition to that all-pervading *genius loci*. It dates from Charles First's time, and was probably a compliment to his Queen, Henrietta Maria. Outside these grounds, still reserved for Royalty and its representatives, stretches to the east and south the free and wind-swept slopes and hollows of the King's Park.

CHAPTER XI

THE KING'S PARK

THE boundaries of this royal domain—this piece of rough nature, turned to the purposes of a public pleasure and exercise-ground—are nearly five miles in circuit; it rises in Arthur Seat to a height of 825 feet above the sea. Thus it has room and diversity of surface, and a bold and spacious outlook beyond any other of its kind. The weather-beaten and time-stained House of the Stewarts seems to crouch under the lee of the central hill and of the great crescent-shaped ridge of precipices—the Salisbury Crags—that rise almost from the Palace gates and reach a height of fully 450 feet above its level. Geologists have found this crumpled square mile of the surface of Scotland one of the most interesting spots in the British Isles. It is a very museum of the igneous rocks; it is eloquent of the upheavals and outbursts of the inconceivably remote period when the site of Edinburgh was a centre of volcanic energies; and it has given clues to the geological past of Scotland.

But the King's Park possesses records of much more recent date and more immediate human interest. It would take a volume to tell its authentic annals and to set forth its traditions. It has been the scene of duels and mutinies, murders and conspiracies. Within it or on its margin are fragments of old

St Anthony's Chapel

religious houses, holy wells and springs, lake and peak and glen. In the "Duke's Walk" the last of the Stewarts who enjoyed his royal heritage was wont to take exercise, and eighteenth-century affairs of honour were sometimes settled on this spot, then made more secluded by oak coppice. It is now part of the parade ground, which has also swallowed up Clockmill House and its trees. Nearer to the eastern entrance of the Park is that still more evil-omened trysting-place, "Mushat's Cairn," known to Jeanie Deans. Hither, while the pious Cameronian's daughter was holding parley in the darkness with the mysterious stranger, came the warning lilt of Madge Wildfire—

> When the gled's in the blue cloud,
>   The laverock lies still;
> When the hound's in the greenwood,
>   The hind keeps the hill.

On a spur above, looking to the north, with St Margaret's Loch spread below and its spring of crystal water welling from under a boulder behind, is "the chapel, cave, and hermitage dedicated to Saint Anthony the Eremite," founded by the Logans of Restalrig, and much esteemed and resorted to by the seafaring community of Leith, but now a mere fragment of ruin perched on a rock. A scrap of ballad minstrelsy clings to this spot also. The forsaken lady sang—

> Now Arthur Seat shall be my bed;
>   The sheets will ne'er be pressed by me;
> St Anton's well will be my drink
>   Since my false love's forsaken me.

In climbing to it from the Palace one passes another "Holy Well"—that named of St Margaret—the

The King's Park

ornamental Gothic stonework of which was removed from the fountain of St Triduana, reputed to be the original Rood Well of many virtues, which had to yield place to the St Margaret's locomotive works of the North British Railway. A rival claim, it should be said, has been put in for the recently restored "Chapter House" (so-called) at Restalrig. Thus are the old and the new, the sacred and the utilitarian, brought into sharp conflict even on the knees of Arthur Seat.

The Hill is provided with a "commodity of good names." We come upon them whatever route we choose in ascending or going round it. Between St Margaret's and St Anton's Well is the "Haggis Knowe." The great hollow scooped out between the main hill and the magnificent buttress of the Salisbury Crags is the "Hunter's Bog," now appropriated as a shooting range. The Young Pretender traversed the Bog on his first coming; mounting a bay gelding at the Haggis Knowe, he was greeted by a cheering crowd in the Duke's Walk and by a cannon-ball from the Castle, which struck James V.'s tower as the Prince alighted in front of Holyrood. The sharp ridge that bounds this valley to the eastward and forms the favourite approach to the summit is the "Lang Raw." Below the ridge are the curious outcrops of volcanic rock known as the "Dasses"; and between it and the whinny heights of the "Crow Hill" is a subsidiary glen ending in the expressively named "Punch Bowl." For those who prefer a steeper ascent, varied by some crag-work, a way will be found by the "Hawse," at the head of Hunter's Bog, and the "Gutted Haddie," under the "Raven Rock" and the "Lion's Haunch," by which the height can be

The Wild M'Craws

escaladed almost on its steepest side. Others again, who prefer roundabout and easy routes, can follow the carriage drive which skirts the eastern slopes of the hill and rises to Dunsappie Crag and Loch, from the bank of which, 370 feet above sea-level, the track is plain and, except for the final scramble, smooth going to the top. It carries us almost over the site of the encampment of the rebels of the '45 ; and higher up, on the knolls and hollows of the Nether Hill or Lion's Haunch, is the spot where the mutineers of the Seaforth Highlanders—the " Wild M'Craws "—entrenched themselves in 1778, after having overpowered their officers on the Castle Esplanade, under the idea that they were about to be sold into slavery in the East Indies.

Around the boulders on the summit, blackened by many a bonfire and rubbed smooth by the exercises of many generations of schoolboys, there is generally a fresh wind blowing to cool the brow of the perspiring climber. The prospect, ranging from Ben Lomond to the May Island and from Lochnagar to the Lammermuirs, is an exceeding great reward for his toil, unless indeed a "haar" had stolen up behind him from the Firth and drawn a veil over the panorama.

Should the line of the drive be pursued past Dunsappie, a scene soon breaks upon us which is scarcely surpassed by that disclosed from the crown of the Hill. The roadway gently ascends until it appears almost to overhang the hollow of the " Windy Gowl " and the snug village of Duddingston and its Loch, spread some 300 feet beneath. The low square tower of the ancient Norman church emerges from among the roofs and trees amidst which it is set, on a knoll projecting into a lake bounded by reeds and crags and covered with swans and other water-fowl. Thomson the landscape painter, was minister of Duddingston; Walter Scott was an elder in the parish church, and the stump of a tree is shown in the manse garden under which he wrote part of the " Heart of Midlothian." At the Kirkgate, beside the "loupin'-on stane," still hang the "jougs"; King James, of sapient renown, is said to have resorted to the Sheephead Inn, hard by, to solace himself with skittles after the cares of state; Prince Charlie lodged in another of the village houses. Beyond are the park trees of Duddingston Lodge, belonging to the Duke of Abercorn, and half-embracing the waters of the loch; and Prestonfield, the seat of the Dicks of Braid, and now of the Dick-Cunynghames, an old house that has entertained Dr Johnson and was familiar to the youth of Henry Cockburn. More apart, Craigmillar Castle rises from amongst its trees, stately even in ruin; and between us and the far blue line of the Pentlands, the Moorfoots and the Lammermuirs, are spread the valleys of the Esk and of the Tyne, and the fairest and richest parts of the Lothians.

Before the carriage-way descends to the lower levels, it passes through a gap where there is a fine echo. Precipices rise on the right hand, and on the left the Hill almost overhangs the " Wells o' Wearie " and the park road to Duddingston, in the grand red basaltic columns known as " Samson's Ribs."

Near the Park gate of St Leonard's, the King's Drive meets the " Radical Road," which, starting from opposite Holyrood, has skirted the base of the Salisbury Crags. This is another Park walk unsurpassable elsewhere in interest and beauty. The "close-built, high-piled city" presses to the base of the steep, smooth

The Inhabiting Spirit

talus of the Crags; and when one has ascended to the summit of the slope—to the "Cat Nick," the immemorial test of the climbing powers of the Auld Reekie callants —the sheer cliffs still rise nearly 100 feet above, although the hollow through which the Drive winds past St Leonard's braes and Dumbiedykes has sunk 400 feet below. Over the city and its smoke, from a height above that of the highest level of the Castle Rock, one can look abroad upon the hills and waters that encircle the "romantic town."

Sir Walter is the inhabiting spirit of the scene. It was, as he tells us, "his favourite evening and morning resort when engaged with a favourite author or new subject of study." It was to him "the scene of much delicious musing when life was young and promised to be happy." His pen can best describe the peculiar fascination of a stroll around the Radical Road. "As the path gently circles around the base of the cliffs," he writes, "the prospect, composed of enchanting and sublime objects, changes at every step, and presents them blended with, or divided from, each other in every possible variety which can gratify the eye and the imagination." His own imagination has encircled it with a fresh and never-fading charm.

It was from this romantic path that Reuben Butler "saw the morning arise" the day after the slaughter of Porteous. One looks down from it almost on the turrets of Holyrood and the thatched roof of "Davie Deans's Cottage." His magic wand created the Radical Road itself; it was built by the hands of the unemployed in the distressful times that followed the Great War, in response to the lament by the author of "Waverley" concerning the impassable state into which the pathway had fallen.

CHAPTER XII

ROUND THE FLODDEN WALL—THE COWGATE

FROM Dan to Beersheba—from the Castle to the Palace
—we have penetrated through the heart of Old Edinburgh, and of its neighbour and vassal, the Canongate.
To pick up the remaining threads of its history and to
glance at what is left of its past, it will be enough to
stroll round the line of the ancient mural defences, built,
or rather renewed, after the calamity of Flodden had
left the "Guid Toun" naked and open to the attack of
a victorious enemy. This Flodden Wall has already
been scanned from the North Bridge and from the
Castle Rock, and we have passed through its principal
gateway and defence at the Netherbow. On its
northern side, the city was content, as we have seen,
with the protection afforded by the waters of the Nor'
Loch, which at one time spread eastward until they
reached to the boundaries of the grounds of the Trinity
College Church and Hospital, at the lower end of Leith
Wynd.

Here, close up against the Craigs of Calton, was
situated a supplementary entrance and barrier of the
city—the Leith Wynd, or "New" Port—designed to
protect it against incursion from the north through the
little burgh of Calton, or St Ninian's Row. On the

TRINITY COLLEGE CHURCH BEFORE 1848.

From a Lithograph.

The "Colledge Kirk"

east side of this gate, as shown on Gordon of Rothie-may's map of 1647, stood "Paul's Work," originally an hospital for the entertainment of aged poor men, founded in 1479, and dedicated to the Virgin, by Bishop Spence of Aberdeen, and afterwards turned into a woollen manufactory and a house of correction. To the west lay the "Colledge Kirk" and its adjoining hospital, with trim gardens extending to the Loch.

Church and charity were the princely foundation of Mary of Gueldres, Queen of James II. of Scots, who, shortly after that monarch's death in 1460, began raising and endowing this collegiate charge, dedicated "to the honour and the praise of the Holy Trinity, to the ever-blessed and glorious Virgin Mary, to Saint Ninian the Confessor, and to all the Saints and elect people of God," and provided with a provost, eight prebendaries, and two clerks, to whom afterwards were added a dean and sub-dean. The foundress died three years later, and her remains—their identity has been disputed—were found enclosed in a leaden coffin close by the high altar when the church was demolished in 1848, and were removed to Holyrood. The building, which, next to St Giles, was the most important of the ecclesiastical antiquities of the city, was removed, along with the Hospital and other ancient landmarks, from the sequestered spot on which it had stood for four hundred years, to make way for the railway. It was a fine specimen of the Scottish style of the decorated Gothic of the fifteenth century, and consisted of a choir, with aisles, apse, and transepts—the nave, though evidently part of the original plan, never having been completed. As has been already noted, part of the structure has been rebuilt with the old stones, and incorporated in the new Trinity College Church in Jeffrey Street, a modern thoroughfare that, along with Colston Street, has superseded the old Leith Wynd, the site of which is now covered by railway platforms, sidings, and signal-boxes.

Beyond the crossing of the Canongate, Leith Wynd was continued southward by St Mary's Wynd, the "Rag Fair" of the Edinburgh of Fergusson's day, lined at one time by rows of booths, full of second-hand clothes, built against the Town Wall, while on the other side were carriers' quarters and places of entertainment for travellers, among them the "White Horse Inn," where Dr Johnson and his biographer put up on their way to the Hebrides. It changed more than its name in becoming St Mary Street, and was made the scene of the first experiment of the City Improvement Trust in clearing away slums and building working-men's houses. Originally it was a road that led by the eastern outskirts of the town to the Convent of St Mary of Placentia, and to the Hospital of St Leonard. At the foot of the Wynd, the Town Wall was pierced on the right by the Cowgate Port; a lane, now the South Back of Canongate, straggled in from the direction of the King's Park; and in front access was had, through the guarded gateway of St Mary's Port, to the faubourg of the Pleasance, a happy corruption of the name of the Convent, bestowed on a suburb which in old deeds is sometimes called "Dear-enough."

Close by, St John's Hill occupies the crest of a ridge overlooking the Canongate closes and breweries and the green hollow under "St Leonard's Crags"; Thomas

St John's Hill

Campbell, while still in early manhood, is said to have written his "Pleasures of Hope" there, before removing to Alison Square, and other notable people have found a quiet retreat in St John's Hill, in the heart of noise and squalor. Nearer to the fringe of the Park lies the district of Dumbiedykes—so named, according to Sir Walter, because a teacher of the deaf and dumb once had a residence in the locality; its streets and terraces run down slopes that are in places so steep that no wheeled vehicle can venture to descend them, and the windows look across the valley to the great glacis and frowning cliffs of the Salisbury Crags.

The Pleasance, too, has its memories, although it has been brought to low social estate. It led to the Gibbet Loan and to St Leonard's Chapel, to which the Douglases repaired to plot the death of James V.—a site that afterwards became the terminus of the "Innocent Railway," and is now occupied by mineral sidings. The Quakers had their refuge in the Pleasance, where still are a little meeting-house and burial-ground of the "Friends." It was the centre of the excursions and adventures of Mr Crockett's "Cleg Kelly." But this poor and crowded district of St Leonard's, crouching at the foot of green hill and naked rock, is associated in our thoughts chiefly with the scenes and characters of the "Heart of Midlothian." On a "kaim," or ridge, on the margin of the Park is a humble thatched dwelling, the "Herd's House" of former days, on which the popular fancy has bestowed the name of "Davie Deans's Cottage." Scott, as we have seen, has often looked down upon the spot, in his rambles round the "Radical Road," and his eye caught the merits of St Leonard's braes as the scene of a romance, as his

Flodden Wall—The Cowgate

ear seized on "Dumbiedykes" as the soubriquet of the Silent Laird.

Through the Cowgate Port, Butler escaped after having been an unwilling witness of the lynching of Jock Porteous in the Grassmarket. Once on a time the cattle of the burgesses were driven afield by the rural lane that led, through this narrow natural defile, from Holyrood to St Cuthbert's Kirk. In the days of the early Stewarts the Cowgate opened upon the country. As late as the middle of the seventeenth century, and later, gardens and cultivated land began where the Town Walls ended. Even in the age of Dr Robertson, the historian, and of Adam Smith, eminent citizens who flitted so far from the centre of society as St Leonard's and the Sciennes were regarded as having gone into Siberian exile. But, down in the hollow of the "Coogait" and in its wynds and closes, "patricians, senators, and princes of the land" were for centuries content to take up their abode; and foreign visitors descanted on its "magnificence."

Some of the Cowgate alleys we have already explored from the High Street and the Canongate. The stumps of a few ancient lanes—such as Forrester's Wynd—continue to hold their place, after their very names have been lost in the thoroughfares above. But the hand of improvement has been busy on the Cowgate frontages, especially at the eastern or "Port" end. Light has been let down into it by the demolition of some of the most striking of the antique houses. We have seen that the Palace of the Beatons, at the foot of the Blackfriars Wynd, has utterly disappeared; the like fate has befallen the house of Gavin Douglas, the poet-bishop of Dunkeld, in the neighbouring

134

THE OLD MINT.

From a water-colour by D. Ritchie.

The Cowgate Port

Robertson's Close; and one may look in vain for any trace of the Scottish Mint or "Cunzie" House, whose sombre and massive turret of polished ashlar-work protruded into the narrow thoroughfare.

In compensation, some of the handsomest of the modern public buildings of the Scottish Capital have their roots in the Cowgate—among them the Sheriff Court-House, the Library of the Solicitors before the Supreme Courts, and the New Free Library, this last on a site once occupied by the residence of Sir Thomas Hope, King's Advocate to Charles I., and nearly opposite that of the masterful and turbulent Earl of Haddington, who is still remembered in the locality as " Tam o' the Coogait."   Other shadows are thrown by the South and George IV. Bridges, whose traffic roars overhead, two or three storeys above the level of the squalid Cowgate pavement.   Yet, with all these changes, in the dim perspective of the tall imposing lands; in what little has been left of gabled end, and timber front, and turnpike stair ; in its " dives," and low moulded doorways, and narrow close-heads, and projecting poles, bearing the dingy washing of the inmates of the degraded thoroughfare, the Cowgate still preserves more of the ancient air of an Edinburgh street than can perhaps elsewhere be found.

The chief of the few remaining antiquities of the street is the Magdalene Chapel, which lies far to the westward near the Cowgatehead, where its modest spire is almost buried from sight among the tall buildings that crowd around.   It was founded nine years before Flodden, on the site of an earlier Maison Dieu, chiefly by a pious burgher, Michael Macqueen, and by his spouse, Janet Rynd, whose tomb, with black-letter inscription still legible, is to be found within. The chapel and charity, for the support of a chaplain and seven bedesmen, were placed under the trust of the Incorporation of Hammermen, and after the Reformation the chapel became the meeting hall of that body, and held the "Blue Blanket," the palladium of the privileges and liberties of the Edinburgh Crafts. In the principal window is one of the few examples of pre-Reformation stained glass left in Scotland, and in the spire is hung an ancient bell. John Craig, Knox's assistant, preached Latin discourses in Magdalene Chapel; in it the National Covenant was prepared for signature in the adjoining Greyfriars Churchyard; and the table is still shown whereon the body of the Earl of Argyle, shortened by the head, was laid after execution. The building is now occupied as a Protestant Medical Mission.

Three famous accesses from the Cowgate to the south were the Horse Wynd, the College Wynd, and the High School Wynd. The first led past the west side of the old College enclosure, once the grounds of the Church of St Mary-in-the-Fields, to the gateway in the wall that opened on the suburb of Potterrow. Horse Wynd, strange as it may seem, was once celebrated for it spaciousness and salubrity as a place of residence. Near the Cowgate corner stood a quaint building in which Andro Symson, successor of Chepman, had his printing-press; further up were dwellings, one or two of them still standing, in which quite a knot of law lords and blue-blooded Jacobite families lived in the period of knee-breeches and sedan-chairs. It is now a steep ascent, partly by steps, to the level of the modern Chambers Street, and forms, in its lower half, a portion of Guthrie Street. College Wynd was also a fashionable locality. Like its neighbour, it gave direct access to the College from the High Street, in days before the South Bridge had been made. Oliver Goldsmith lived in it, and ran up tailors' bills, while attending medical classes in the neighbouring place of learning. But a greater title to fame belongs to it, for in a house at the wynd-head, close to North College Street, opposite the dwelling of Dr Joseph Black, the great chemist, and under the same roof as Lord Henderland, Walter Scott was born. Up this narrow way, as James Grant notes, Boswell and Principal Robertson conducted Dr Johnson to view the "Town's College," when the author of "Waverley" was a baby.

Some distance further east was the High School Wynd. It was not many years after the Black Friary, which had occupied the site, had been wrecked and its stones used "in the bigging of dykes," that the Grammar School of the burgh was finally settled in the "High School Yards." For two centuries it was housed in a narrow turreted building, over the porch of which was a carved stone with the date 1578, and the words "Musis Respublica Floret." The wishes of the founders were not belied. The original High School, and its more spacious successor erected in 1777, became a home of many illustrious memories. Some of its teachers and of its scholars have prominent places in the history of Scottish learning and literature. Drummond of Hawthornden was taught his letters, no doubt with the aid of the birch, in the High School; Thomas Ruddiman, the grammarian, was a prop of the institution; Allan Masterton — Burns's Allan, who composed " Willie brewed a peck o' maut "—was one of its lesser lights as writing-master; David Mallet, or Malloch as he was then content to be called, was at one time its janitor. Three Lord Chancellors of England, it has been noted—Erskine, Loughborough, and Brougham—received their schooling in this famous place of learning, and other "old boys" who were taught under the benignant sway of Adam or of Pillans, were Walter Scott, Francis Jeffrey, and Francis Horner. Of an earlier generation, when the pupils were expected to turn up for their Latin exercises at 7 A.M., was Henry Mackenzie, who recalls with pride his invitations to drink tea with the Rector in a house "at the country end of the suburb called Pleasance," named, in remembrance of the ambition of an aspiring tailor, the "Castle of Clouts." Still more cherished and inspiring than the recollections of the class-room and the tea-table were those that clung to the games and battles in the "Yards," which perpetuated the traditions of the more tumultuous and often bloody "barrings-out" of earlier times; the "alarms and excursions" between the High School boys and the "gamins" of the adjoining Cowgate and Pleasance, and the visits to the "Jib House" at the wynd-head. Scott himself, notwithstanding his genius and his lameness, "made a brighter figure in the Yards than in the class."

In 1829 the Royal High School flitted to the slopes of the Calton, and the disused edifice was appropriated for the purposes of a Surgical Hospital in connection with the neighbouring Royal Infirmary. This is another institution of which Edinburgh has just reason to be proud. Its nucleus had been formed exactly a hundred years before the High School removal. Ten

High School and Infirmary

years after it had taken imposing and beneficent shape, in a building, in Infirmary Street, which did honour to the charity and public spirit of " Edinburgh before the '45." Whigs and Tories exerted themselves nobly in the rearing of a structure surpassed at the time by none in Europe as a place of healing and tendance. The zealous Whig Lord Provost, George Drummond, was its chief promoter; the Jacobite Lord Cromarty, attainted later for his share in the Rebellion, laid its foundation-stone; the first of the great surgical dynasty of the Monros was active in its organisation; and the institution was not long in working order when it was turned into a military hospital for the wounded, both Highlanders and Hanoverians, from Prestonpans. The fame and success of Edinburgh as a medical school has depended on the growth and efficiency of the Infirmary; and after the institution had moved to a roomier and more convenient site between Lauriston and the Meadows, the old building continued for long to serve a great and blessed purpose as the City Fever Hospital, which has now taken up new and airy ground on the southern side of Wester Craiglockhart Hill. Part of the former Infirmary buildings has been turned to the purposes of laboratories and class-rooms of the Engineering Faculty; the neighbouring Old Surgeon's Hall— home of many memories since it was first built in 1697—still stands within the south-eastern angle of the Blackfriars ground, but is marked for early destruction.

In close proximity to these temples of healing stands Lady Yester's, one of the oldest of the city churches. It was founded in 1644 by a pious ancestress of the Marquis of Tweeddale, and has had among its distinguished ministers Principals Robertson, Lee, and Caird. Here, too, are Corporation Baths and other public buildings, while bounding the Old Infirmary ground and the site of Old Surgeon Square to the south, there may still be seen the massive remains of the Town Wall extending from the Pleasance along the northern side of Drummond Street.

All this intra-mural space once formed part of the gardens of the Dominican Monastery. In these grounds, secluded yet airy, placed between the city and the fields without, Cardinal Bagimont, John of Gaunt, Archbishop Beaton, and John Knox had walked and meditated. They originally embraced the site of the Church of the "Blessed Mary-in-the-Fields," lying to the westward. By 1567, the church, like the neighbouring monastery, had fallen into ruins. Queen Mary had just before granted a charter for the foundation of a University, in fulfilment of a purpose for which a public-spirited citizen, Robert Reid, Bishop of Orkney, had left a sum of 8000 merks. Not until several years later, however, in the time of Mary's son, James, did these good intentions begin to bear fruit, and academic buildings of a humble kind to rise on the mouldered and shattered religious foundation. The times were too troubled for the peaceful pursuits of learning. In particular, in the year after the drafting of the charter of the "Oure Townis College," there happened, on this very spot, a tragic event that shook the whole land, and ultimately drove the Queen from her throne and kingdom—the "mystery of Kirk o' Field."

The scene of this dark and epoch-making crime lay between the line of the older defences and the later Flodden Wall. It partook of the character both of

Kirk of Field

town and country, and has been represented as a place suitable for an invalid, such as Darnley was, recovering from grievous sickness—salubrious and retired, and yet convenient of access from Holyrood. Buchanan, a prejudiced witness—but who is not?—describes it as "a house not commodious for a sick man, nor comely for a King, for it was both riven and ruinous, and had stood empty without any dweller for divers years before, in a place of small resort, between old falling walls of two kirks, near a few almshouses for poor beggars."

The building—"Robert Balfour's ludging"—probably stood on or near the corner of the present Drummond Street and South Bridge, the fabric of the Kirk of Field occupying, it is supposed, part of what is now the College Quadrangle. A postern gate entered through the Town Wall, and while Darnley lay in an upper chamber, a room below was reserved for the Queen; and in this Mary slept on the two nights preceding the murder. No sooner had she left it late on the night of the 9th February 1567, to be present at the bridal banquet and masque of her servant Sebastian, than the gunpowder was stored in this apartment by the minions of Bothwell, who himself kept hovering near the scene, clad in "the loose cloak of a Black Reiter"; and at "two hours after midnight," when dancing had barely ceased at Holyrood, came the shock for which, according to the Queen's enemies, she had been listening as impatiently as her lover. Not the least mysterious part of this black business is the fact that, while the house was blown to fragments —"not one stone left upon another"—the bodies of Darnley and his page Taylor were found, in their nightgear, some distance off in the orchard, with scarce a mark of violence on them.

CHAPTER XIII

ROUND THE FLODDEN WALL—THE UNIVERSITY

NOT until 1582 did the Town's College—the latest but not the least illustrious of the Scottish Universities—begin to rise on its appointed site. King James bestowed upon it his name and his "special approbation." But it does not appear that the College was indebted to him for more substantial favours; the gift promised by the Modern Solomon to his "God-bairn" came to naught. The University owes, indeed, little to royal favour; and an endowment of £200 annually, granted by Cromwell, was rescinded at the Restoration. It managed to grow and thrive for centuries under the auspices and control of the City Fathers; and although there were quarrels between Town and Gown influences, and blunders were committed on both sides, the University has, on the whole, reason to feel grateful for the fostering care bestowed on it by the Council and Magistrates, with whom its connection is by no means entirely severed.

For long, the Faculties had to be content to house meanly in scattered and incommodious buildings, which served both as class-rooms for the students and dwellings for the professors. The College Library may almost be said to have had a separate beginning; in

THE UNIVERSITY.

"Oure Tounis College"

the bequest made by Clement Little of his collection of 300 books; it received, among other reinforcements, the volumes that had been gathered by Drummond of Hawthornden, and has gradually developed into the magnificent collection of over 150,000 volumes, including many precious MSS., accommodated in the spacious and beautiful Library Hall of the University, after having long been cribbed, cabined, and confined in an antique building which continued to hold its place—the last relic of the Old College—for some years after it had been enclosed within the present Quadrangle. One of the most recent benefactors of the Library has been the late Sir William Fraser.

As it stands to-day, the University building was begun in 1789, and was not completed until forty-five years later. Indeed, the copestone was not put upon the original design of Robert Adam until fully a century after the laying of the foundation-stone, by the addition of the dome and cupola, crowned by a golden figure of "Youth" bearing aloft the lighted torch of knowledge, which contribute materially to the dignity of the structure. Wanting this feature, even the front elevation, towards South Bridge had an air of massiveness that approached heaviness; while the face presented towards South College Street, and also that towards Chambers Street—the latter now opened freely to the light by the removal of the old buildings that screened the College flank—had, and still have, in their monotonous lines and dull grey tones, a decidedly sombre and oppressive effect, suggestive rather of the burdens and toils of learning than of the inspiring influences of knowledge.

But if a somewhat lowering and repellent front be

Flodden Wall—The University

presented to the outer world, compensation will be found by those who enter boldly, through the lofty gateway of three arches, supported by six monolithic Doric columns of Craigleith stone, into the heart of this great mass of academic buildings—the Quadrangle. Certainly there is nothing to encourage the frivolous tastes and rash aspirations of the youthful student, in the stairways and balustrades, the arcades and galleries, the columns and pediments, all of massive grey stone, that surround this spacious central court. They teach rather the useful truth that solid and sustained effort is a condition of high attainment. The style is Græco-Italian, and bears evidence of the improving touches made by Playfair on Adam's design ; and these interior façades possess a severe beauty and noble serenity that well accord with the spirit of the place. Yet the Quadrangle is reminiscent of the sport and high spirits at least, as much as of the labours and meditations, of the neophytes of this temple of Scottish learning. It has witnessed College rows and rejoicings ; it has been the scene of furious and well-sustained snowball fights ; it has been the starting-place or the goal of torchlight processions. The students have here given demonstrative welcome to a long succession of illustrious Lord Rectors of their own choosing, Thomas Carlyle among the number ; John Stuart Blackie has stalked through its piazzas, humming a lilt, and swinging his " kail runt " ; R. L. Stevenson, an idle student of law, but already a keen observer of human nature, has dangled his legs from the balustrade, while taking malicious delight in the tumult beneath him.

A thousand memories, grave and gay, start up in the hearts and minds of Edinburgh alumni at the mention of

The Old College Quadrangle

the Old College Quadrangle. How many more inhabit the corridors and class-rooms, reading-room and library! The statue of Sir David Brewster, in white marble, facing the entrance gateway, is a reminder not only of the man, but of the services which Edinburgh University has rendered to Science. Busts, and portraits, and medallions, in the Library Hall and elsewhere, seem by preserving the features to perpetuate the influence of the "mighty dead," in Literature, in Divinity, in Law, in Classical Learning, who once taught or studied within these walls. But chiefly, perhaps, Medicine has here received and bestowed distinction, under a long line of eminent and famous men. Latterly, the old University buildings became too straitened to contain, along with the other Faculties, the Edinburgh Medical School, and it moved to new and well-appointed quarters on the margin of the Meadows, and in contiguity to the new Royal Infirmary.

The Healing Art has not wholly deserted the precincts of the Old College. In Nicolson Street, not many paces from the line of the Flodden Wall and the site of Kirk o' Field, and opposite to the Empire Theatre, is the graceful classic front, supported on Ionic columns, of Surgeons' Hall—the Museum of the Royal College of Surgeons—successor to the old building in Surgeon Square which was associated in the popular mind with "Burke and Hare" and the resurrectionists. Large additions have recently been made to meet the growing wants in the matter of class-room and labora-tory accommodation of the School of Medicine of the Royal College. Other institutions, including the Heriot-Watt College and School of Art, ministering to the mental or bodily wants of the public have arisen in the broad thoroughfare that has taken the place of the narrow and darkened alley of North College Street, now bearing the name and adorned with the statue of William Chambers, who was a chief agent in the improvement. An edifice that, in all senses, bulks more largely in the eye of the public is the Royal Scottish Museum. This spacious and handsome building, in Venetian Renaissance style, forms an effective contrast in tone and architectural effect to the sombre University block, lying immediately to the east, and connected with it by a bridge thrown across West College Street.

The Museum is on a site once partly occupied by the Trades Maidens Hospital, now removed to the southern side of the Meadows. Begun in 1861, when the foundation-stone was laid by the Prince Consort, it was not completed until 1888. For the purpose of enlargement and security against fire, ground formerly occupied by spirit stores and other buildings lying south of the Museum and of the remains of the Town Wall, which runs immediately behind it, has recently been acquired. Originally a branch of South Kensington, whence it has drawn large part of its treasures illustrative of art, science, industry, and natural history, the Museum may be described as containing an epitome of human knowledge and progress. In the Great Hall, 200 feet in length and 80 feet in height, and in the wings and adjuncts of the building, there may be studied the annals of the earth from the earliest geological epoch down to the newest discovery in science, and the advance of man in the arts of war and peace as illustrated by the rude weapons of palæolithic times and by models of the latest type of ironclad or lighthouse. The processes of manufacture, of all kinds and in all stages from the raw material to the finished product, are exhibited to the inquiring eye and mind; examples, or models, of the most renowned works of art of our own and of foreign countries have the place and prominence due to them; and in the Natural History Department are stuffed or prepared specimens of nearly all the tribes of birds and beasts and creeping things that inhabit the planet.

For such as take an interest in the dust and shadows of local traditions, as well as in the achievements of modern industry and science, the western end of Chambers Street will have its attractions. For here, in close proximity to the entrance to Greyfriars Churchyard, on ground long known as " The Society," there still linger some traces of Brown Square, which, with the adjacent Argyle Square, represented one of the first attempts of Old Edinburgh fashion to " break bounds " and enjoy more freedom and elbow-room in its domestic life than were possible in the pends and closes. The North Bridge was hardly in contemplation when the building of Brown Square was begun in 1763, and " diminutive and obscure " as it appeared to later eyes, it was at the time hailed, as the author of " Redgauntlet " tells us, " as an extremely elegant improvement upon the style of designing and erecting Edinburgh residences." The families which flitted thither felt, for the first time, the comfort and convenience of living " self-contained," or as the phrase then ran, " entire within themselves." One remembers how Saunders Fairford— father of Allan Fairford and the prototype of the father of Walter Scott—was persuaded, after a wrench like that of " divorcing soul from body," to abandon his old quarters in the Luckenbooths, on the plea that " the better air of this new district was more favourable to the

Flodden Wall—The University

health" of his growing and weakly son; and the parallel is irresistibly suggested of the other stern old Edinburgh lawyer who, for a similar reason, left the purlieus of the Old College to go yet further afield to George Square.

Out of the house in Brown Square (usually identified with Lord Glenlee's handsome dwelling, afterwards a Dental Hospital, which continues to make some outward show on the south side of Chambers Street) issued the fair apparition of "Lady Green Mantle," and "walking along the pavement turned down the close at the north-west end of Brown Square, leading to the Cowgate"—by the line, that is, of the modern George IV. Bridge—and, to the eyes of her lover, "put the sun in her pocket when she disappeared." But we cannot halt to call up the ghosts that haunt a nook in which, a century ago, the "literary muses" found congenial refuge and company. Jean Elliot, the writer of "The Flowers of the Forest," is one of them; the "Man of Feeling" also, whose lively shade seems to flit before us all over Old Edinburgh. He was an occupant of the house next to the Fairfords, before it became associated with Robert Burns's acquaintance and neighbour on the banks of the Ayr, Lord Glenlee, a gentleman of the old school, who is described as "walking daily to Court, hat in hand, with a powdered wig, through Brown Square, down Crombie's Close, across the Cowgate, and up the Back Stairs to the Parliament House, attended by his valet, and always scrupulously dressed in black," until age compelled him to take to a sedan-chair.

Other lawyers and "law lords" herded on this new "South Side"; among them Henry Dundas, first Lord Melville, Lord Cullen, and three Lord Presidents of the Court—Sir Ilay Campbell, Robert Blair of Avontoun,

GOSFORD'S CLOSE, ON SITE OF GEORGE IV. BRIDGE.

(From a water-colour by W. Geikie.)

[*To face page* 148.

Brown Square

and Miller, father of Lord Glenlee. Not a few of them afterwards moved, with fashion, to the extra-mural George Square. The locality was convenient for the College as well as for the Courts. That ponderous authority on port and mathematics, Sir John Leslie, lived in Brown Square; and a house in Argyle Square, which had belonged to Dr Hugh Blair, was possessed later by another great magnate of letters and divinity whose fame is also, it may be feared, beginning to fade —Dr Thomas Chalmers. Nor should it be forgotten that, among the many South-Country visitors who put up at the George Inn—the "Hole in the Wall"—just within the Bristo Port and close to the western end of Chambers Street, were Colonel Mannering and Dandie Dinmont.

Near Bristo Port, at the back of the Museum, as has been noted, there may still be discovered a portion of the Town Wall. It is part of the section which extended between the Potterrow and the Bristo Ports—the two city exits to the south. They led into the suburb of Easter Portsburgh, of which the main thoroughfare was the Potterrow, spoken of by Hugo Arnot, 130 years ago, as a "mean street," and although its northern entrance has lately been widened, the description applies to it to-day. Before and after Arnot's time, however, it housed persons of note. If the Regent Morton's tale is to be trusted—a bold supposition—it was in a lodging in the Potterrow that the notorious "Casket Letters" were discovered, having been smuggled thither from the Castle by Bothwell's henchman, Dalgleish. The Duke of Douglas and the Earls of Moray and Stair had town residences in it. The Stair house, near the southern extremity, was known as the "General's Entry," and tradition has assigned it as the residence of General Monk while he was Governor of Scotland. A more authentic and more romantic association is that connected with Burns and Mrs Maclehose; up the turn-pike of the General's Entry, now removed, "Sylvander" mounted to visit his "Clarinda." "Chloris," another of the fair ones who caught the wayward fancy of the poet and inspired some of his sweetest songs, was a dweller in Potterrow. Lothian Street, which crosses it under the shadow of the University, has had among its student lodgers Thomas de Quincey, Charles Darwin, and Robert Louis Stevenson; and Thomas Campbell lived several years in Alison Square, a tributary of this lower-ing lane, one of the last places where one would dream of searching for traces of the Lyric Muse.

Strolling back towards the Bristo Port, from the junction of Potterrow and Bristo Street, one is still on classic ground. Not many yards off is the Buccleuch Parish Church, formerly known as the St Cuthbert's Chapel of Ease; in it the Marquis of Bute has placed a fine memorial window to his ancestress, Miss Macleod of Raasay; while in the little God's acre beside it rest the blind poet, Dr Blacklock, who encouraged Burns to print his first volume of poetry; Mrs Cockburn, another acquantance of the ploughman bard, and author of the more modernised version of "The Flowers of the Forest"; David Herd, the ballad collector; Dr Adam of the High School, and Deacon Brodie. The space in front of the Chapel was the field of fray in the "bickers," in which Walter Scott took active part, between the Potterrow callants, led by "Green Breeks," and the more aristocratic youth of George Square.

The whole neighbourhood, indeed, is redolent of the

George Square

early years of Scott. Is not George Square within a stone-throw? In No. 25 lived for many years the practical, sober-minded Writer to the Signet, who saw with dismay his son steeping himself in worthless balladry and romance, and following "gangrel" courses, in place of taking kindly to the law; yet had in himself such an indignant soul of honour that when the Secretary Murray of Broughton came on one occasion to George Square to transact some necessary law business, and had obtained the entertainment which politeness demanded, Walter Scott, the elder, flung out of the window the teacup from which the traitor to his Prince had drunk. It was equally characteristic of the son that he should have preserved "Broughton's Saucer" among his "auld nicknackets." From George Square young Walter trudged to his first school—in Hamilton's Entry, Bristo Street—and afterwards to the High School and the College; and went volunteering, rambling, and sweethearting in those years—not unhappy ones, he acknowledges, in spite of some pangs of disappointed love and ambition—which he spent under his father's roof.

It would take a volume to exhaust the historical and literary memories that cling to George Square, of which we may still say, with Lord Cockburn, that "with its pleasant trim-kept gardens it has an air of antiquated grandeur about it, and retains not a few traces of its former dignity and seclusion." Every other house has been the home of an Edinburgh celebrity. Admiral Lord Duncan, the hero of Camperdown, came to anchor in No. 5; Sir Ralph Abercrombie, the victor of Alexandria, rested on his laurels in No. 27; "Timothy Tickler," of the "Noctes"—otherwise Robert Sym, W.S., and uncle of Christopher North—dwelt in No. 20; Sir Francis Grant, the Academician, was born in No. 32; and in No. 39, the gentle Rector of the High School, Dr Adam, parted from life with the murmured words, "It grows dark, boys; you can go; the rest to-morrow." Nor must one forget among the many legal lights of the Square the brilliant Henry Erskine and Lord Braxfield, "the Hanging Judge."

In a flat at No. 7 Charles Street, leading out of the Square into Bristo Street, Francis Jeffrey was born in 1773; and twenty-nine years later, in 18 Buccleuch Place, opening off the other side of the Square, was founded the *Edinburgh Review*, of which Jeffrey was a leading spirit. Sydney Smith, describing the circumstances with perhaps more humour than accuracy, informs us that "Brougham, Jeffrey, and himself happened to meet on the eighth or ninth flat in Buccleuch Place"—Brougham reduces the height to three storeys—"the then elevated residence of Jeffrey"; Smith proposed and it was "carried by acclamation" that the three literary adventurers should set up a review, the suggested motto of which was, "We cultivate literature on a little oatmeal"—a free translation of Virgil's "Tenui musam meditaris avena."

The Bristo Street associations are of an older and more sombre cast. Up an entry in the neighbourhood of Charles Street and Marshall Street is the church which is the successor to that ministered to last century by those uncompromising champions of Secession, Ralph Erskine and "Pope" Adam Gib. Nearer to the "Port," bordering, in fact, on "Society" and the Town Wall, stood the old Darien House, for generations a sad memorial to Scottish eyes of

Bristo

a national misfortune and a national injury, the last, or nearly the last, wrong done by "the auld enemy," England. Later it became a "bridewell" or pauper asylum, and in one of the rooms died poor Robert Fergusson, a raving maniac, at the early age of twenty-four.

With the Darien House, the City Poor House and the Merchant Maidens Hospital have disappeared from Bristo, and new academic buildings lend their more inspiriting and ornamental presence to the locality. Many old houses, among them the Jewish Synagogue, have been cleared away to make room for the Students' Union and the School of Music, and to remove obstructions of view and access to the M'Ewan Hall, itself part and complement of the New University Buildings, or Medical School. The group now occupies nearly the whole space between Charles Street, Bristo, Teviot Place, and the Middle Meadow Walk. The class-rooms and laboratories of the Medical Faculty are accommodated on a scale and in a manner worthy of their purpose, in the fine edifice of the Early Italian style of architecture, designed by Sir Rowand Anderson, which has already, although the lofty campanile tower has not yet risen to complete the work, cost a sum of over £300,000. Fully a third of this amount has been laid out, by the munificence of Mr William M'Ewan, M.P., upon the University Hall, which is a grand domed room, magnificent in its proportions and rich and elaborate in its mural decorations, set apart for academic functions and other great occasions when the interest of the public touches closely the life of the "Town's College."

Separated from the New Medical School only by

the tree-shaded and unicorn-guarded Meadow Walk, is another noble institution in which the city takes just pride—the New Royal Infirmary. The central block and the group of connected pavilions cover many acres of ground between Lauriston and the site of the old "Burgh Loch," long since turned into a park and playfield; and the sheaf of spires and baronial turrets rising above the trees is a feature in the prospects of Edinburgh from the south. But it is not so much on account of its external appearance as of the objects it fulfils and the spirit that sustains it that the Royal Infirmary bulks largely in the eyes of the citizens. It has been built by voluntary contributions; it is maintained by public benevolence; it ministers to the needs of some 8000 in-patients annually, not to mention a much larger host of out-patients; here, if anywhere, Science has joined hands with Mercy and Charity.

The broad Meadows to the south, which now form the chief southern lung of the city, were once covered by a marshy lake, which extended from Lochrin on the west to the grounds of the Convent of St Catherine of Sienna, or the "Sciennes." Elk and urus had once disported themselves in the fields now dedicated to cricket, archery, and other forms of recreation, and have left their bones as evidence. The "Burgh Loch" and the "Goose Dub" were dried up by aid of the windmill which waved its arms near the street that bears its name, and which raised the water for the Brewers' Society, an incorporation commemorated by the "Society Port." Drainage and improvement on more systematic lines were undertaken by a Fife laird, Hope of Rankeillor, in the period before the '45, and

The Meadows

the title of Hope Park is witness that the services of the chief reclaimer of the marsh are not forgotten.

About the middle of last century Hope Park became a place of "fashionable promenade" for beaux and belles. Was not David Balfour taking the air here, with bucks of greater skill and experience, when he sustained the affront from Lieutenant Hector Duncansby which led to the famous duel? "A poor thing, but mine own," Old Edinburgh might have said of its damp and rheumatic "Rotten Row." "There has never, in my life," says Lord Cockburn, "been any single place in or near Edinburgh which has so distinctly been the resort at once of our philosophy and our fashion. Under these poor trees walked and talked and meditated all our literary, and many of our legal, worthies of the eighteenth and beginning of the nineteenth century."

CHAPTER XIV

ROUND THE FLODDEN WALL—THE GREYFRIARS AND GRASSMARKET

OVER against the chief entrance to the New Infirmary in Lauriston, and alongside the grounds of George Heriot's Hospital, reaches a narrow arm of the Greyfriars Churchyard, that "infelix campus" wherein has been raked the dust of so many generations of the great and the gifted who strolled in the Meadows and walked the streets of Old Edinburgh. The "Yairds of the Gray Freiris"—the grounds of the Franciscan Convent founded by James I. of Scots—lay just within the embrace of the Flodden Wall, but "sumquhat distant fra our toune," when Queen Mary, in 1562, gifted the pleasant, open spot, on the supplication of the magistrates, to be a place of burial in lieu of the overcrowded St Giles Kirkyard—"Sua that the air within oure said toune may be the maire puire and clene." Since then, the Greyfriars has grown into a very mound of mortality, so that the access from the foot of the Candlemaker Row, once the main entrance, is by a flight of upward steps, instead of by the descent represented on old plans; and that ancient thoroughfare to the Grassmarket has recently had to be protected by a strong retaining wall and battlement, to keep the dead from breaking bounds upon the living.

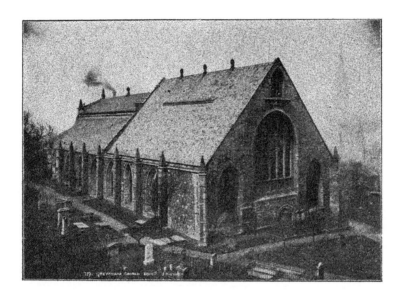

OLD GREYFRIARS.

HERIOT'S HOSPITAL.

A "Theatre of Mortality"

The Greyfriars is one of the most doleful, as it is undoubtedly the most interesting, of Scottish church-yards. Many pens have described its "quaint and smoke-encrusted tombs, its many headstones sunk deep in the long rank grass"—which, by the way, is now more trimly kept—and its strange medley of associations, grim, and sad, and heroic. R. L. Stevenson has, once for all, condensed the spirit of this historic graveyard, into the pages of his "Picturesque Notes." Nowhere are "the quick and the dead" brought into such intimate juxtaposition and dramatic contrast.

"Here a window is partly blocked up by the pediment of a tomb; there, where the street falls far below the level of the graves, a chimney has been trained up the back of a monument, and a red pot looks vulgarly over from behind. A damp smell of the graveyard finds its way into houses where workmen sit at meat. Domestic life on a small scale goes on visibly at the windows. The very solitude and stillness of the enclosure, which lies apart from the town's traffic, serves to accentuate the contrast. As you walk upon the graves, you see children scattering crumbs to feed the sparrows; you hear people singing or washing dishes, or the sounds of tears or castigation; the linen on a clothes-pole flaps against funereal sculpture; or a cat slips over the lintel and descends on a memorial urn."

It is a Theatre of Mortality, whose walls are "appallingly adorned" with the insignia and mottoes of death, peculiarly rich in those "traditional ingenuities in which it pleased our fathers to set forth their sorrow and their sense of earthly mutability." One such grim and grotesque emblem faces you on entering through

The Greyfriars and Grassmarket

the gateway opposite Bristo Port—a skeleton Death,
life-sized (if one may employ a paradox), capering
against the eastern gable of Old Greyfriars Church.

That singularly plain fabric has no history behind
the year 1612, when the magistrates ordered a church
to be built on the spot; it is divided only by a common
wall from New Greyfriars—a structure equally frugal of
outward adornment—which came into existence more
than a century later. But Old Greyfriars, especially,
has reason to be proud of its associations with eminent
men who have preached or worshipped in it, of whom a
multitude sleep their last sleep under the shadow of its
walls. Of its eighteenth-century ministers, perhaps the
most distinguished was Principal Robertson, whose
mausoleum, next to that of William Adam, the architect,
is a prominent object on the western side of the churchyard. He had as his colleague Dr John Erskine, a
shining light of Evangelicism, while the historian was a
staunch pillar of Moderatism; and, as Colonel Mannering had opportunity of discovering on his visit to Old
Greyfriars, the afternoon service was sometimes devoted
to destroying the impression made by the prelection of
the morning.

Scott's own early impressions of the solemnity of
spirit and baldness of form of the Scottish Presbyterian
service were obtained here; "every Sabbath, when well
and at home," Sir Walter's father and mother, "attended
by their fine young family of children and their domestic
servants," filed through the gate on their way from the
adjoining George Square to their pew in Old Greyfriars;
and no doubt visits were paid to the family burying-plot,
where Scott the elder is now laid, near the entrance to
the Heriot grounds. It was here too, on a rainy Sunday,

Old Greyfriars

that the author of "Guy Mannering" made his first plunge into love, by offering his umbrella and his escort home to the beautiful young lady, Miss Belches Stuart, who nearly broke his heart when she married Sir William Forbes, the banker—by no means the only idyll begun under the frowning and grinning effigies of Death and Time in Greyfriars Churchyard.

The most memorable historical incident connected with the scene was the signing, on the flat gravestones around, of the National Covenant of 1638, renewed later as the Solemn League and Covenant. The flock of the Greyfriars took the lead in entering upon this compact between the people and their God, which cost afterwards so much "blood and tears"; and Montrose, who was to become the fiercest foe of the Covenanters, was one of the first to sign the bond. A bitter sequel to the signing—a later act in the national tragedy—was witnessed on the same spot forty years later, after Montrose's and many a noble head besides had fallen in the struggle between "Kirk and King." In 1679, the prisoners, some 1200 in number, captured after Bothwell Brig, were cooped up in the long and narrow branch of the churchyard which stretches to Lauriston, herded together under the open sky, in inclement winter weather, and watched over night and day by guards who had to render, by lot, "life for life" if any of their charges escaped. Death, who had so many memorials around, must have seemed a kind releaser to these wretched people; comparatively few survived the terrible five months' ordeal of camping in the Greyfriars; and the ship, chartered to carry the residue to the Barbados plantations, perished in a storm off the Orkneys.

The Greyfriars and Grassmarket

A gloomy tale, well according with the furniture and surroundings of the scene! The grief and anger and bitterness worked into the soul of the nation during the "Killing Time" break out in the inscription, uncouth as poetry, but expressive of the spirit of an age and people, upon the "Martyrs' Monument," one of the pedimented tablets that overlook the Candlemaker Row. The passenger is asked to "halt and take heed," for

> Here lies interred the dust of those who stood
> 'Gainst perjury, resisting unto blood ;
> Adhering to the covenants and laws
> Establishing the same ; which was the cause
> Their lives were sacrificed unto the lust
> Of Prelatists abjured.

From Argyle to Renwick, according to this grim record —the original tablet now stands over against the frame containing the National Covenant in the Municipal Museum—there perished of the excellent of the earth, "one way or another, murdered and destroyed for the same cause, about eighteen thousand, of whom were executed at Edinburgh about a hundred noblemen and gentlemen, ministers and others." "The most of them lie here."

Greyfriars, indeed, is a very battlefield of old creeds and factions, strewn and heaped with the corpses of those, who, while in life, hated each other "to the death." Over against the "Martyrs' Monument" is the once splendid, but now tarnished and smoke - grimed, mausoleum of Sir George Mackenzie, an accomplished gentleman and "author of some pleasing sentiments on toleration," but King's Advocate in the persecuting times, and abhorred by the Covenanters only next after

Martyrs and Persecutors

Claverhouse. Heriot boys used to snatch a shuddering pleasure by crying defiance through the grating behind which, in a vault with others of his kin, lies "Bluidy Mackenzie" much chapfallen—

> Bluidy Mackenzie, come out if ye daur,
> Lift the sneck and draw the bar.

Under a tall monument against the west wall rests Principal Carstares, friend and chaplain of William of Orange and minister of St Giles and of Greyfriars, a moving spirit in the Revolution of 1688; and in front of it is the tomb of Alexander Henderson, the leader of the National Covenant Movement, who had a chief hand in the drafting of the "Shorter Catechism." The headless body of the Regent Morton was huddled underground in Greyfriars, and a bust of George Buchanan commemorates the fact that this eminent scholar found here a nameless grave. "Jock Porteous," captain of the Town Guard, had his "lair" near "Pope Gib"; Allan Ramsay and Dr Hugh Blair are buried against the wall of New Greyfriars; not far away lies Duncan Ban Macintyre, the sweet singer of "Ben Dorein"; Duncan Forbes of Culloden, Dr Archibald Pitcairn, and Creech the publisher, have graves within the same hallowed ground; and we have our last glimpse of the "Man of Feeling," whose tomb on the terraced eastern slope of the churchyard faces his birthplace in Candlemaker Row. A number of the old urban and suburban families notable in Edinburgh annals—the Littles of Craigmillar, the Byreses of Coates, the Trotters of Mortonhall, the Chiesleys of Dalry, the Foulises of Ravelston—have imposing tombs and vaults in the Greyfriars. And tally has been taken of thirty-seven chief magistrates

The Greyfriars and Grassmarket

of the city; twenty-three principals and professors of the University, many of them of more than European fame; thirty-three of the most distinguished lawyers of their day, including a Vice-Chancellor of England, six Lords President of the Court of Session, and twenty-two senators of the College of Justice, who have been gathered into this dust-bin of celebrities.

Nor are the humbler and mechanical arts less well represented than poetry and piety and learning. Beside the entrance gate, and near the spot traditionally associated with the signing of the Covenant, is the quaintly inscribed tomb of the Mylnes, for generations "Master Masons" to the Scottish Kings, as the epitaph of the sixth of the line records—

> Reader, John Mylne, who maketh the fourth John,
> And, by descent, from father unto son,
> Sixth Master Mason to a royal race
> Of seven successive Kings, lies in this place.

Pride of pedigree has never been set forth with more terseness and circumstance. Behind the old Candlemakers' Hall, which in this age of gas and electric light has declined into a public-house, are epitaphs to other men prominent in their time in the affairs of the town and of the State—among them a "King's Ambassador, for thirty years Conservator of the Scottish Priviledges in Holland," who "behaved with glory among the English and Spaniards"; a "Chief Chirurgeon to His Most Serene Majesty, and to the King of France's troop of Guards from Scotland"; and a worthy magistrate of the same early Jacobean age, who proclaims from the grave his forgotten honours—

> Twice Treasurer, twice Dean of Gild I was,
> To Edinburgh's fair town and publick cause.

A Dust-bin of Celebrities

The fame of all has "fallen dumb," but the munificence of his greater son and successor has kept alive something of the memory of the elder George Heriot—goldsmith to James V., as was the younger Heriot to James VI.—whose half-effaced inscription, one of the oldest in Greyfriars, is not far from the Martyrs' Monument. The son's own memorial is the great Hospital hard by.

George Heriot, the younger—"Jingling Geordie" of the "Fortunes of Nigel"—died in 1624, predeceasing by a year his royal master and kindly gossip, James, whom he had followed from Edinburgh to London. Fortune smiled still more constantly upon the prudent merchant and jeweller and worthy citizen in Cornhill than in his booth under the shadow of St Giles Kirk; and he bequeathed all his wealth, save some legacies to friends and relatives, for the foundation of a hospital "for the education, nursing, and upbringing of youth, being puir orphans and fatherless children of decayit burgesses and freemen" of his native town, "destitute and left without means," in testimony of the honour and regard he bore to his "native soil and mother City."

Nobly has the trust been fulfilled; and ever since the death of the pious founder, Heriot's great Charity has been gratefully recognised as a blessing and ornament to Edinburgh. It has grown and prospered with the progress of the city. Its landed property alone, chiefly in the form of "superiorities," extends over something approaching a moiety of the whole area of the burgh, and its annual income now amounts to about half as much again as the capital value of Heriot's original bequest, which, after deduction of many charges and leakages, was found to come short of £24,000.

The Greyfriars and Grassmarket

Time and changed conditions have made it not only desirable but necessary to widen the interpretation of Heriot's will, while adhering to its spirit. A considerable part of the large revenues are now devoted to the encouragement of higher education by means of University bursaries, to the maintenance of the Heriot-Watt College and School of Art in Chambers Street, and to other educational and charitable purposes.

The chief centre of the beneficent activities of the Heriot Trust continues, however, to be the noble and now venerable Hospital, which began to rise in the fourth decade of the seventeenth century, on the open ridge above the Grassmarket, then known as the "High Riggs." The great quadrangular building, enclosing a central court, has a grave and stately dignity of its own, according with its date and origin. It was the wonder of the age in which it was built; and holds its own, as an example of the architecture of the period, with any Scottish edifice that has come down to us from Jacobean times. Curiously enough, although tradition has named Inigo Jones as the architect, it is not known with any certainty who planned this elaborate and symmetrical structure, with its wealth of ornament, in the form of corbelled turrets and cupolas and pedimented windows with architraves rich in scrolls and devices. The front is towards the north and the Grassmarket, where under the tower there is a quaintly pillared entrance door to the inner court ; but the most familiar façade is that which is turned towards the thoroughfare of Lauriston and has in its centre the Gothic windows of the Hospital Chapel, originally decorated with the material taken from the Kirk of the Citadel at Leith.

The building now accommodates a highly-equipped

Heriot's Hospital

Technical School; in its time it has sheltered the wounded from the "Dunbar Drove," and has been turned to other and more incongruous purposes. It still stands well aloof from neighbours on a clear space surrounded by stone terraces and green lawns, that look across to the Castle; and on "Heriot's Green" the Herioters of all ages still assemble on the "Founder's Day"—the first Monday in June—to decorate the statue of George Heriot with flowers, and to engage in sports on ground which has witnessed Lunardi's balloon ascents, and the parades of the Edinburgh Volunteers, of the time of the Great War, in which Walter Scott was one of the most zealous officers.

Bounding Heriot's grounds towards the west are some remains of the Town Wall, the lines of which we have been loosely following in our survey of the Old Town. This fragment of the fortified *enceinte* is of considerably later date than the Flodden Wall—the foundations of which, however, are traceable under the line of new buildings to the north of the Hospital—and is still in a fair state of preservation. It contains one of the quadrangular battlemented towers with which the outer line of the Wall was broken; and outside of it runs a narrow and ancient thoroughfare, named the Vennel, descending by a steep flight of steps into the Grassmarket.

Grim and many are the associations of this great open Place, lying under the shadow of the Castle Rock. It is a quadrangle, 230 yards in length and of goodly breadth; and from each of its corners issue one or more streets of old and somewhat sinister renown in Edinburgh annals. At the south-east angle the Cowgate and the Candlemaker Row join at the Cowgatehead, where up many steps in a high and dingy building overlooking the Grassmarket, latterly a nest of the poorest of poor tenements and now marked for demolition, Henry Brougham's parents first set up house. Down a steep and winding descent on the north-east comes in Victoria Street, occupying in part the "sanctified bends" of the Old West Bow. It was the Via Dolorosa of Edinburgh—the way, steep and crooked, to the "gallows tree," which rose, from the seventeenth till nearly the close of the eighteenth century, at the eastern end of the Grassmarket. Here, where handsome piazzaed terraces look down upon the street, and flights of stairs descend to it from the level of the Lawnmarket, stood "Major Weir's Land," once the haunt of a brood of gruesome memories and superstitions. Here was the house wherein Prince Charlie was feasted by the Lord Provost of the day, and, according to unfounded tradition, escaped through a trap-door into the Grassmarket from a sally of the Hanoverian garrison of the Castle.

Moving back to the neighbourhood of the Vennel and the Town Wall, the West Port will be seen leading out of the western end of the market-place—a somewhat darkling and ill-savoured way still, although there have been widening and improving at the expense of the older buildings. The West Port was the chief entrance to the walled city from the west. Its gateway had to be guarded as assiduously against surprise and assault as the Netherbow itself; it witnessed nearly as many sallies, brawls, and State pageants, and its spikes never wanted the same ghastly garniture of the heads and limbs of traitors, malefactors, and martyrs. Mary of Guise made her first entry through the West Port on St Margaret's Day, 1538; Anne of Denmark was received

CROMBIE'S LAND, WESTER PORTSBURGH.

From a water colour by James Drummond

The West Port

here with long Latin orations and with volleys and waving flags from the Castle; Charles I. was symbolically welcomed by the "Nymph Edina," who read to him loyal and laudatory lines composed by Drummond of Hawthornden; and through the gate the recalcitrant General Assembly of the Kirk were "drummed" by Cromwell's troops in 1653.

Outside the "Port" lay Wester Portsburgh, a community whose organisation and whose interests were in many respects distinct from those of the dwellers within the walls. It was "pre-eminently the Trades' suburb of Old Edinburgh, as the burgh of Canongate, outside the Netherbow Port, was its Court suburb." In conjunction with the "Easter" Portsburgh, lying outside of the Potterrow and Bristo Gates, it had its distinct municipality, its own courts and mills, and its own incorporated trades. Traces of the insignia of these extra-mural crafts may still be seen on house-fronts between the Grassmarket and the Main Point—the meeting-place, in Portsburgh, of the highways from north, south, and west. But they and their privileges have long since departed the scene—merged in the larger institutions and industrial interests of the city. Wester Portsburgh, never an aristocratic quarter, suffered social deterioration from incursions of the "Irishry," and became a camping-ground for the hosts of unskilled labour. It had always had a dubious reputation as a refuge and rallying ground of schism and faction. Its public "green" on the unoccupied part of the "High Riggs," was a great meeting and preaching place of the sects of religious and political dissent who were refused or who could not afford a covered temple. But Portsburgh's recreation ground was latterly appropriated

The Greyfriars and Grassmarket

for the purposes of a Cattle Market. The Market is now shifted to the city outskirts at Gorgie, and its place is in part occupied by the handsome and spacious new Municipal School of Arts; while on the margin of the old Portsburgh green—near the junction of Lauriston and Lady Lawson's Wynd—a Fire Station, surmounted by a lofty campanile of red stone, has arisen near the site of the venerable crow-stepped mansion of the Lawsons of High Riggs.

The last and heaviest stroke was dealt to the reputation of the West Port when discovery was made of the hideous series of crimes perpetrated in 1827 and 1828, in Log's Lodgings, Tanner's Close, by those "Irish Thugs," William Burke and William Hare. The death trap, baited and sprung by these miscreants on the wretched victims whose bodies were afterwards sold for dissection in Surgeon Square, was a low tramp lodging-house in an alley on the north side of the thoroughfare, which had convenient access behind into the King's Stables Road. The den of infamy has long ago been swept away; not so the extraordinary impression which the "West Port Murders" made upon the popular imagination.

The King's Stables Road is the last of the main highways tributary to the Grassmarket, which it leaves at the point where the Town Wall met the foot of the Castle Rock, whose battlements frown down from a height of 300 feet on the "plainstanes" below. By the road winding at the lowest level round the base of the acclivity, you can make your way to the West Princes Street Gardens, to the West Kirk, and to the New Town. It is not a cheerful way, and the airs wafted from the carts of the Cleansing Department, which has

PLAINSTANES CLOSE, GRASSMARKET.

From a water colour by R. Noble

The Burke and Hare Murders

here its headquarters, are not as the spices of Araby.
But there was a time when "all the King's horses and
all the King's men" found accommodation in this
convenient spot outside the walls, especially when there
were jousts or trials by combat in the "Barras"—the
green meadow beyond—and when that "vain knight-
errant," James the Fourth, viewing the sports from the
windows of the Banqueting Hall in the Castle overhead,
would "cast his hat over the wall," in sign that it was
time for the tilting to cease.

The Grassmarket houses have lost much of the air
of individuality and the picturesqueness of grouping
which they possessed earlier in the century, more
especially those on the south side of the Place. Gone
are the Temple Lands, which Scott describes as bearing
on their fronts and gables the iron cross of the Orders
of the Templar and Hospitaller Knights who owned
them. They stood not far from the "Bow-foot Well"
and the site of the scaffold, marked by a St Andrew's
Cross in the causey. From an adjoining dyer's pole,
Captain Porteous was hanged by the mob of 1736, what
time the Grassmarket presented a wild scene, "crimson
with torchlight, spectators filling every window of the
tall houses, the Castle standing high above the tumult,
amid the blue midnight and the stars." Close by, but
swept away in the earlier storm of the Reformation,
once rose the monastery of the Greyfriars, wherein
Mary of Gueldres was lodged before her marriage with
James II. of Scots; it gave hospitable entertainment, a
dozen years later, to Henry VI. of England, his Queen,
Margaret of Anjou, and their son, Prince Edward, who
had fled hither from the victorious Yorkists, after
Towton fight.

The Greyfriars and Grassmarket

It is a long stride from those times and scenes to the modern political events associated with the Corn Exchange in the Grassmarket, within which, to mention but one personage and incident, Disraeli spoke his famous phrase about "educating his party." The north side of the Grassmarket has preserved more of its antique features than the south, and there are doorways with dates and inscriptions going back to the decades immediately following the Union of the Crowns, in the tall and irregular tenements ranged in line under the great ridge of the Castle Esplanade. One of these dwellings is the Old White Hart Inn, the rendezvous, in its day, of the West-Country gentry and of Highland lairds and drovers whom business or pleasure brought to town, and who found in the Grassmarket their nearest and most convenient landfall. It was the goal and starting-place also of a number of the carriers' carts and lumbering coaches, by means of which the traffic and intercourse between the country and the capital were conducted in the age before steam. William and Dorothy Wordsworth put up at the White Hart on their tour in 1803, and found it cheap and noisy.

Coaches and carriages now make only fleeting and accidental appearances in the Grassmarket. But it is still a resort of the country carter and carrier, the drover and the shepherd, the farmer and the horse-couper. So long ago as 1477, it was ordained that a weekly market should be held here for wood and timber; while on Fridays "old graith and gear" were to be sold in it, opposite the Greyfriars, "like as is usit in uthir cuntries." In 1560 the Cornmarket was shifted from the old site at the Tron to ground where there was more room for meeting and bargaining; and from that time until of recent years agriculture may be said to have centred its movements and interests in the Grassmarket.

In ordinary times only a moderate current of life flows through the great square. The central space is often deserted; and about the corners of the Cowgate and of the West Port there hang melancholy little groups of the "submerged" of the city population, gathered out of the neighbouring stairs and closes. If the stones could speak they might tell of strange things and sad—strangest and saddest of all, of those scenes of the "Killing Times," when the martyrs of the Covenant, the Men of the Moss Hags, mounted the scaffold opposite the Bow-foot, and "glorified God in the Grassmarket."

CHAPTER XV

NEWINGTON AND GRANGE

SCARCELY less important in the evolution of Modern Edinburgh than the making of the North Bridge was the formation of the street which, by continuing the line of that thoroughfare across the Cowgate valley, opened the way to the sunny fields lying south of the Flodden Wall. Until the South Bridge was built, Auld Reekie society was hemmed in almost as much in this direction as towards the north. It had trenches and walls to pass and narrow alleys to thread before it could breathe country air. True, as has been seen, there had been some earlier colonising of the trans-Cowgate region in the neighbourhood of "Society" and Brown Square; and by and by fashion and letters began to find congenial settlement in George Square and to perambulate the margin of the Burgh Loch. But to reach these mild and remote regions from the centre of the city, a plunge had to be made down into the depths of the guarding valley, and a corresponding ascent through some strait and steep wynd or close to meet again the light of day. A troublesome passage this, on foot or by sedan-chair; and the Old Edinburgh aristocracy of birth and learning were gregarious and avoided trouble in locomotion. They waited for a broad

The South Bridge

and level path to be laid out for them sunwards; and this came with the building of the South Bridge.

That work, completed in 1788, largely under the stimulus of the Lord Provost, Sir James Hunter Blair, made a curious change in the ideas of distance and propinquity entertained by the citizens of the age. When Adam Smith returned from London to Edinburgh in 1776, and took up his quarters in the house in Panmure Close, which William Wyndham noted in his diary as "magnificent," taste and philosophy, as Mr Rae, the biographer of the author of the "Wealth of Nations," reminds us, "still found their sanctuary in the smoke and leisure of the Canongate." Robertson, the historian, had indeed flitted out to Grange House, in the far-away territory beyond the Burgh Muir. Joseph Black, the chemist, Smith's special crony at this period, had taken up his abode at a country villa, on the site, in Nicolson Street, of the Royal Blind Asylum, which has planted a branch for the housing of the female blind a mile and a half further out. Adam Ferguson had gone to "a house in the Sciennes, which, though scarce two miles from the Cross, was thought so outrageously remote by the compact little Edinburgh of those days, that his friends always called it Kamtschatka, as if it lay in the ends of the earth." It may be remembered that it was at this house of Sciennes Hill, standing near the modern Braid Place, that Walter Scott, a boy of fifteen, met, for the first and only time, Robert Burns, then moving as a bright, new, particular light among the *literati* of Edinburgh.

The South Bridge was then approaching completion. Henry Cockburn remembered crossing it on planks in 1787; and a year later the carriage-way was finished, and so traffic and population moved smoothly over it, until streets and rows of villa houses have flooded all the southern slopes, and are now climbing and annexing the hill of Liberton, three miles in a straight line from the Post Office. The Bridge was carried across the hollow to the College and the Town Wall by nineteen arches, of which the principal spanned the Cowgate, into whose murky abysses the pedestrian or the outsider on the street car—an excellent means of surveying Edinburgh's South Side—gets a brief but impressive glimpse in passing.

The old Poultry Market and other obscure localities behind the line of the High Street were invaded and occupied by the new street, which at once became, and still remains, an important centre of business and avenue of traffic. Here was built the Goldsmiths' Hall, as also the Merchants' House, since flitted elsewhere. In the recess of Adam Square, now obliterated, the Watt School of Arts, founded by Leonard Horner, first stood; it has been removed to Chambers Street, along with the seated statue of the great engineer, which was placed in front of the earlier building, originally erected by Robert Adam, the architect of its neighbour, the University. At No. 49 South Bridge was the antiquarian bookshop of David Laing, celebrated in "Peter's Letters," where Scott and Lockhart and other lovers of old authors and rare editions were wont to drop in, and where the owner gathered the vast and curious store of literary and bibliographic knowledge which served him in such good stead when he became Secretary of the Bannatyne Club and Librarian of the Signet Library.

Booksellers still flourish on the South Bridge, but

Nicolson Street

the Royal Riding School, the resort of another class of Edinburgh citizens of the period, has its place taken by the School of Medicine and Surgeons' Hall already mentioned. Here, just without the former city bounds, Nicolson Street begins to "draw its slow length along" towards the south. It was thought a handsome and spacious thoroughfare a hundred years ago. Now its aspect grows almost antique and a little shabby. Its architecture, otherwise void of distinction, preserves a typical feature of the street frontage of the date in the gabled ends that break the monotonous lines of roof and chimney. This "New Road" was originally drawn through the park and pleasure - grounds of Lady Nicolson, a well-endowed widow, who named it after her husband, and raised a fluted column to his memory in the neighbourhood of Nicolson Square, a locality that became, until fashion changed again, a favourite residence of persons of rank and gentility. The Wesleyan Methodists built their chapel in the Square in the year before Waterloo; in the eyes of many visitors the building may derive interest from the fact that President Grant repeatedly worshipped in it; while the Nicolson Street United Presbyterian Church will seem more venerable, when they know that the learned and genial Dr John Jamieson, of Scottish Dictionary fame, was its pastor.

A somewhat squalid labouring quarter now bounds Nicolson Street, especially towards the east. From Ecclefechan to the depressing shades of Simon Square, reached through Gibb's Entry, came Thomas Carlyle, a poor and friendless student, who looked in vain for an encouraging word from his teachers to cheer him on his way. The adjoining alley of Paul Street

Newington and Grange

had a tenant as lonely as the gaunt Annandale scholar, and still more scant of coin, in David Wilkie, the great *genre* painter, who settled in this humble quarter in 1799, removing later to a room in Palmer's Lane, West Nicolson Street, where Robert Fergusson, the poet, had sat for Alexander Runciman as the model for the picture of the "Prodigal Son." Genius and Poverty have kept close company in the purlieus of Nicolson Street. So have high birth and ill fortune. In a garret in East Crosscauseway lodged the once beautiful and courted Lady Jane Douglas, sister of the last Duke of Douglas, wife of Sir John Stewart of Grandtully, and the mother of the successful claimant in the celebrated "Douglas Cause," a litigation which gave rise to unexampled expense and excitement, and to popular riots almost rivalling those of the Porteous Mob.

As one moves southward, the vistas that open on the left hand out of West Newington and Clerk Streets are seen ending in the beetling cliffs above the Radical Road, and the crest of Arthur Seat rears itself over the roofs and chimney-pots of St Leonard's. On the right, beyond the Newington Parish Church, there is a peep of the trees and greensward of the Meadows at Hope Park End; and then, a little way past the church in which preached for many a day the Rev. Dr Begg, type and pillar of the Free Church "Stalwarts," begins the long, smooth declivity of Newington, falling away to the hidden and buried Pow burn and the Suburban line, and to the still lower level of the burn of Braid and Liberton Toll. Straight ahead rises the square tower of Liberton Kirk, crowning a hill where suburban residences already mingle with the village houses and trees; there come

The City's Sunny Side

in sight also thè green knolls and folds of the Blackford and Braid Hills, bearing upon their shoulders embodiments of the mediæval and the modern spirits in the shape of the square, grey Keep of Liberton and the New Royal Observatory; while to the east, where the country opens towards the sea, Craigmillar Castle stands high and aloof, "a very stronghold of Old Romance."

From Craigmillar to Craiglockhart, the city has spread in one continuous suburb bearing different names—Newington, Grange, Morningside, Merchiston —and files and videttes of villadom keep pushing out and annexing new ground on this milder flank of Edinburgh. That has happened which Sir Walter Scott wondered had not, by natural law, come to pass in his day, as he watched a growth which then set mainly to the north; a "New Town has occupied the extensive plain on the south side of the College," and has long overpassed the wide bounds of the Burgh Muir. In the Grange district especially, town and country intermingle, and the region is one of parks, and gardens, and villa residences.

When the century began, the ground thus appropriated was country, almost unadulterated; a few scattered mansions, a few groups of poor cottages at tolls and crossways, represented nearly all of the city that had "burst its steiks" in this direction. As yet the broad thoroughfare that descends southward, in the line of South Bridge, under the names of Clerk Street, Minto Street, Mayfield, and Craigmillar Park, was not. The old country ways of a hundred years ago followed what then, as now, were known as Causewayside and the Old Dalkeith Road. The former, after passing the eastern end of the Burgh Loch and the breweries of Summer-hall, traversed the "Sciennes," called after the Convent of St Catherine of Sienna, built by a pious dame, Janet, Lady Seton, after the "dowie day" of Flodden had left her a widow, and attached to an older chaplainry dedicated to St John the Baptist. The nuns of the Sciennes escaped the tongue of scandal, and won the praise even of the satirists of their day. But neither their good works nor their annual processions to the "Balm Well" of their patron saint at Liberton, the virtues of which had been gratefully acknowledged by the crowned of the earth, availed to save their convent from Hertford's invasion and the tempest of the Reformation. A fragment of it exists, built into a garden wall in the neighbourhood; and the modern Convent of St Catherine, in Lauriston, is erected upon an outlying part of its former lands on the South Side.

The Old Dalkeith Road still keeps close to the eastern fringe of the city, and under the lee of Arthur Seat. Upon it stand the Parkside works of Messrs Nelson & Sons; and in Salisbury Road was an early residence of the head of another great publishing house, William Blackwood, which witnessed social gatherings of the contributors of "Maga" in the palmiest days of that Nestor of monthly magazines. Newington House—long the home of the late Duncan M'Laren, M.P.—and many other residences in this pleasant neighbourhood have also their literary and political memories. More than one cemetery, with names of note on the tombstones, open into Dalkeith Road. Close at hand, too, is a lodge, leading to the old house of the Dicks of Prestonfield, by a way known to

The Old Dalkeith Road

Johnson and Boswell and other celebrities. Peffermill, a neighbouring old baronial mansion, gabled and escutcheoned, but abandoned, like many of its kind, to the "waistrie" of small tenants, stands lonely and neglected near ¦the highway which branches off from the Dalkeith Road by the Duddingston distilleries and breweries, past the gate of Niddrie Marischal towards Musselburgh and the sea.

Niddrie has belonged to the Wauchopes, lately represented by General Wauchope of the Black Watch, for more than five hundred years. Hugh Miller, while a stone mason, helped to build the modern addition to the house, and in his walks in the neighbourhood " often saw the sun sink over the picturesque ruins of Craig-millar Castle." Neither Niddrie, nor any of the other old family seats in the vicinity, can compare for a moment in historical interest or in dominating position with Craigmillar, whose towers and battlements, " bosomed high on tufted trees," look down upon them and the surrounding fields.

The story of this impressive and well-preserved ruin is worthy of its site and aspect; but it cannot be told here in full. Its owners have been the Prestons, and the Little-Gilmours who still possess it along with the adjoining lands of the Inch and Liberton. These families have been closely connected with the annals of Edinburgh, and have mingled prominently at times in national affairs. But Craigmillar is chiefly remembered as the scene of the sudden and mysterious death of John, Earl of Mar, the high-spirited brother of James III., while confined in the castle under a charge of treason; as the occasional residence of James V. and of his daughter Mary, Queen of Scots, when in quest of

Newington and Grange

country air and retirement, and as the place first
appointed for the lodging of Darnley, when he was
brought sick from Glasgow to die of violence at Kirk of
Field. At Craigmillar, too, the Sixth James, "without
the aid of his council," came to the resolution to
espouse Anne of Denmark. It may almost be said to
have been a country residence of royalty during these
reigns. Nor does its appearance belie its reputation.
Its massive walls and gateways; its vaulted hall,
mullioned windows, and sculptured arms; its crumbling
turrets and battlements; the grass-grown courts, where
protrudes the living rock, and the venerable trees that
surround the place, make it easy for the imagination to
repeople it with the warriors and courtiers of the time
of Mary and Bothwell.

Memories and traditions of the Queen of Scots are
rife in and around Craigmillar. "Little France," on the
neighbouring Old Dalkeith Road, is supposed to have
derived its name from having sheltered her retinue;
the great old sycamore, known as "Queen Mary's tree,"
still stands sturdily by the wayside. At Craigmillar
Walter Scott caught part of his love of the "old
unhappy far-off times." His Reuben Butler was school-
master at Liberton; Peffermill looks the part of the
"House of Dumbiedykes." All the low ground
between Liberton and Arthur Seat was once occupied
by dense wood and marsh—part of the ancient "Forest
of Drumselch"—in which lurked beasts of the chase
and occasionally outlaws, among whom legend has
placed the "Wight Wallace" himself. Near Bridgend
was a royal hunting-seat, to which James V. occasionally
resorted. A stone bearing the Royal arms, removed
from Bridgend, is one of the antiquities of the Inch,

Craigmillar Castle

which, as the name helps us to know, was a moated grange, reached by its possessors, the Monks of Holyrood, by a drawbridge. They had mill and columbarium rights at Liberton Dam reaching back to the beginning of the twelfth century, and still visible to the eye in the form of dovecot and millwheel. The property and the whole barony of Liberton, which is thought to have taken its name from a leper foundation, came into possession of the family of the Littles, so honourably associated with the beginnings of Edinburgh University, and passed, by marriage, to the Gilmours.

The Littles it was who built Over Liberton House, which has been so restored, internally as well as externally, as to be an almost perfect example of a seventeenth-century Scottish mansion, of a period when the necessity for defence could not be left out of consideration even by those who lived within a three-mile radius of Edinburgh Cross. The neighbouring Tower, a keep of the grimmest and simplest type, belongs to a far earlier date, when defence was all in all. Its original builders and occupants—the Dalmahoys of that Ilk—must have reached the living-rooms of their "craw's nest" by a ladder which they could draw in after them.

We have here wandered as far as the lower slopes of the Braid Hills. These charming southern environs of Edinburgh we have loosely surveyed rather than investigated, and the guide through them is fain to adopt the words in "Marmion"—

Hill, brook, nor dell, nor rock, nor stone,
Lies on the path to me unknown.
Much might it boast of storied lore;
But, passing such digression o'er,

Newington and Grange

Suffice it that the route was laid
Across the furzy hills of Braid.
They passed the glen and scanty rill,
They climbed the opposing bank, until
They gained the top of Blackford Hill.

The "scanty rill" is the Braid burn, cutting its way from the Pentlands towards Duddingston Loch and the sea; and the steep "glen" is partly choked with the trees of the Hermitage of Braid, the residence for many years of John Skelton—"Shirley"—the biographer of Mary Stewart and of Maitland of Lethington. The "opposing bank" of the Blackford Hill is now also, like the Braids, public property, and the red sandstone gateway on the east makes grateful acknowledgment of the services of Sir George Harrison, the Lord Provost of the day, in obtaining the boon of this noble park for the citizens. In the well-appointed Observatory, stationed high and aloof from the town and its smoke on a site over 400 feet above sea-level, the great Dunecht Telescope, bequeathed to the Government by the late Earl of Crawford and Balcarres, has been housed.

From the crest of the hill, a hundred feet higher, Marmion looked down upon the Flodden host encamped on the Burgh Muir and on "mine own romantic town." That brave and warlike show—the white pavilions pitched on "the bent so brown," and the gay banners streaming above the clumps of old oak wood, and over all, set in the Bore Stone, the lion standard of Scotland, which was so soon to go down in the dust with its defenders—came like a ghost and went like a ghost. Sir Walter himself had seen changes from the time when, a truant boy, he had

182

Blackford Hill

bird-nested "among the broom, the thorn, and whin" of Blackford, and listened to the bells of St Giles. Rude nature had given way before husbandry; the hill waved with yellow grain—

> And o'er the landscape, as I look,
> Nought do I see unchanged remain,
> Save the rude cliffs and chiming brook.

Now, as by another wave of an enchanter's wand, the scene is changed once more. The advancing lines of villas and tenements climb the lower flanks of Blackford Hill. The Pow burn, or Jordan, has disappeared, and its place has been taken by the trailing smoke of the Surburban line which occupies its former bed. Blackford House, the secluded old mansion girt about with noble trees and shaven turf and flower-plots, has had a railway station thrust upon it; barely possible is it to imagine the time when the venerable old lady who occupied it—Sir Thomas Dick Lauder's friend—"every morning bathed in the Jordan, which then ran, pure and sparkling, through her garden." The once wide and empty space of the Burgh Muir is filled with houses, rising from among trees and lawns. But there still remain the chief glories of the prospect—the "dusky grandeur" of the height "where the huge Castle holds its state"; the "ridgy back heaved to the sky" of the Old Town; the distant Ochils and Grampians; and the "gallant Firth" with its islands, spread between the shores of Fife and Lothian, as drawn for us in the word-picture which is in the memory of every schoolboy.

The Circular Route of the tramway, which traverses the Grange, Morningside, and Bruntsfield districts,

Newington and Grange

carries one past, or within easy reach of, most of the spots in that locality that are of any historic or other note. The round is also made pleasant, especially in fine summer weather, by the glimpses of the handsome houses and of the gardens, flowers, and greenery of this the more sunny and smiling side of Edinburgh, and by the frequent peeps of the hills and the country beyond. The way leaves the main thoroughfare of Newington by Salisbury Place and the Longmore Hospital for Incurables and follows the broad avenue of Grange Road. This passes through and takes its name from the lands of the Grange of St Giles — "Sanct Geilis Grange" as it appears in the old documents—bestowed as far back as the days of David I. on the monks of Holm Cultram, in Cumberland, but held and cultivated, on an oasis in the waste of the Burgh Muir, by the vicars of St Giles Kirk. Early in the sixteenth century the lands came into the possession of the merchant family of Cant — the owners of Cant's Close in the High Street—and from inscribed stones, arms, and dates, it appears that the oldest part of the existing baronial manor-house of Grange was built by them before that century was out. Part of the Grange was assigned, along with a grant from Sir John Crawford, for founding the House of the Sisters of the Sciennes, the site of which has already been indicated. The "Ladies' Well," and the " Penny Well" in Grange Loan, once held to be a sovereign cure for sore eyes, are supposed to have, like the Liberton "Balm Well," associations with St Catherine's Convent, and, of course, with Mary, Queen of Scots.

At the western end of the Grange property was another famous mediæval foundation — St Roque's

The Grange of St Giles

Chapel. Did not the clamour of war notes, heard on the neighbouring Blackford Hill, portend that

> The King to mass his way had ta'en,
> Or to St Katherine's of Sienne,
> Or Chapel of St Roque?

The Chapel has entirely disappeared, although a few carved fragments of it have been built into walls in a neighbouring laundry. Seven years after Flodden the victims of the Black Death were gathered upon the Common around St Roque; the bodies of the dead were buried in its consecrated ground, and the clothes of the plague-stricken were washed in the Burgh Loch.

The story of Grange House is more cheerful and not less romantic; it is told in detail by Mrs Stewart Smith, in " The Grange of St-Giles." House and lands passed out of the hands of the Cants into those of the Dicks of Braid, in 1631, the bargain being struck, according to tradition, during a game of golf on the Braid Hills. The new owner was that too loyal and generous " Sir William Dick of Braid, Knight " — David Deans's " worthy, faithfu' Provost Dick "—who was accounted the wealthiest man of his day. He had dealt out his money like " sclate stanes," in the cause, first of the Covenant and then of the Stewarts. " Douce Davie's " father had seen men " toom the sacks o' dollars out o' Provost Dick's window " into the carts that carried them to the army at Duns Law; and there was " the window itsel' still standing in the Luckenbooths, at the airn stanchells, five doors abune Advocates' Close," in witness of the fact. He had his reward by dying in a debtor's prison in Westminster, after the Restoration.

The Grange was saved from the wreck by Dick's

daughter-in-law Janet M'Math, whose mural tomb may be found in the Greyfriars; and, as the Dicks married into the Loyalist families of the Setons and the Lauders, the associations of Grange House continued strongly Jacobite during the seventeenth and eighteenth centuries. There is shown among its precious relics a thistle taken from the bonnet of Prince Charlie when " he honoured the House of Grange by visiting William Dick, its third baron, and Anne Seton, his lady, and her sisters, Jane and Isabel"; it was given in exchange for a·white rose, offered to him by these loyal ladies, and to " mark the regard of his family, from Queen Mary downward, for that of Seton," as further evidenced by another Grange heirloom — the watch presented by her mistress to Mary Seton, of the Queen's Maries. One of its last-century occupants was the venerable Principal Robertson. Young Henry Brougham, the historian's grand-nephew, had the run of the place, along with Henry Cockburn, who draws for us a pleasing picture of the Doctor in his declining years pottering about the old garden and orchard, in his powdered·wig, brown corduroy knee-breeches, and resplendent coat and waistcoat of bright blue and scarlet, with his ear trumpet dangling from a button-hole, as he encouraged the boys to climb the cherry trees, or made plans with them for keeping the tame rabbits within bounds.

Another and later literary character, who not only lived in Grange House, but was its owner and renovator, was Sir Thomas Dick Lauder, seventh baronet of Fountainhall, the author of the " Wolf of Badenoch" and other works, famous in their day, some of them written in the library of the old manor-house, which he turned from " a tall grey keep" into a baronial residence. The place has its "haunted chamber" and its "monk's walk," but of more genuine interest than either is the "Griffin Gateway," which a little lame urchin, Walter Scott by name, climbed in order to discover whether the tongues of the heraldic monsters were "veritable paint or veritable flame."

The "Lovers' Loan," the scene of many a tryst, skirts the Grange House grounds on the west; its hedgerows are replaced in part by high walls, including that of the Grange Cemetery, a necropolis within which rest from their labours many of the "Disruption worthies," among them Dr Cunningham and Dr Guthrie, Hugh Miller, and, foremost of all, Dr Chalmers. A Chalmers Memorial Church rises on one side of the cemetery, and a Robertson Memorial Church on the other, erected by rival Presbyterian bodies in memory of men mighty in works and in faith.

Still following the tramway line westward, we cross the shady Whitehouse Loan, which preserves the name of an old country residence where, it is said, Dr Robertson wrote his "Charles V.," John Home his "Douglas," and Dr Blair his "Lectures." St Margaret's Convent, "the first religious house built in Scotland after the Reformation," also opens into the Loan, which gives access besides to the house and grounds of Bruntsfield or Bruntisfield. Miss Warrender, in her "Walks near Edinburgh," speaks of Bruntsfield as "the last of the old houses in the immediate vicinity of Edinburgh which is still inhabited by its owners." "In spite of recent additions and alterations"—in spite also of the feuing plan, which is annexing its parks and hemming it in with new streets and terraces—"it still preserves much of the character of the semi-fortified

Newington and Grange

mansion, with protecting outworks which, centuries ago, frowned over the Burgh Muir"; and "its antiquity is even more apparent inside than outside, from the thickness of the walls, the diversity of the levels, and the steep little turret stairs." The oldest date it bears is 1605, when it belonged to the Fairlies of Braid, but there is evidence that a mansion stood here as early as 1457. It came into the hands of George Warrender of Lochend, a merchant burgess, and afterwards a Lord Provost and a baronet, in 1695, and has remained in the family since. It has a "secret room," discovered in the present century, and known as the Ghost Room, "although nothing has been seen, at any rate for many years."

Building and street-making operations have caused the removal of the mound on which James IV. is reputed to have stood to review the Scottish host. A mysterious gravestone in the park at Bruntsfield, bearing the date 1645, is supposed by Wilson to be that of some gentleman and scholar who had fallen a victim to "the last and most fatal visitation of the plague." Within a walled enclosure in Chamberlain Road is another stone, bearing the same date and a curious rhymed inscription, and probably recording a similar tragedy in the family of the Livingstones of Greenhill.

CHAPTER XVI

FROM MORNINGSIDE TO THE WEST KIRK

NEAR where the Circular Route meets, at Churchhill, the long slope of Morningside Road and the tramway line ascending from the furthest outskirts of the city, is another memorial of the early history of the Burgh Muir, and of King James's fatal enterprise. This is the "Bore Stone," a rough slab of red sandstone, built into a wall beside the Morningside Parish Church, and bearing an inscription and quotation from "Marmion" to indicate that it was here, on the crest of the ridge, that the royal standard was raised at the muster of 1513. Recent building operations, on the spacious grounds of Falcon Hall, have obliterated the last relics of the row of lowly one-storey cottages which, along with the neighbouring village of Tipperlinn, also swept away, represented nearly all of Morningside that was inhabited at the beginning of last century. A generation ago the town ended at the bottom of the slope, and through Morningside toll-bar you entered the country. Across the Jordan burn you passed into Egypt farm; for in this quarter the Bible divides with Scott romance the local nomenclature, and Goshen, and Eden, and Canaan border upon Marmion Terraces and Abbotsford Parks.

From Morningside to the West Kirk

The toll-bar has, of course, disappeared. New houses, shops, and churches have sprung up like mushrooms in the land beyond Jordan. The growing town has spread southward to the skirts of the Braids, eastward to the base of Blackford, and westward to the slopes of the Craiglockhart Hills. The tramway line extends for a mile along the road leading to the Carlops, and to Penicuik and Roslin. There is an older road, also now bordered by houses for the greater part of the way, which dips down to the Braid burn, before rising to join the other on the hither side of Fairmilehead. By this route Stevenson's "pleasant gauger" fluted his way towards the Bowbridge, in the next hollow, playing "Over the Hills and Far Away" to warn his smuggling friends of his coming. "R. L. S." himself often followed the same route, when bound to his father's summer home at Swanston, which can be seen nestling snugly among its trees in a pastoral and secluded nook—the old grange of the monks of White-kirk—at the base of the steep scaurs of Cairketton.

The Pentlands stretch away westward, fold after fold, and height beyond height; every glen has its story, and every hill its magnificent prospect of the Lothians and of the Firth. You can descry the trees round Bonally Tower, where Henry Cockburn spent the quiet autumn of his days, and rising from the woods of Dreghorn and Redford, the "glen of Howden," up which St Ives escaped with the drovers; and you can trace part of the route pursued in the snow by the "Westland Whigs" of the Pentland rising, on their way to ruin at Rullion Green.

Looking nearer at hand, from the shoulder of the "furzy hills of Braid," the lover of nature and of old

SWANSTON.

ROSLIN CHAPEL.

[*To face page* 190.

Swanston and the Pentlands

romance will find many spots worth noting. Screened by the trees of Comiston, once the domain of the old merchant family of Forrest, is Hunters' Tryst, the "howf" of the athletic Six-Foot Club, of which Scott and the Ettrick Shepherd were active members; and the tall monolith of the Kay Stone, marking the site of a forgotten battle or the grave of some forgotten hero, stands on the margin of a supposed Roman Camp. Another camp, that of the Gallachlaw, where Cromwell lay entrenched for weeks, waiting in vain for David Leslie to make a mistake of generalship, lies on the eastern side of the road, with the shale-mounds of Straiton and the graveyard of Old Pentland crouching below them, for background. Close behind the Braid Hills is Mortonhall, which for many generations has belonged to the Trotters. They were successors of the St Clairs of Roslin, who, according to tradition, received these lands and the neighbouring "Forest of Pentland" as the reward for their ancestor saving the life of The Bruce when assailed during the hunt by a savage and giant buck, and who held them on condition of winding three blasts of a horn from the "Buck Stane" when the King visited the neighbourhood.

The game of golf has now taken possession of both slopes of the Braids. The northern side is one of the breeziest of public parks, and most hazardous of courses. From the teeing-grounds and putting-greens glorious views are had of the city and its fair surroundings; peeps may be had, when skies are favourable, of Ben Lomond in the west, and of the Bass and the May in the east. The southern declivities and hollows are similarly occupied as a private course by the Mortonhall Club; rubber balls are now lost where the fairies danced around the Elf Loch, and long drives are made from beside the Buck Stane.

Returning townwards by the tramway line, after this brief country excursion, one passes the entrance to the City Poorhouse, which obscures the mouldering old keep of the Lockharts of the Craig, now a mere ivy-clad shell, set in the hollow or saddle between the Craiglockhart Hills. The abrupt green Wester Hill has been annexed by golf, and carries a Hydropathic Establishment on one of the flanks; on the other flank, not far from the Poorhouse, the new City Fever Hospital has risen. The Easter Hill has skating ponds sheltering under the wood and coppice of its western side. Near its crest, conspicuous in situation and architecture, are the new buildings of the Royal Lunatic Asylum, which has outgrown the space and accommodation of the original site in Morningside; and lower down there is a cemetery. Truly the ills and the recreations of life are well represented on Craiglockhart.

The new Asylum has appropriated and transformed old Craig House, and has destroyed the air of mystery and antiquity which used to hang around this once solitary mansion. The glimpses caught of its grey gables and narrow windows through its avenue of great lime and beech trees did not belie the reputation of the old mansion of being haunted by a "Phantom Lady," who, while in life, had been so stricken by grief for the loss of her husband—slaughtered, says Robert Chambers, by Moubray of Barnbougle, on Bruntsfield Links—that she shut herself up for the remainder of her days "in a room all hung with black, into which the light of heaven was never permitted to enter," and studied deadly revenge.

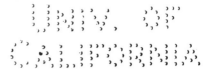

CRAIGMILLAR CASTLE.

MERCHISTON CASTLE

Craig House

Sorrow and distress of mind still inhabit Craig House. But it has had its cheerful and stirring days. Three hundred years ago it was the scene of a characteristic feat of rescue, achieved by the sapient King Jamie. Discovering, while riding in the neighbourhood, that the owner of the house, John Kincaid, held in durance a buxom and well-dowered widow, whom he had abducted from Water of Leith, James sent two of his retinue with a threat that Craig House would be burned if the lady were not delivered up. Kincaid was tried for the offence, and it seemed accordant with the ideas of justice prevailing at the time that he should be ordered to hand over to the King his "brown horse." Craig House became at a later date the possession of the ill-starred "Knight of Braid"; and the learned Dr John Hill Burton was long a tenant of the mansion. It appears from a carved date and initials to have been built about the middle of the sixteenth century by a laird named Symson; but the historian of Scotland was disposed to believe that its "secret subterranean passage" uncovered anew, together with some interesting wall-paintings, during recent changes, was "as old as the Romans."

Returning to the "Boroughmuirhead" by way of Myreside and Colinton Road, one passes another historic house. This is Merchiston Castle, which remained for four and a half centuries a possession of the name and race of Alexander Napier, Provost of the city, who acquired it in 1438. To the square battlemented tower, surmounted by gables, turrets, and chimneys, modern additions have been made; and the building has been long occupied and well known as Merchiston Castle School. Formerly it was moated, and, like Craig

House, it had an underground avenue of escape. It was garrisoned and besieged during the civil war that followed the flight of Mary Stewart; and Merchiston and the Burgh Muir became a centre of the struggle between the "Queen's men" and the "King's men." A pear tree, said to have been planted by the ubiquitous Queen of Scots, used to be shown in the Castle garden, and a bedroom in the tower bears her name. At the date of those quarrels, young John Napier of Merchiston, the inventor of logarithms, who was born in 1550 in the Castle, was pursuing his mathematical studies. Like other men whose knowledge was in advance of his age, he obtained the popular reputation of being a warlock, who, in his little study in the tower, consulted as his familiar a black cock. His son married a sister of the "Great Marquis"; and it was the wife of his grandson, Sir Archibald, the first Lord Napier, who, as told in Mark Napier's Life of Montrose, had Graham's heart secretly abstracted from the body, which had been buried in the criminals' place of interment, and enclosed it in a casket, made of the hero's sword-blade, that passed through many adventures and is still a treasured possession of the Lords Napier and Ettrick. The castle contains a room with a fine ceiling of Charles II.'s time, bearing medallions of early Scottish kings.

A separate branch of the Napiers lived at Wrychtis-housis, or Wright's Houses, the strangely named and picturesque old edifice, with "peel tower, turrets, and crowstepped gables and gablets, encrusted with legends, dates, and coats of arms," which was cleared away in the first year of the nineteenth century to make room for Gillespie's Hospital, a charitable institution—founded by a celebrated High Street snuff merchant—since con-

Homes of the Napiers

verted into one of the Merchant Company's Schools. Of the original Wright's Houses, a strange and apparently well-authenticated ghost story is told of how a black servant, brought home after the American war by a tenant of the house, General Robertson of Lawers, was disturbed nightly by the apparition of a headless woman carrying a child in her arms; and how long afterwards there was discovered, buried in a closet off the room, a box containing the skeletons of a mother and infant, the former with the head separated from the trunk, along with papers which pointed to a secret family crime and tragedy of early date. Some of the old Napier sculptured and heraldic stones are built into the enclosing walk of the school grounds; others, including the fine lectern sundial, are at Woodhouselee; still others at North Queensferry.

The group of buildings, terminating in the scaly and amorphous body and lofty spire of the Barclay Free Church, that now bears the name of Wright's Houses, has lost nearly every trace of the rusticity and quaintness it possessed, when golf flourished on the adjoining Bruntsfield Links, and when some of the oldest of the Edinburgh golfing clubs—the Honourable Company, the Burgess, and the Bruntsfield among them—held convivial meetings in the Golfer's Rest. The royal and ancient game, played for centuries on this part of the Burgh Muir, has been banished the spot, and its exponents have migrated to the Braids, Musselburgh, Barnton, or Gullane. The old wars have left deeper dints on the Links than have cleek and brassy. On this piece of undulating ground, lying high and dry above the South or Burgh Loch, was fought the battle of the Burgh Muir, where Guy of Namur and his Flem-

From Morningside to the West Kirk

ings were put to the rout; from its vantage Cromwell trained his guns on the Castle; and in its hollows the troops watching the attempt of the Covenanters of the Pentland Raid to enter the city were bivouacked. Peaceful, and even a little prosaic, is now the scene, surrounded as it is by terraces of many-storeyed tenements; and Bruntsfield—no longer disturbed even by the cry of "Fore!"—has become a safe promenade for the nursery maid.

The streets converging from Bruntsfield and other quarters on the Toll Cross retain, in their names, but almost in these alone, a reminiscence of the time when this locality, outside of the Portsburgh, was open ground, intersected by rural roads, with here and there a family mansion. Valleyfield Street preserves the memory of an ancient house in which legend affirms that the Regent Morton once lay ill; Leven Street contained—until its place was appropriated by the King's Theatre—Leven Lodge—a country seat, in the eighteenth century, of the Earls of Leven; Drumdryan Street is on the site of another old mansion; Lochrin House—a handsome square building in its own grounds, at the corner of Gilmour Place—has vanished before the modern builder; Thorneybauk, once a footpath and hedgerow, has been appropriated by the new Power Station of the Cable Tramways. The High Riggs—a gloomy continuation of the West Port—bears the name that in former times was applied to the bare ridge which extended from Greyfriars to the Toll Cross, or "Two-penny Custom," where the dues on goods entering the town were taken.

Fountainbridge—the long thoroughfare into which Thorneybauk once led—only recalls by its narrowness,

The Union Canal

and by an occasional begrimed and old-fashioned cottage still awaiting removal, the fact that, two or three generations ago, it belonged to the country rather than the city, and had, adjoining it, fields and pleasure grounds, and a " Grove," the site of which is still fixed by the local nomenclature. It is now a crowded workmen's quarter, and has a theatre, a working-man's institute, and a circus among its institutions. It crosses the Union Canal by a double-leaved drawbridge a little above the Canal Basin of Port Hopetoun.

The Canal, now an almost deserted channel of traffic, was finished in 1822, and completed a line of inland water communication between Edinburgh and Glasgow by forming a connection with the Forth and Clyde Canal above Grangemouth. Passenger boats made their slow journey, by the aid of towing-horses, from the capital to the metropolis of the West; travellers had their choice of the "canal express" and the stage coach. A few coal and manure barges now represent the traffic on the Union Canal; and channel and towing-path are deserted, except when frost binds the waters and troops of skaters skim its surface, making their way past the single gate-pillar and the sundial which mark, on the right hand and on the left, the site of the old house of Meggetland, and across the Slateford viaduct, towards Linlithgow. Rubber and vulcanite works are ranged on its banks, and empty their waste into it, and the waters are fouled with many impurities. It has witnessed many tragedies, best remembered of which is the sad death of George Meikle Kemp, the gifted designer of the Scott Monument, who, one dark night before he had an opportunity of seeing his completed work, accidentally fell into the canal. Ritchie Moni-

From Morningside to the West Kirk

plies's Castle Collop is supposed to have stood near the Canal banks; the Public Slaughter-houses, which may be supposed to contain the traditions of that "old and honourable house weel kenned at the West Port of Edinburgh," have removed to a site near the canal bank a couple of miles to the westward.

Past the Canal Basin of Port Hopetoun, once a pretty park sprinkled with trees, now a muddy and deserted pool, surrounded by coal stores, in which decaying water-craft are laid up, runs the broad thoroughfare of Lothian Road. In "Kay's Portraits" it is told that the street was made in a single day, towards the end of the eighteenth century, in fulfilment of a bet made by Sir John Clerk of Penicuik, who wagered that he would drive his carriage before sunset over ground then covered by "barns, sheds, and cowhouses." He duly fulfilled his promise, to the astonishment and dismay of one aged cowfeeder, who had gone out to milk her kine in the morning, and, on her return at nightfall, found that her cottage had disappeared and the whole neighbourhood changed, as by the rubbing of Aladdin's lamp.

In its gentle dip and rise to the west end of Princes Street, Lothian Road skirts, on the left hand, the Goods and Passenger Stations of the Caledonian Railway, which, in the year 1848, formed its terminus here—on the site of the Castle Barns or grange—alongside the Canal landing-place, and at once struck the slow waterway out of the running for the passenger traffic to the West. The lofty new West Princes Street Station and Hotel has risen on ground through which St Cuthbert's Loan meandered through fields to meet, at the Kirkbraehead the Kirk Loan climbing the northern slope

198

Lothian Road

from Stockbridge and the Dean. Both of them were country lanes, bordered by hedgerows, before Lothian Road was built, and their point of junction has become one of the two great confluences of traffic of the New Town. Their destination was St Cuthbert's, the old West Kirk, still sheltering, as it is believed to have done for eleven centuries past, under the west front of the Castle Rock.

Street improvements and railway alterations have made, and continue to make, great changes in the locality of the old Castle Barns and around the West Kirk. The "tall narrow, three-storey country villa" called Kirkbraehead House, where resided the Lieutenant-Governor of the Castle, Lord Elphinstone, in the last decade of the eighteenth century; the church in which that doughty champion of Free Church principles, Dr Candlish, preached after the Disruption; and the St Cuthbert Poorhouse, have successively had to make place, and rails and platforms and booking-offices cover their sites. The church has been transported to Stockbridge, and there set up again, stone for stone; the Poorhouse has removed well out into the country to the north, where, in spite of the growth of St Cuthbert's Parish, it has been found too spacious for the shrunken number of its inmates. The ridge above the King's Stables Road and the West Churchyard, facing the Castle, is occupied by a handsome terrace, which numbers among its edifices the School Board and Parochial Board Offices and a building which before the Church Union was the Synod Hall of the United Presbyterian Church and earlier still the New Edinburgh Theatre, but now a possesion of the Town and let as a hall for public entertainment, studios and offices, including those of the Royal Scottish Geographical Society; while in Grindlay Street, adjoining Castle Terrace, is the Lyceum Theatre, where already have gathered a goodly number of those traditions and memories of the drama in which we have found the town to be so rife. The block of buildings between these sites, including what has been a public school, is the spot finally fixed upon as the site of the Usher Hall, for the erection of which the late Mr Andrew Usher, so long ago as 1896, left the sum of £100,000. Operations have at length begun for giving form and substance to this long-delayed boon to the musical public of Edinburgh.

"St Cuthbert's-under-castle" itself has suffered change. But, in spite of the fact that one railway rears a stony front almost threateningly over it, while another, the North British, mines under its territory in a double tunnel, it has managed to retain its consecrated space and to grow in bulk. At no date, from the period of the first erection on this spot of a cell or house of prayer of the Columban Church dedicated to the great Apostle of Northumberland, does the architecture of the West Kirk appear to have been of a type worthy of the age of the foundation and the spacious extent of its charge of souls. Its date, as a sacred site, conjectured to be of the eighth century, is, perhaps, older than can be assigned to any other parish church in Scotland. The original area of the parish was the largest in Midlothian, and well-nigh enclosed the city, stretching almost to Leith on the east side of Edinburgh as well as on the west. Out of it a whole group of subsidiary parishes have since been cut.

In the early centuries, before gunpowder, the Castle, near though it was, does not appear to have been so ill

The West Kirk

a neighbour to St Cuthbert's. Afterwards, however, the Church received many hard dunts from the Rock—and occasionally returned them. In David I.'s time, the West Kirk and its emoluments were made over to the monks of Holyrood; and we have seen that these holy men were wont to visit their possessions be-west the Castle by following the route of the "Cowgait" and the West Port. On the northern side of the Rock, the marsh or loch came up to the borders of the West Kirkyard; although there was a "kittle" track, of which mention has been made, creeping under the brow of the cliffs and defended by the Wellhouse Tower. Beyond the hollow and its bogs, the "Lang Gait," so frequently spoken off, ran along the bare ridge, among furze and broom, towards the Kirkbraehead.

Of the period of the erection of the Church which stood on the spot at the date of the Reformation, and which was pulled down in 1775, nothing definite can be said. Old prints and descriptions show that it was a long and narrow building, with a southern aisle or transept, a nave which latterly fell into ruins, and a square tower. Barnlike additions were made to it; and the interior is spoken of as "formed after no plan, and presenting a multitude of petty galleries stuck one above another to the very rafters, like so many pigeons' nests." It had been badly battered in the wars, especially during the visits of Cromwell. The General Assembly met in it while David Leslie was following the Protector to Dunbar, and passed the West Kirk Act, which "lifted up a testimony against the sin and guilt of the King and his house"; and when Noll returned and made the building into barracks, what with the Ironsides within and the play upon it of the

From Morningside to the West Kirk

Castle guns from without, the walls alone were soon all that was left standing. Another shower of shot and shell fell upon St Cuthbert's from the Rock after the Revolution, when the Castle held out for James although Kirk and Country had declared for William. Yet the Old West Kirk held together for nearly a century longer, and then, at the nadir of taste, made way for a structure, big enough in all conscience, but looking, as Professor Blackie or some other wag described it, "like the packing-case out of which the neighbouring beautiful, toy-like structure of St John's Episcopal Church had been lifted." If it had a redeeming feature, it was the steeple, 170 feet in height, which has been preserved and forms part of the fabric of the existing St Cuthbert's planned by Mr Hippolyte Blanc.

The West Church has had some noteworthy pastors. One of the earliest, after the Reformation, was Mr Robert Pont, of a family of eminent Presbyterian ecclesiastics. An inscribed stone, bearing his initials and taken from his " manse," is built into St Cuthbert's Church Hall, and his tomb is in the Churchyard. The Rev. David Williamson, the "Dainty Davie" of the ribald song-writers, was minister at the time of the Revolution Settlement, and is perhaps best remembered on account of his large allowance of seven wives, the last of whom survived him. Another occupant of St Cuthbert's Manse was the intrepid Rev. Neil M'Vicar, who, with Prince Charlie's Highlanders as auditors, prayed for "that young man" at Holyrood, who had come seeking an earthly throne—"We beseech Thee take him to Thyself and give him a crown of glory." A later minister of the collegiate charge, Dr David Dickson, is commemorated by a fine piece of sculpture,

West Kirk Worthies

built into the steeple, the work of Handyside Ritchie.
The Rev. Sir Henry Wellwood Moncrieff, Dr Paul,
and Dr Veitch were all of them divines of antique
mould in a past generation; and the late senior minister,
Dr James MacGregor, was a preacher of note.

In the churchyard may be read, among other distinguished names, those of Thomas De Quincy, the
"Opium-eater," and of Sir Henry Raeburn, the painter.
The old family of the Nisbets of Dean had their vault
adjacent to the Church, and it is still easily discoverable.
Divided only by a wall from St Cuthbert's burial-ground
is the cemetery around St John's Church; and here
also rests the dust of many well-known Edinburgh
citizens. One of them was the genial Dean Ramsay,
the preserver from oblivion of a fund of Scottish
anecdote and humour, who was long the incumbent of
St John's, and whose memory is kept alive by a monument, in the form of a Celtic cross, on the line and level
of Princes Street.

CHAPTER XVII

THE NEW TOWN—PRINCES STREET

FROM circumambulation of the Older Edinburgh, from exploration of the southerly latitudes of its suburbs, we return to the parallel whence we set out. The "short mile" of Princes Street, from the North Bridge to Lothian Road, from the Register House to St John's Church, is the ground-line of Modern Athens; it is the score from which the New Town started on its race down the declivities to the north, and westward towards the roots of the Corstorphine Hills. To hosts of Edinburgh's visitors, it is the base they lay down in measuring and regulating their excursions and in taking their bearings. To not a few, it is not only the first and the last picture of the city that strikes the eye—it is the sole one that is left engraved in the memory. Peeps of its palace fronts and monuments, rising above the turf and trees of the gardens, are revealed to them as they emerge from the tunnels that form the dark prelude of the railway approach; and it stretches before them, in all its shining length, when they ascend from the depths of the Waverley platforms, or pass out of the portals of the West Princes Street Station.

Nor has Edinburgh, or its "New Town," much

PRINCES STREET, LOOKING WESTWARD.

[*To face page* 204.

reason to complain if the impression of its beauty be
drawn from the aspect and situation of the street which
is at once its favourite promenade and the centre of its
business life. "Her face is her fortune," someone had
said of the Scottish capital; and if High Street be the
deep heart, Princes Street is the fair face of Edinburgh.
"The most magnificent esplanade in Europe," the
citizens are fond of thinking it; and many widely-
travelled strangers have promptly granted the claim.
It may be that the architecture is not quite worthy of
the site. Certainly, since the dull, flat monotony of the
original Princes Street elevation, of three plain storeys
and a sunk area protected by railings, has almost disappeared, there is no longer any pretence of regularity
of features or harmony of style. But uniformity is not
an element of picturesque beauty; and there are times
when Princes Street, the mere frontage of it, with the
broken lights and varied outlines of its long perspective,
looks sparklingly beautiful. There are many handsome
buildings among its hotels, clubs, insurance offices, and
other business or public edifices; and nothing could be
finer in themselves, or more in harmony with their
situation, than the Scott Monument and the temples of
classic art on The Mound. Closing the vista eastward
are the white columns and monuments of the Calton
Hill, while in the opposite direction rise the group of
West End spires and towers.

But the glory of Princes Street, that which gives it
charm and distinction above other thoroughfares, is its
prospect towards the south, its outlook over the valley
which once held the Nor' Loch, to the Old Town and
the Castle. It was happy in being saved from the fate,
destined for it by the vandals of a century ago, of being

The New Town—Princes Street

"built on both sides." A mere beginning was made with this obstruction, now represented by the new Railway Hotel which is erected at the east end. By doubling its front Princes Street would not merely have spoiled, it would have completely destroyed its character. As it is, the guests at its hotel windows and the passengers on its crowded foot pavements and on the broad stream of its cars and carriages look across, as from a platform built to yield them the prospect, to the huge and shadowy bulk of the Rock, the long verdant sweep of the Castle Braes, and the sky-climbing broken masses of the High Street houses crowned by spire and dome and pinnacle, and separated from them only by a quarter of a mile of air and a light screen of foliage.

Every one has his own favourite Princes Street view. Some prefer the great confluence of traffic at the Register House; others the green spaces and wider vistas of the West End; still others the head of Waverley Bridge, the foot of the Mound, or the junction of Castle Street, where the grey citadel towers almost threateningly overhead. Alexander Smith preferred "the corner of St Andrew Street looking west," to gaze upon "the poem of Princes Street." "The puppets of the busy, many-coloured hour move about on its pavement, while across the ravine, time has piled the Old Town ridge on ridge, grey as a rocky coast, washed and worn by the foam of centuries; peaked and jagged by gable and roof; windowed from basement to cope; the whole surmounted by St Giles's airy crown. The New is there looking to the Old. Two times are brought face to face, and are yet separated by a thousand years." Could only a river be rolled down the ravine, or a lake

The Old and the New

lie in the lap between Old and New! Instead, there is a smear of engine-smoke.

Princes Street "beiks in the sun," and catches all the light and warmth that visit the chilly, grey metropolis of the North. "Seen in its glory," says R. L. Stevenson—"with soft air coming from the inland hills, military music sounding bravely from the hollow of the Gardens, the flags all waving on its palaces"—it is "what Paris ought to be." But a shift of wind or a slight drop in the weather-glass, and all is changed— the mists choke the valley, "the rain is splashing on the window, and the passengers flee along Princes Street before the galloping squalls." It may be that in this inconstancy of mood, in the evanescence of its smiles, resides one of the chief charms of this famous thoroughfare. After all, gay and garish sunshine is neither its most characteristic nor its most becoming dress. When the rosy morning light, stealing past the shoulder of Arthur Seat, strikes upon the Old Town projections and the buttresses of the Castle, and slowly gilds the sleeping front and deserted pavement of Princes Street, the effect is magical. The scene is not less lovely when flooded with mellow evening radiance. But most entrancing of all, perhaps, is the spectacle on a clear star-lit night, when the moon has just gone down behind the Castle battlements, and Old Edinburgh's "ridged and chimneyed bulk of blackness" is silhouetted against the midnight sky like the ragged edge of a thunder-cloud.

The New Town, and Princes Street in particular, are gathering to themselves a considerable stock of years and of venerable associations. Yet there are those still alive who have spoken to men who could remember when the ground was chiefly pasture and waste; and

The New Town—Princes Street

highway robberies were committed among the whins of the Lang Dykes after George the Third became king. Along this high ground beyond the Nor' Loch, David Leslie had deployed his army in the direction of Corstorphine, when he made his masterly defence of the capital against Cromwell in 1650; and the English and Scottish hosts exchanged iron salutes — the "Gogar Flashes"—across the marshes to the westward. We have seen Dundee and his horsemen galloping along this Lang Gait in the Revolution year to rouse the Highlands to the help of King James. Another scene in the drama of the Stewart dynasty was witnessed on the spot in the '45; for it was by the same ridge, running along the line of the present George Street, that the citizens saw Gardiner's Dragoons fleeing before the advancing Highlanders towards Leith Links and Musselburgh after the "Canter of Coltbrig."

For many years after the last Jacobite Rebellion, hares and partridges were shot, and crops were grown on the site of the New Town. The reputation of the place was none of the best. Readers of "David Balfour" will remember how suspiciously he looked about him for spy or footpad, as he made his way by furze and broom and standing grain down to the hollow of the Dean. Two farmhouses stood on the ground—the one, Bearford Parks, near where stands St George's Church; and the other in the dip that now forms the Queen Street and Heriot Row gardens. One or two country lanes meandered down towards the Water of Leith. The Kirk Loan has been mentioned. It was a country road, screened in summer-time by flowering hawthorn, and gave the good folks living on the north side of the parish access to the West Kirk after they had crossed the wooden bridge at Stockbridge. It is lamely translated in Church Lane.

A more frequented way was the Old Queensferry Road, followed by the "Antiquary," which dipped down to the stream in that steep part of the glen where the grain mills and houses of Water of Leith were congregated, and climbed the opposing bank making for the Ferry and the Hawes Inn. Gabriel's Road was another rural pathway that slanted down the slope leaving the Lang Gait at the hamlet of Moultrie Hill, long displaced by the Register House and St James's Square, and crossing the little river by a ford beyond the Silvermills lades. At the head of it, in what is now West Register Street, afterwards stood Ambrose's Tavern, the scene of the "Noctes Ambrosianæ," which rang so often to the mirth of Christopher North and the sallies of the "Shepherd" and "Tickler." Further down was a cottage in which "ambulative citizens regaled themselves with curds and cream" when making long country excursions to Broughton or to St Bernard's Well. So bare was the ground of houses or other obstructions in the early part of the eighteenth century, that spectators on the Castle Hill were witnesses in part to a terrible murder which was committed in Gabriel's Road in 1717, when a young tutor named Irvine—a Scottish Eugene Aram, who had unhinged his mind by brooding on predestination—cut the throats of two boys, who were his pupils, with a penknife.

The Broughton Loan was a more direct road to the little barony burgh of Broughton, which stood beside the loch and mills of the Holyrood Canons—the Canonmills—and boasted of its own courts and tolbooth and burned its own witches. The way led past the village

The New Town—Princes Street

of Picardy, colonised by Picard silk-weavers, to whom
the Governors of Heriot's Hospital granted five acres
of land to settle upon, after the revocation of the Edict
of Nantes. The line of Leslie's old entrenchments,
which became Leith Walk and the favourite path by
which the citizens strolled when bent on an oyster feast
and taking the air on Leith Pier, bounded the New
Town site towards the east; it passed the Gallowlee
—an eerie spot in a failing light; under the shadow of
the "fatal tree" a spaewife sat and croaked as David
Balfour tramped by on his way to Pilrig. Further
afield, on the western side of the great open space, were
a few old manor-houses; among them Easter Coates,
which, little changed in externals, survives to this day,
almost the only relic left of the period when the New
Town was country; and Wester Coates, built upon by
the houses of Grosvenor Street. The trees of Randolph
Crescent represent the rookery of the departed
Drumsheugh House, where the Jacobite Chevalier
Johnstone found shelter in the guise of a packman; and
on the other bank of the Water was the mansion
of the Dean, the ancestral home of the old family of
Nisbet.

The aspect of the scene was rural, and not a little
lonesome and desolate when James Craig, sister's son
to Thomson of the "Seasons," drew his plan of the New
Town, which received the compliments and approval of
the magistrates, in 1767. On the plan were inscribed
his uncle's lines—

> August, around, what public works I see!
> Lo, stately streets! lo, squares that court the breeze!
> See long canals and deepened rivers join,
> Each part with each and with the circling main,
> The whole entwined isle.

Princes Street Prospects

For, as has been mentioned, it was part of the original design, first conceived by Earl Mar of the '15, that a branch stream should be drawn from the Water of Leith and made to flow into the Nor' Loch, which, thus kept fresh and clean, should discharge its waters into the sea round the eastern base of the Calton Hill. Alas that the ambitious and happy idea of the "entwined isle" never got beyond the stage of project! And residents and visitors have sometimes lamented that the New Town streets and squares "court the breeze" only too successfully. Its wind-swept terraces and "draughty parallelograms" must have been a trying change to those who flitted out hither from the sheltered crannies and havens of the Old Town closes; air they got in plenty, but no "bield." It was complained also that the familiar neighbourliness and cosiness of home life fled when Edinburgh fashion camped out in the northern fields; formality came into manners as well as into street architecture; the "good old times" were at an end.

Yet this Modern Athens, as the first dwellers in it were fond of calling it, has both prospects and memories. It is the later Edinburgh of Walter Scott and Lockhart, of the "Blackwood Group" and the Edinburgh Reviewers. David Hume came to live at the north-west corner of St Andrew Square—was not St David Street named after him in jest? Robert Burns lodged in St James's Square and penned epistles to Clarinda in a high upper room looking down upon the green space behind the Register House. The bulk of the "Waverley Novels" were written at No. 39 North Castle Street, neighbours across the way marvelling at the daily vision of the hand that travelled ceaselessly across the paper. The "Chaldee Manuscript" was concocted in John Wilson's house in Queen Street. William Ewart Gladstone, a little boy of five, looked out wonderingly from the window of a Princess Street hotel, and listened while the Castle guns fired salutes for the victory of Waterloo. From St Andrew's Church, after severing themselves from the Establishment, the Fathers of the "Disruption," with Dr Chalmers at their head, marched down Hanover Street to the Tanfield Hall at Canonmills, there to form the Free Church and begin a new era in Scottish ecclesiasticism. In the Heriot Row gardens, and by the banks of the Water of Leith, Robert Louis Stevenson played and dreamed and gathered memories that were to be background to the stories of Catriona, and Alan Breck Stewart, and St Ives, and Weir of Hermiston. Princes Street was long familiar with the breezy figure, with plaid and "kail runt," of Professor Blackie; and with the portly form and leonine look—"the head of Jove on the body of Bacchus"—of Sir James Young Simpson, the discoverer of chloroform.

A long procession, of eminent judges and advocates, of weighty and eloquent divines, of men learned and illustrious in science, medicine, and philosophy, have streamed down the Mound and spread through the New Town streets and places when work was over in the Law Courts, the Assemblies, and the University. It is needless to go back to the time of Cockburn and Jeffrey, of Chalmers, or of Gregory, and to go over the long list. Enough has been said to show how varied as well as brilliant are the New Town memories of the past. As to its prospects, it may be that more might have been made of the site, but at least it succeeds, as few cities drawn and built by plan and

PRINCES STREET IN 1837.

From a water-colour by J. D. Swarbreck.

rule have done, in combining the stately and the picturesque. Handsome in itself, it is more magnificent in its outlook. Of the Princes Street view we have spoken ; it embraces the Salisbury Crags, and from upper windows takes in glimpses of the Pentlands and the shores of East Lothian. From the platform of Queen Street, or from the crossings on the swelling ridge of George Street, one gazes down upon peeps of the Firth, and across these to the hills of Fife. It is curious, says the author of " Picturesque Notes," how much description would apply commonly to the Old and New Town—

" The same sudden accidents of ground, a similar domineering site above the plain, and the same super-position of one rank of society over another, are to be observed in both. Thus, the broad and comely approach to Princes Street from the east, lined with hotels and public offices, makes a leap over the gorge at Low Calton ; if you cast a glance over the parapet, you look direct into that sunless and disreputable confluent of Leith Street, and the same tall houses open upon both thoroughfares. This is only the New Town passing overhead above its own cellars ; walking, so to speak, over its own children, as is the way of cities and the human race."

Every city, too, swallows country hamlets in its growth ; and fragments of them will lie undigested for generations. It is so, at least, with the New Town of Edinburgh. For not only does it look down, from the Regent's Bridge, on what was once the extra-mural burgh of Calton, and from the parapet of the Dean Bridge, survey the mills and foaming weir and huddled crowd of old houses of the village of Water of Leith :

but the explorer may still, as in Stevenson's boyhood, come upon relics of an earlier age—fossils, as it were, of the period before the ground was given over to the architect and builder to work their will upon—in corners like Silvermills, or Canonmills, or Water Lane, or "the nugget of cottages at Broughton market," which represents all that is left of Broughton burgh. "Antiques" these forlorn old houses may be, "with a quaint air of having wandered far from their own place," like Robert Fergusson's butterfly; abashed and homely enough with "their gables and their creeping plants and their outside stairs." But it can no longer be said of any of them, as a couple of generations ago, that they are "more rural than the open country"; that there are corners that "smell like the end of a country garden in April"; or that the inhabitants stand and gossip at the doors, after the manner of the village folks of Colinton or Cramond—from which also, in turn, the idyllic air, the "haunting flavour of the country," is being chased. They are closely sealed and prisoned in stone. The mill stream runs no longer past the door. Since "the last elm died in Elm Row," a score of country mansions that then stood well out of town, in their own grounds, have been pulled down or portioned off among small tenants, and their groves and avenues cut down to make way for streets and crescents; "the villas and the workmen's quarters spread apace" on this as on other borders of the city.

The New Town was slow in making a start. A premium of £20, it is said, was offered to the first builder on the site; and it went to the bold speculator who laid his foundation in "Rose Court, George Street." The first of the Princes Street houses to rise was the

New Town Beginnings

most easterly of the line—that which bears the number "10," and is occupied by the Crown Hotel. It was built by John Neale, a silk-mercer, who obtained the ground at a nominal feu, with exemption from burghal taxes. Of another early house of the row, erected in 1769 by a person bearing the Hebraic name of Shadrach Moyes, it is recorded that the owner made a condition that someone must build to westward of him, to shield him from the winds from that quarter which blew shrewdly along the bare hillside. Archibald Constable, Mr Neale's son-in-law, came from High Street to No. 10 in 1822, and there for a time he played the part of a "publisher-Mæcenas," and embarked in the grand and rash schemes that brought himself and Scott to ruin. "If I should break my magic wand in the fall from this elephant, and lose my popularity with my fortune!" was the thought that wrung the heart of the great master of Romance, as he set himself "doggedly" to retrieve the disaster.

Constable's shop, as Mr Giles points out in his Princes Street Notes, was "situated at a point visible from the lower end of North Bridge to anyone strolling down from the High Street and Old Town," as the Edinburgh Reviewers and the other *literati* of the day would likely do. At an earlier date, William Blackwood had established himself at No. 17, and this spot (still dedicated to literature) became "the great lounging bookshop of the New Town," whence issued, in 1817, the first pages of "Maga." From the corner of Hanover Street, facing the Mound, began to appear, in 1833, *Tait's Magazine;* and at the same time the House of Chambers—its magazine a weakly plant in its second year—moved to 19 Waterloo Place, at the east end of

The New Town—Princes Street

the thoroughfare. By this date more than half of the booksellers and publishers of the city had flitted to or started business in the New Town; Princes Street had established its claim to be the birthplace of magazine literature—the Paternoster Row as well as the Oxford Street of Edinburgh.

With the dealers in literary wares came the mercers, the jewellers, and other caterers to fashion, and took up position on the front line. Princes Street grew and changed apace; but for long Hanover Street, and afterwards Frederick Street and Castle Street, were bounds beyond which the world of shops did not extend. The stately George Street set up as a rival early in last century, when, too, an extended New Town was planned, and moving down the slope, began to obtain footholds on the further bank of the Water of Leith. The great affluents of Lothian Road and Leith Street had already been formed, and Waterloo Place was planned in the Waterloo Year. Through these and other channels an ever greater flood of traffic poured into Princes Street; and gradually it took its present shape—an almost continuous line of hotels, clubs, cafés, bank and insurance offices, and great drapery establishments, rising above a glittering array of shop fronts.

The Princes Street edifices are in many styles, and among them are fine buildings—the New Club, on the site of the Old Stamp Office; the Liberal and Conservative Clubs; the Life Association Office; the new buildings of the North British and Mercantile Insurance Company, set up at the close of a century of business life, the earlier years of which had been spent in the Royal Exchange, in the Old Parliament Close, at the corner of Bank Street and High Street, and in Hanover

Princes Street Edifices

Street; "Jenner's," opposite the Scott Monument; several of the hotels. Last, not least, and first in date, there is the Old Register House, begun on Adam's plans as early as 1774, but not completed until many years afterwards, and reinforced in 1860 by the New Register House, as a repository of the National Records of Scotland. On the opposite side of the way are the General Post Office, which with the growth of business has undergone successive extension and heightening, and, occupying the whole block between the Waverley Market and the North Bridge, the towering mass of the North British Station Hotel.

Of West and East Princes Street Gardens something has been said already. They are green and beautiful spots in the heart of the city that derive even greater charm from their bold and striking natural features—the Castle cliffs and the steep dip of the Old Town ridge—than from their groves of trees, their stretches of greensward, their fountains, their monuments. The West Gardens—once filled by a Slough of Despond—have become, but for the trail of the railway, an ideal Town Park. They are seen at the best on a bright summer day, when military music rises from the depths of the hollow or floats down from the Esplanade, and gay groups stroll or rest on the turf. The ground became public property in 1876, when a slice was taken from it to increase the width of the Princes Street roadway.

Greater and more grievous are the parings to which the East Gardens have been subjected, in order to provide more space for railway sidings and platforms. But, as consolation, there is always the Scott Monument, a work of art that by its grace and beauty and harmony of proportion has stood, and is likely to stand, the test of time and criticism, and to give delight to generations to come. It was designed by an almost self-taught hand—that of George Meikle Kemp, son of a Moorfoot shepherd, whose genius had been kindled by personal study of Melrose Abbey and other examples of Gothic architecture, and by love of the works and character of Sir Walter. In niches of the monument are placed figures, from the chisels of different sculptors, of characters in the Waverley Novels; under the groined and open canopy is a seated statue of Scott with his dog Maida, by Sir John Steell; and overhead is a small Scott Museum. To many not the least wonderful thing about this "pride and ornament of Princes Street" is its cost—less than £16,000.

To one or two of the other Princes Street monuments and statues, Lord Rosebery's prayer—that the spirits that possessed the Gadarene swine might enter into them, so that they might "run down a steep place into the sea"—may seem not uncalled for; but others, again, are worthy of their subjects and their honourable position. The list includes Steell's equestrian statue of the Duke of Wellington, in front of the Register House, and monuments to David Livingstone, Adam Black, M.P., Christopher North, Allan Ramsay, Thomas Guthrie, and Sir James Young Simpson, marshalled in line parallel to Princes Street. A colossal seated statue of Her Majesty the Queen also surmounts the Princes Street façade of the Royal Institution, a building which, with the National Picture Gallery, crowns the conspicuous site of the Mound with classic Grecian pillar and architrave, and gives to the scene, whether viewed from near at hand or from a distance, one of its strongest architectural

THE SCOTT MONUMENT.

Princes Street Monuments

notes. The Institution, the older of these companion structures by a quarter of a century, is in "the Doric style of Pericles." The School of Art, the Board of Manufactures, and a sculpture gallery were formerly accommodated here; they have flitted elsewhere, and the whole building is now set aside for the Royal Scottish Academy, which has given up its share in the tenancy of the neighbouring edifice, the National Picture Gallery. This, a beautiful copy of an Ionic temple, contains two ranges of picture galleries, holding the fine national collection, which includes, in addition to many rare and precious examples of English and foreign, and notably old French, masters, a full and admirable representation of works of the Scottish school in landscape and portraiture—from Jameson to Raeburn, and from Raeburn to Sir George Reid and Sir James Guthrie.

CHAPTER XVIII

THE CALTON

THE Calton Hill and its monuments might be claimed as among the ornaments of Princes Street. They close its vista eastwards with the group of columns that have been said to give to Edinburgh "the false air of a Modern Athens." They "enfilade" the whole length of the street, which, whether glittering in the sunshine or showing its long perspective of gleaming lamps under a canopy of darkness, is one of the most striking features in that "Calton Hill prospect," which has been truly called one of the finest in Europe. The Calton Hill bears Edinburgh's uncompleted sketch of its Parthenon. It would, doubtless, have been its Acropolis had there not happened to be a still more commanding site for a citadel. Indeed, the country visitor and the tourist from the South, emerging from the darkness of the Calton tunnel, are wont to "joyously hail" the much-turreted and battlemented Calton Jail, perched upon the Dow or Dhu Craig—the precipitous side of the Hill—as the veritable Castle on its Rock.

Until Waterloo Place and Regent's Bridge were opened, the Calton Hill was reached by descending into the depths of Low Calton and climbing up the steep and narrow path of Craigend. Princes Street,

Calton Views

says Lord Cockburn, was closed in this direction by "a mean line of houses running north and south," beyond which was a burying-ground; and through the heart of this the new and wide access to the Hill and round its southern flanks to the country lying east and south had to be cut. The route, to the base of the rocky hill, is lined on both sides by stately buildings—which George IV., on his entrance, condescended to admire—save where it is bounded by the retaining walls of the divided graveyard. Here the monuments of the dead lean over and look down on the pavements and the tram-cars. The burial-ground of Calton was granted to their vassals of the Calton burgh by its superiors, the Lords Balmerino, the last of whom lost his head in the '45 Rebellion. A peep down upon the site of the ancient extra-mural barony burgh from the Regent's Bridge is still impressive, although the features of the scene have been so completely changed. St Ninian's, or Beggars', Row, leading past St Ninian's Chapel to the country and to Leith, was its main street, and, like the neighbouring Canongate, it had its Baron Bailie, its Trade Incorporation, and its High Constables, whose staves of office dropped from their grasp only with the municipal reform of 1856, when the Calton insignia were deposited with the Society of Antiquaries. St Ninian's Row, under another name, now serves in part as a side access to the Waverley Station.

It is worth while turning aside for a little into the "City of the Dead" built aloft on the Calton Craigs, from which, in the days of civil war, ordnance has repeatedly been planted to "ding and siege" the quarrelsome town of Edinburgh. Young Stevenson was among those who loved to haunt this commanding yet

The Calton

secluded spot, when he was "in an unhappy mood"; the dust of his own people lay near by in the New Calton, which overlooks Fergusson's grave in the Canongate, and Holyrood, the "House of Kings." May he not be regarded as successor of the "Fairy Boy," the old *genius loci* of the Calton Hill? In a circular mausoleum, reminding one, by its shape, of an ancient "broch," reposes David Hume; near it is a monument, crowned by a life-sized figure of Abraham Lincoln in bronze, to the memory of the Scottish soldiers who fell in the American Civil War. William Blackwood and Archibald Constable are placed not far apart and close to the brink below which runs the stream of the Waterloo Place traffic, as if they would still listen, as they did so eagerly when they were old neighbours and rivals in business in Princes Street, to the hum and whisper of the world. The gentle Dr John Brown, author of "Rab and his Friends," and Robert Burns's great crony, William Nichol, of the High School, sleep peacefully in this haven of rest, which, like Greyfriars, has its Martyrs' Monument, in the shape of a tall white obelisk, commemorative of Muir, Palmer, and their companions, banished for their early efforts in the cause of Reform. In the corner of Old Calton Churchyard which has been cut off from the rest by the thoroughfare of Waterloo Place, rest, as the stones record, members of the Cordwainers' Craft of the burgh, under the windows of the new offices of the Gas Commissioners.

Escaping from the shadow of Graveyard and Prison, one who chooses to reconnoitre the shoulders of the Calton before climbing to its crown finds himself on a broad sweep of terraced road, with the Hill and its trees and monuments rising on his left, the dingy, smoke-

Old Calton

canopied Canongate huddled at his feet, and over against him the forms of Arthur Seat and the Salisbury Crags. This would be a famous "view-point" were there not other and still better vantage-ground above. On the right side of the way, where "Jacob's Ladder" climbs up out of the abysses of the North Back of Canongate, there is a monument to Robert Burns—"a Corinthian cyclostyle of twelve columns and a cupola," a copy of the Choragic monument of Lysicrates. The collection of Burns's relics, it has been seen, has been removed to the Municipal Museum. The eye is even better satisfied with the beautiful lines and proportions of the classic edifice on the terrace opposite—the Royal High School of many memories—a gem of modern Edinburgh architecture. It was designed by Thomas Hamilton, an old High School boy, and rose on this airy and commanding site when the time came, towards the end of the third decade of the century, for removing the Burgh School from its shady and unhealthy environment of the Cowgate and the "Yards."

By Regent, Carlton, and Royal Terraces, which enclose, with a noble range of houses and a screen of trees and gardens, the eastern front of the Hill, and afford, along their whole length, fine prospects of the Abbey quarter, the Queen's Park, Leith, and the sea, one is brought back again to the neighbourhood of Leith Street and High Calton, at Greenside. Once, on this north-western spur of the Hill, there stood a Carmelite Monastery, converted at the Reformation into a Lepers' Hospital. The savage rules of the time, dictated by fear, ordained that any of the wretched inmates who escaped out of bounds, or who even opened the door between sunset and sunrise, should be hanged

223

on the gallows beside the gate. The "Rood of Green-side," set apart for burnings for heresy and sorcery, stood under the Hill in this quarter; and in curious juxtaposition was the "Playfield," the scene of tournaments, sports, and out-of-doors dramatic performances, described in a grant by James II. of Scots as in "the valley or low ground lying betwixt the rock called Craigingalt on the east and the common way, or passage, on the west." Sir David Lyndsay's "Pleasant Satyre of the Three Estaits" was played on this spot, until its free handling of the vices of the clergy provoked the prelates of the Ancient Church to interdict it; and tradition asserts that Bothwell succeeded in first taking the eye of Mary by his bold horsemanship in riding down the steep bank and leaping his steed into the tilting-yard.

It is time to leave the skirts of the Hill and ascend to its summit. This can be done by the flight of steps cut through the brown basalt rock at the end of Waterloo Place; by the carriage-way that rises from Regent Road behind the High School playground; or by the footpath that climbs the steep from Greenside Church. On the green crown of Calton, high above the city houses, and clear even of their smoke, we find monuments—and monuments. On the highest platform is a column, erected to the memory of the great sailor Nelson. In shape it has been likened to a Dutch skipper's telescope, and it has been described, perhaps with a touch of extravagance, as "among the vilest of man's handiworks." A time-ball drops on the head of Nelson's Monument, to give warning, through the signal-gun at the Castle, that it is one hour after noon on the Greenwich meridian, and to this top-gallant level

THE CALTON HILL FROM THE SOUTH-WEST.

[To face page 224.

The Calton Monuments

the visitor can painfully ascend if he wishes to get more of a bird's-eye view than can be had from the turf and rocks at its base.

Twelve great fluted columns of white Craigleith stone, founded on a temple base and crowned by Doric capitals and frieze, rise hard by, and front, from the centre of the Hill, the line of Princes Street. The original idea was to raise a Modern Parthenon on the spot, " as a memorial of the past and an incentive to the future heroism of the men of Scotland," and in particular as " the tribute of a grateful country to her gallant and illustrious sons" who fell in the battles, by sea and land, of the great war with France. The foundation-stone was laid, with much state and ceremony in 1822, by George the Magnificent in person. But money and enthusiasm gave out when this fragment of the work had been erected, at a cost of some £12,000; and the " National Monument" has been made the subject of many mocks and girds as the " National Disgrace" or " Folly." In point of picturesque effect, the part is perhaps better than the whole. These graceful, far-shining Calton columns come finely into the picture of the Hill and of the city, from whatever side they are viewed; the Scottish Valhalla is a "splendid failure."

Classic memorials of Dugald Stewart, the philosopher, and of John Playfair, the astronomer, both of them designed by the nephew of the latter, W. H. Playfair, adorn the hill; and here, too, are the quaint irregular form of the Old Observatory—an early home of Scottish astronomy—and the white domes of the New or City Observatory, containing the Cox and Crawford telescopes. It is not, however, for the sake of its monuments but for its prospects—not for what is to be

The Calton

seen on it, but for what can be seen from it—that the Calton is chiefly famed and frequented. R. L. Stevenson —a good authority on a point of the kind—gave it the praise of being perhaps the best of all places for viewing Edinburgh—"since you can see the Castle, which you lose from the Castle, and Arthur Seat, which you cannot see from Arthur Seat." To be sure, you lose the Calton Hill, which is no small loss. Certainly the spectacle of Edinburgh from the Calton Hill rivals, if it does not surpass, that from Mons Meg, from the Radical Road, or from the Blackford Hill.

It is not one, but many. For the old city and the new encircle the Calton braes and cliffs, and present towards them their most romantic aspects. Some may prefer the wide and glorious prospect from the northern slopes over the New Town, the Port of Leith, and the Firth of Forth, to the hills of Fife. It is true, it is to some extent a repetition, as to background, of the view from the Bomb Battery of the Castle; but all the details are altered. For foreground there is the steep plunge into the valley of Greenside; and out of it spring gaunt and grim ranges of tenements that, for height and dinginess, will endure comparison with any of the Old Town lands —buildings that, starting from "three storeys below the street pavement," rise six or seven storeys above it. Other admirers there are who will take most delight in the lovely vista, best seen from the base of Nelson's Monument, of Princes Street with its traffic, overhung by the mass of the Castle, and made still more enchanting after nightfall, when interminable lines of light twinkle away into the distance. But the majority will give the chief praise to the magical scene—whether viewed by day or night—from the southern crest or

Calton Views

flank of the hill, where you look upon the high-piled houses of Old Edinburgh, rearing themselves in weird shapes against the sky, or hiding in the murky shadows of the narrowing gulf between you and Arthur Seat.

An infinite variety of charm comes to the Calton Hill prospects with changes of the season, of weather and of light. Stevenson gave his voice for "one of those days of sunshine and east wind which are so common in our more than temperate summer"—when, along with the coolness and freshness drawn in from the North Sea, there is a faint floating haze, enough to obscure but not to hide Aberlady Sands, and Berwick Law, and the hump of the Bass—as a choice time for a stroll on the Calton Hill. Among a hundred other objects you can pick out Leith and its forest of masts, the ships at anchor in the Roads, the white pharos on Inchkeith, the Fife towns, sitting "each in its bank of blowing-smoke" on the coast opposite, and the sea-way to "Norrowa over the faem." "You turn to the city, and see children dwarfed by distance into pigmies, at play about suburban doorsteps; you have a glimpse upon a thoroughfare where people are densely moving; you note ridge after ridge of chimney-stalks running down-hill, one behind another, and church spires rising bravely from the sea of roofs. And here you are on this pastoral hillside, among nibbling sheep and looked down upon by monumental buildings."

Return again, "on some clear, dark, moonless night, with a ring of frost in the air," and you will find "a sight as stimulating as the hoariest summit of the Alps." For though the town "lies blue and darkling on her hills, innumerable spots of light shine far and near along the pavements and upon the high façades. Moving

The Calton

lights of the railway pass and repass below the stationary lights upon the bridge. Lights burn in the jail. Lights burn high up in the tall lands and on the Castle turrets; they burn low in Greenside along the Park. They run out one beyond another into the dark country. They walk in procession down to Leith, and shine singly far along Leith pier. Thus the plan of the city and its suburbs is mapped out upon the ground of blackness, as when a child pricks a drawing full of pin-holes and exposes it before a candle; not the darkest night of winter can conceal her high station and fanciful design." Such are a few of the city enchantments to be seen from the Calton Hill.

CHAPTER XIX

GEORGE STREET AND ITS ENVIRONS

" THE great enemy of the good is the better." George
Street would be the pride and centre of life of Edinburgh
New Town if there were no Princes Street. Even as it
is, George Street may challenge comparison with its
more famous rival on many points of situation, architecture, and history. It can look down from its higher
site upon the Princes Street throng, and out and away
to the green country, the sea, and the hills. It has its
monuments and architectural ornaments; its vistas
closed by the two magnificent open spaces, each in its
own way almost unrivalled, of St Andrew and Charlotte
Squares—on the one hand the lofty pillar of the
Melville column and the needle-like spire of St Andrew's
Church; on the other the fine dome of St George's. In
age, even, it can compete with the other; the foundation-stone of the New Town, as we have seen, was
practically laid in Rose Court, behind the church of St
Andrew. Of the memories, literary, artistic, and even
romantic, that cling to the "city of a thousand associations," George Street and its environs have more than
their share.

Like these associations, the stately beauty of which
George Street and its Squares can now boast has come
to them gradually. In the early decades of last century

George Street and its Environs

George Street was described as "comparatively mean" in aspect; nay, "as the most melancholy and gloomy street that can well be imagined." It was originally designed for residence rather than business. Even yet, commerce has only begun to intrude its foot or display its wares in the serene atmosphere and under the gaze of the watching sphinxes of Charlotte Square—one of the most dignified "places" in Europe.

It is quite otherwise with its "marrow" to the east —St Andrew Square—and with the thoroughfare between. The headquarters of Scottish banking are in and near St Andrew Square. Here also is the Stock Exchange; and several of the principal insurance offices —the Edinburgh, the Standard, the Royal, the Prudential among them—have raised, of late, imposing structures, within gunshot of the great fluted column (a copy of that of Trajan at Rome), from the summit of which a colossal statue of Henry Dundas, first Lord Melville, the friend of Pitt and in his time the "King of Scotland," looks down upon the city whose political liberties he erstwhile ruled with a rod of iron. The mansion-house of another Dundas of mark—Sir Laurence, a merchant prince and a Lord Provost, who was ancestor of the Earls of Zetland—stands somewhat back from the Square, and is now occupied by the Royal Bank, once obscurely housed in the Old Bank Close. Next neighbours are the British Linen Company Bank—an ornate building with projecting Corinthian columns, and symbolic figures crowning its entablature—and the National Bank; the head office of the Commercial Bank rears a classic front a few doors along George Street, where likewise the Union Bank, long located beside the Courts of Law in Parliament Square, has latterly taken up its station. The

MONS MEG.

GEORGE STREET, LOOKING EAST.

[To face page 230.

Banks and Monuments

Music Hall and the new headquarters of the Grand Lodge
—successors of St Cecilia's Hall and Mary's Chapel, in
Niddry Wynd, as centres of Edinburgh Music and
Scottish Masonry; the offices of the Royal Society and
of the United Free Church, do not exhaust the list of
public buildings which range themselves on the line of
George Street.

The statues and monumental groups that preside
over its squares and guard its crossways number
seven, reckoning that which surmounts the Melville
column. John, Earl of Hopetoun, the Peninsular hero,
stands leaning on his war-steed in front of the Royal
Bank; and on the other side of the Melville column is
the group of Alexander and Bucephalus, designed and
cast in bronze at dates fifty years apart, and so repre-
senting the life-work of Sir John Steell. George IV.,
sceptred and robed, at the intersection of Hanover
Street, bears eloquent testimony to Scotland's loyalty
under difficulties. The great statesman, William Pitt,
from the chisel of Chantrey, also looks towards Princes
Street, from where the ridge is traversed by Frederick
Street. In a similar position, with regard to Castle
Street, stands a figure of the great Chalmers, a latter-day
Knox, clad in his doctor's gown, his massive face turned
towards the Castle Rock and his finger upon Holy
Writ. Last, not least, in the centre of Charlotte
Square, surrounded by its greenery, and with the
pillared façade, the dome, and the gilded cupola of St
George's Church—the St Paul's of Edinburgh—as back-
ground, is an equestrian statue of the Prince Consort,
the granite pedestal surrounded by emblematic groups
in bronze offering " Albert the Good " the tribute of all
ranks and conditions of men.

George Street and its Environs

George Street and its approaches, and the streets that lie below it to the north, echo faintly to the lost footsteps of the men who, after the building of the New Town, made Edinburgh a shrine for the pilgrim of letters, philosophy, and science. Literary lions paced its pavements in groups in the period of the Great War and of the rule of the Dundases. Every other door has its association with some name or event of note in the social life or literature of the time.

We can only glance here and there, and take cognisance of an outstanding figure, or incident, or site of "Modern Athens." Henry Brougham was born in No. 21 St Andrew Square, two years after the death of Hume, whose last years in Edinburgh were spent in the house, on the corner of which a wag of the day chalked the name "St David Street." "Many a better man has been called a saint," was the philosopher's placid comment; "many a worse man also," posterity may add. Lord Buchan, a literary bore of the first calibre, who sought to patronise Burns and Scott, and played at reviving classic tastes and costumes, was afterwards a dweller in No. 21; and next door lived "Cocked-hat Hamilton," who carried down to his death in 1835, the practice of wearing the three-cornered head-covering and the other articles of fashionable attire of the vanished generation who figure in "Kay's Portraits."

But it is easy to find closer local links with Burns—and especially with Scott. It has been noted that, from an airy "poet's lodging" behind the Royal Bank, in St James's Square (where St Ives and his Rowley some time quartered with Mrs M'Rankine), Sylvander spied his Clarinda. Creech, the bookseller, had his residence

Lost Footsteps

in No. 5 George Street, where now is the Standard Insurance Office; at 25, the home of the Ferriers—parents of Susan, the novelist, and grand-parents of James Frederick, "the last of the philosophers"—Burns and Mrs Piozzi have been guests; and from the company that were wont to assemble for whist and supper the author of "Marriage" and "Inheritance" drew the materials of her pictures of the Edinburgh society and characters of the day.

As for Sir Walter, did not his widowed mother live and die in 75 George Street? Was it not in No. 108 that he took lodgings and brought home his newly-wedded wife, not so many doors apart from No. 86, where dwelt his friend, Sir William Forbes, the banker, whose marriage to Scott's "first love," Miss Stuart, went near to break his heart? Above all, did he not times innumerable limp up the steps of No. 39 Castle Street—a few yards below the corner of George Street—the home in town where he lived and worked for eight-and-twenty years; the magician's cave whence issued mysteriously the bright array of the Waverley Novels, to astonish and delight the world? However hard might be the strain on the busy hand and brain, Scott's stock of time, patience, and good-humour never seemed to fail; and the Ettrick Shepherd naively tells us—"Many a time have I been sorry for him, for I have remained in his study in Castle Street, in hopes to get a quiet word out of him, and witnessed the admission of ten intruders forbye myself." A number of his familiar friends lived or lodged near by—Skene of Rubislaw in Castle Street; Lord Chief-Commissioner Adam in Charlotte Square; Captain Basil Hall in St Colme St. His own brave heart was his support when,

George Street and its Environs

after his financial collapse, he moved to "Mrs Brown's lodgings, 6 St David Street," opposite to where Sir David Brewster began the writing of his "Encyclopædia"—and wrote in his Journal, "Here I am in Arden; when I was at home I was in a better place." Saddest passage of all, it was to the Douglas Hotel in St Andrew Square—long the chief hostelry of the New Town—that he was brought home, utterly broken in health and unconscious of what was happening around him, to spend his last night in Edinburgh. There is no scene more sacred to the memory of Scott than George Street.

It can lay claim also, if not to the birth, to the fostering and the growth of the rival literary forces that inspired and guided *Blackwood* and the *Edinburgh Review*. We have seen how early Brougham's connection with the locality began. Sydney Smith preached in Charlotte Chapel, Rose Street, and edited the first number of the famous *Review* in No. 46 George Street. Francis Jeffrey flitted in 1810 to No. 92 from "third-rate apartments" in Queen Street; and there abode for seventeen years, during which he did some of his best work as critic and reviewer, before removing his household gods to more palatial quarters in Moray Place. Carlyle found him seated at his "big baize-covered table loaded with bookrows and paper-bundles, and cheerfully lighted by five pairs of candles," and was received by the "famous little gentleman" in a "perfectly human manner." Jeffrey's friend and biographer, Lord Cockburn, was a contemporary dweller in 14 Charlotte Square, when not sheltering at Bonally, his green retreat in the Pentlands. The men and manners of the time—a time when "society and literature adorned each other; the war sparkled us with military gaiety and parade; and London had not absorbed the whole of our aristocracy either of wealth or rank"—live again in the genial pages of his "Memorials." Carlyle found in him a wholesome contrast to Wilson; "a bright, cheery, large-eyed man, a Scotch dialect with plenty of good logic in it, and plenty of practical sagacity; veracious, too; a gentleman, I should say, perfectly in the Scotch type, perhaps the very last of that peculiar species."

It must not be imagined that the opposites of all these qualities and endowments were to be found in "Great Christopher," whom the crusty philosopher of Cheyne Row has himself described as "a broad, sincere man of six feet, with long, dishevelled hair, and two blue eyes, keen as an eagle's." Wilson was the giant of the "Blackwood group," and laid about him lustily, and with a fine boyish impetuosity, although Lockhart's spear may have been keener and thrust more sure. It was in his mother's house, 53 Queen Street—next door to that in which Sir James Young Simpson, at a later date, lived and pondered the secret of anæsthetics —that these Tory free-lances prepared their first audacious sally on the Whig camp. But the saloon of the celebrated "No. 45," in George Street, was the centre of counsel and operations of the band of writers —Aytoun, Hogg, De Quincey, "Delta," and a host beside—who gathered round the House of Blackwood, and made of "Maga" a power, and somewhat of a terror, in the realm of letters.

The literary and other reminiscences connected with George Street and its precincts are far from exhausted. A number of them gather about the shop of Stillie, the

George Street and its Environs

bookseller, who was fond of telling to Mr Gladstone and other visitors that as a printer's boy he had carried proofs to Sir Walter Scott. The publishing house of Mr David Douglas, in South Castle Street, was itself for a time the residence of the great novelist. Audubon, the naturalist, prepared, in 26 George Street, a number of the marvellous drawings of his "Birds of America," which were engraved for him by Lizars, and plunged, with the ardour of a wild man of the woods, who was also a genius and a gentleman, into the delights of Edinburgh society. In Charlotte Square dwelt the witty Lord Neaves; and two doors off, Syme, the great surgeon. Sir William Fettes, a successful merchant and public-minded citizen, whose fortune, accumulated to a quarter of a million sterling, was devoted to the raising of the College bearing his name, standing on the northern outskirts of the city, was another inhabitant of the Square. So, too, was Sir John Sinclair of Ulbster, patriot and economist, among whose family of thirteen gigantic sons and daughters was Catherine Sinclair, whose novels, now forgotten, were almost more popular in their day than those of Scott himself. A monument to this philanthropic lady stands at the corner of North Charlotte Street, and she is worthy of being remembered, if not for her literary work, as being the introducer to Edinburgh of cooking depôts, cabmen's shelters, and public seats and fountains.

Sir Archibald Alison began his "History of Europe" in St Colme Street. But this, like the Sinclair monument, is on the line of Queen Street, which, as we have already seen, possesses almost as many memories of the "Augustan age" of the New Town as George Street itself. Standing on its airy terrace, with its fine gardens

The Augustan Age

filling the hollow between it and Heriot Row and Abercromby Place, the tall, plain, substantial line of the Queen Street houses must present much of the aspect which Princes Street did early in the century. But it faces the north, and has its back usually turned to the sun; the east wind rakes it along its whole length, and except where York Place overlaps it there is no protection against the direct assault of the Borean blasts of winter. In compensation, its upper windows provide magnificent prospects of the Firth and of its bounding hills from Largo Law to the Ochils. The Ladies' College; the official headquarters of the Church of Scotland; the Hall of the Royal College of Physicians, removed hither from the site now occupied by the Commercial Bank in George Street; the Philosophical Institution, associated with a long and brilliant list of literary men and events; the Queen Street Hall—these are among its buildings.

But the structure that chiefly arrests attention is the Scottish National Portrait Gallery. It is a monument of the liberality and public spirit of the late Mr J. R. Findlay of Aberlour, who built it at a cost of over £60,000, on a site provided by the Government at the east end of Queen Street, and presented it to the nation. The architecture is fourteenth-century Gothic, designed by Sir Rowand Anderson; the warm red sandstone of which it is built gives it a distinctive note of colour of its own among the prevailing greys and whites of the New Town houses; and in niches in its front and eastern gable, under crocketed Gothic canopies, with heraldic adornments, there are sculptured figures and groups from Scottish history. Spacious accommodation is found for the Museum of the Society of Antiquaries, a collection rich in the " material documents " of Scotland's past, from the Stone Age downward, and including among its relics of later historic times Knox's Pulpit, Morton's "Maiden," and Jenny Geddes's Stool. Here also are the new quarters of the Board of Manufactures reconstituted as the National Gallery Board. But the prime purpose of the donor may be regarded as fulfilled in the collection of national portraits, handsomely housed in the rooms upstairs. In no small measure the collection, with its setting, bodies forth the wish expressed by Thomas Carlyle in a letter written in 1854 to David Laing, that by help from among "the wealthier and wiser classes of Scotchmen," there might be provided in the capital a Gallery of Portraits containing "what the best-informed and most ingenuous Scottish soul would like most to see for illuminating and verifying Scottish history to himself."

Several of the portraits in this National Collection are from the brush of Sir Henry Raeburn, the "Scottish Reynolds." They remind us that the studio where Raeburn painted—where he is said to have met and courted his wife in the course of two sittings—was in the adjoining York Place, No. 32. Law and conviviality share with painting and the tender sentiment in the associations of this locality; for Charles Hay, Lord Newton, the hero of many drinking bouts in the Crochallan Club and of sharp encounters of wit in the Courts, had his house in York Place, and John Clerk, Lord Eldin, was a dweller in its continuation, Picardy Place. But art has the upper hand. Alexander Nasmyth, who is regarded as the originator of the Scottish School of landscape painting, lived in the same street as Raeburn; George Watson, the first

Portraits and Antiquities

President of the Royal Scottish Academy, had his house in Forth Street; William Douglas, the miniature painter, was a resident in the neighbouring Hart Street; and David Martin and Alexander Geddes in St James's Square.

For a time the New Town of Edinburgh halted at Queen Street. Its Terrace, Lord Cockburn tells us, was the favourite Mall of the residents, and here they walked to and fro under the trees and enjoyed "the open prospect over the Firth and the north-western mountains." Immediately below were undulating woods and lawns—Lord Moray's seat, Drumsheugh, to the west, and Bellevue, the villa of General Scott of Balcomie, to the east. Bellevue embraced nearly all the land between York Place and Canonmills, and Bellevue House became for a time the headquarters of the King's Customs and Excise, before these were removed to what has become the Royal Bank in St Andrew Square. "The mansion-house stood near the eastern side of the central enclosure of what is now Drummond Place; a luxurious house it was. The whole place waved with wood, and was diversified by undulations of surface, and adorned by seats and bowers and summer-houses. Nothing within a town could be more delightful than the sea of the Bellevue foliage gilded by the evening sun, or the tumult of blackbirds and thrushes sending their notes into all the adjoining houses in the blue of a summer morning."

It was hoped that the city would grow round these open spaces. But the century had not long begun when Bellevue was sold and the axe was busy in its woods. About 1822 came the turn of Drumsheugh. Again let us quote the author of the "Memorials." "It

239

George Street and its Environs

was an open field of as green turf as Scotland could boast, with a few respectable trees on the flat, and thickly wooded on the bank along the Water of Leith. Moray Place and Ainslie Place stand there now." It has been told that the trees in Randolph Crescent preserve the rookery of old Drumsheugh House. The ground was "the most beautiful in immediate connection with the town, and led the eye agreeably over to our distant northern scenery."

"How glorious," says Cockburn, "the prospect on a summer evening from Queen Street! We had got into the habit of believing that the mere charm of the ground would keep it sacred, and were inclined to cling to our conviction even after we saw the foundations digging. We then thought with despair of our lost verdure, our banished peacefulness, our gorgeous sunsets. But how can I forget the glory of that scene! on the still nights in which, with Rutherford, and Richardson, and Jeffrey, I have stood in Queen Street, or the opening at the north-west corner of Charlotte Square, and listened to the ceaseless rural corncraiks nestling happily in the dewy grass."

The houses that now cover this enchanted ground are stately enough; but "they are turned the wrong way"—with their backs to the valley of the Water of Leith—"everything sacrificed to the multiplication of feuing feet."

Milestones in the downhill progress of this newer Edinburgh, ruefully regarded by Cockburn, are its prominent parish churches, St Mary's and St Stephen's, built within a few years of each other, while George the Fourth was King. St Mary's, crowned by a spire and fronted with a classic portico, stands in Bellevue

New Town Prospects and Churches

Crescent, at the foot of Broughton Street. It is one of the many churches ranged in line along this thoroughfare. Several of them have either architectural features of note or some place in ecclesiastical history. Near neighbour to St Mary's is the massive Norman pile of the Catholic Apostolic Church, decorated inside with a fine series of mural paintings by Mrs Traquair. The church is a memento of the abiding influence of Edward Irving, who delivered his Apocalyptic messages to crowded audiences while living in Great King Street—"in one of those doleful lines of handsome houses," writes Mrs Oliphant (speaking, doubtless, from the biographer's own impressions, gathered while a tenant in the adjoining Fettes Row), "which weigh down the cheerful hillside under tons of monotonous stone." Higher up are the rich Gothic spire of Free St Mary's and the pinnacles of St Paul's Episcopal Church; while joined to the fabric of the New Theatre Royal—the latest of many—is the Roman Catholic Cathedral of St Mary's. Nor in this list of Broughton denominations and denominational buildings can mention be omitted of the Secession House of Prayer, long in the charge of the learned Rev. Dr John Brown, father of the author of "Horæ Subsecivæ."

The lofty, square, white tower of St Stephen's Church commands, even from its inferior level, the downward sweep of the broad thoroughfare of Frederick Street and Howe Street, descending towards Stockbridge and the Water of Leith. It was designed by Playfair, whose handiwork is writ large over the New Town. Thomas Stevenson, of the engineering "dynasty of the Northern Lights," and father of "R. L. S.," was a devout and regular attender of St Stephen's. His house, just round the corner of Howe Street, in 17 Heriot Row, held most of the early home memories of his son. "'Leerie' will always light his lamps in Heriot Row; many of the fancies of 'a Child's Garden of Verses' first grew in Queen Street Gardens."

Behind the Church, where a maze of workshops have displaced the ancient village of Silvermills, were born the brother painters, the two Lauders; in Howe Street, and also in Great King Street, where De Quincey for a time occupied furnished lodgings, and where Sir William Allan, the painter, had his house, lived Sir William Hamilton, of metaphysical prowess; John Gibson Lockhart, son-in-law of Scott, before he went to London to edit the *Quarterly*, dwelt in Northumberland Street, which was also the place of residence of Mr Hogarth, the father-in-law of Dickens.

Thus could we move northward and westward from street to street and from terrace to terrace of this "cheerful hillside," and in each find some door familiar to the feet of the great ones of the period when Edinburgh was beyond all challenge "a city of Goshen," the second in the Empire for literature, learning, and science—some window behind which genius fared sumptuously, or starved. Beyond Royal Circus, for instance, in Gloucester Place, Professor Wilson spent some of his palmiest days, a very nabob of letters; in a poverty-stricken old tenement in Church Lane, some yards below, was born David Roberts, the painter. In the spacious Moray Place dwelt Dugald Stewart and Francis Jeffrey, when growing age had brought growth of prosperity. Dean Ramsay had his home for a time in Ainslie Place; and Aytoun's house, in his latter years, was in Great Stuart Street. Bright and cherished names these; and not less memorable were the meetings at which the choicest of Edinburgh literary society assembled to welcome some renowned pilgrim from the south—Thackeray, it might be, or George Eliot—at Robert Chambers's house in Doune Terrace, at William Blackwood's in Moray Place, or at John Blackwood's in Randolph Crescent.

CHAPTER XX

THE WEST END

By common consent, Queensferry Street and Road are regarded as the line separating the New Town, in the more restricted sense, from Edinburgh's "West End." It makes no sharp division of social spheres or of architectural styles. For to the west, as to the east of the line, are crescents and terraces where a great part of the wealth and fashion of the city—senators of the Court and dignitaries of the Church and the University, eminent lawyers and doctors, and successful merchants—have taken up abode; and the buildings, if belonging to a later period, are not free from the reproach brought against the monumental structures of Gillespie Graham in Moray Place and its neighbourhood, of being monotonously regular and "magnificently dull."

The Queensferry Road carries us back, in its origin, to the archaic age of Edinburgh history. By a track leading in this direction, from the narrows of the Forth to the Castle Rock, Queen Margaret must often have travelled between Dunfermline and the future capital. By this way her body was secretly smuggled off by night from the power of the usurper; and long before Jonathan Oldbuck and Sir Arthur Wardour drove out

The Ferry Road

to the Hawes Inn by the fly, or David Balfour tramped into town by a devious route from that historic hostelry —parting with Alan Breck Stewart at "Rest-and-be-thankful"—pilgrims to St Margaret's shrine travelled painfully the road to the Ferry and rested at the Pilgrim's Cross, when they came in view of the spire of Dunfermline Abbey, at the spot where the modern tourist, bowling smoothly along on motor-bus, char-a-banc, or "bike," catches his first glimpse of the Forth Bridge.

It is a road that crops up frequently in history, from the day that Alexander III. spurred along it, on his way to his death, and to the ruin of the kingdom, at Kinghorn. When it comes fairly into our view it is seen to leave the end of the Lang Gait at the Kirkbraehead. Skirting a line of low cottages that ran along the site of Queensferry Street, it dipped steeply to the bed of the Water of Leith at the village of Lower Dean, where the Incorporated Baxters of the burgh had their mills, the gaunt shells of which, bearing quaintly carved insignia and mottoes of the craft, and dates going back to the beginning of the seventeenth century, stand to this day beside the rushing stream.

The late Miss Alison Dunlop, among the pleasant memories of the olden time preserved in her little book, "Anent Old Edinburgh," draws for us a picture of the deacons and members of the Baxters' Incorporation marching on their "gaudé day," in the spring weather of 1716, to the village mills by the Ferry Road, and marching back again by the same route, after feeing the millers and feasting on "beef and veall, and broth and breid," followed by "pypes and tobacko," in William Gordon's change-house. With the help of the records of the craft and a little fancy, we see those "douce, staid, vigorous, old or elderly" baxters, as, "with their three-cornered hats just a thought awry, and their Sunday kirk wigs just a trifle ajee, they climb up the steep Bell's Brae, now spanned by the Dean Bridge." They turn in the clear evening light, "not to view the far Forth, with its softened shores and sleeping islands, but each and all pause and look down for a parting glance on their property and prosperity, their great granary still bearing its legend, 'God bless the Baxters o' Edinburgh, wha Built this house'; then turning their faces citywards, past Meldrumsheugh, past the West Kirk, past the now darkening Castle Rock—to quote the *owerword* of one of their own old songs—'they gang toddlin' hame.'"

At a later date the plunge down Bell's Brae was avoided by carrying what is now known as the Old Queensferry Road round by Sunbury and the Belford Bridge, higher up the water; and finally, in 1832, Telford's fine work, the Dean Bridge, spanned the chasm at a height of 106 feet above the rocky bed of the stream. It was built to give direct access to the lands of Dean, till then cut off by the gorge of the Water of Leith from the growing New Town and West End. By its help Edinburgh got sure footing on the left bank of the Water, whence it has spread and is spreading far to the north and west, while across it, in the tourist season, pours a tide of holiday traffic which the modest width of the structure can barely accommodate. From Randolph Cliff, at its southern end, or from where Trinity Episcopal Church abuts on the northmost pier, "many thousands of foot passengers have leaned over the parapet and gazed down into the hollow, divided in mind as to whether the palm for

The Dean Bridge

picturesque effect should be assigned to the up-stream view, into murky depths out of which rise the grey gables and red roofs of the Lower Dean, or Water of Leith village, fronted by its sheet of falling water and backed by masses of foliage and buildings, broken by many spires and pinnacles, and ending in the wooded crest of Corstorphine Hill; or to the prospect seaward, through the green and winding jaws of the gorge and across Leith and its smoke to the Firth, Inchkeith, and Largo Law."

The valley below we shall examine by and by with somewhat greater care. Meanwhile, we but peep down into its depths in passing, like the travellers seated behind the red-coated drivers of the Forth Bridge 'buses. Like these, also, we can spare only a glance at the spreading suburbs and the fair country beyond, bounding the Ferry Road at Buckingham, Clarendon, and Learmonth Terraces, which form so handsome a western approach to the city; at the site of the lost village of Upper Dean—once the refuge of Catriona—beside which the new parish church of Dean has been erected; at Daniel Stewart's College, one of the Merchant Company's Schools, housed in a building which finely combines the Tudor and Scottish castellated styles; and across the hollow opposite, at Fettes College, a richly-endowed institution on the model of the English Public Schools, surrounded by spacious grounds and with the houses of the Masters grouped round the tall spire and terraced front of the central structure.

Still further afield, and beyond the Victoria Hospital for Consumptives and the St Cuthbert's Poorhouse, are the yawning jaws of Craigleith quarry, now flooded and abandoned, out of which the New Town may be said to

The West End

have been built. Beyond come the village of Blackhall; and the house of Ravelston, the old home of the Foulises and Keiths, whose old-fashioned garden, filled with carved relics of the demolished seventeenth-century mansion, Sir Walter Scott, a familiar guest in the time of his grand-aunt, Mrs Keith, made the model of that of Tullyveolan in "Waverley." Under the wooded brow of Corstorphine Hill is ivy-clad Craigcrook Castle where, in Jeffrey's time, Dickens and hosts of other brilliant visitors found hospitable entertainment. And so, in succession, one passes, or glimpses, Lauriston Castle, once the family possession of John Law, of Bank of England and Mississippi Bubble fame; Barnton, with its early associations with the Bartons, the great sea captains, and its later associations with golf; Cammo, where Alexander III. is said to have halted on his fatal ride Fifeward, also devoted in these latter days to the chase of the flying rubber-ball; Cramond Brig, sacred to the exploits of Jock Howieson and the "gudeman of Ballengeich," where the Almond Water is crossed into West Lothian, until finally, having skirted Lord Rosebery's demesne of Dalmeny, one reaches the Hawes Brae, the Ferry, and the Forth Bridge.

From this westward excursus, let us return to the Kirkbraehead, or, heeding new rather than old and obliterated landmarks, to the west end of Princes Street. That thoroughfare is continued, with a slight deflection from the straight line, along the route followed by the high road to Glasgow, by streets, some of which had already come into existence while George the Third was on the throne. Here again we are in the footprints of Sir Walter. No 6 Shandwick Place was his last fixed residence in Edinburgh. In Maitland

Sir Walter again

Street opposite—both sides of the way have been renamed West Princes Street—his son-in-law Lockhart wrote "Peter's Letters." In lodgings in the adjoining Walker Street the worn old soldier of literature laboured like a galley-slave at his "Napoleon," the toughest piece of work to which he ever set his hand. In Atholl Crescent—No. 6, the house of his publisher Cadell—he stayed and made his will before setting out on his last sad journey to Italy.

There is no lack of other literary and historic memories in the locality. In No. 23 Rutland Street, for the thirty years preceding his death, lived the "good physician," Dr John Brown; here he entertained Thackeray, and wrote the story of the immortal "Rab." Melville Street, which possesses a statue of the second Lord Melville, and preserves at its doorways some of the "link extinguishers" of the days before gas, was a residence of Dr Andrew Thomson, the famous Edinburgh preacher and divine; of Fraser Tytler, the historian; and of Sir David Brewster. In Manor Place Sir William Hamilton set up house on his marriage; here, too, lived Mrs Grant of Laggan, the poetess; and in Torphichen Street, near by, Mrs Ferrier, daughter of Professor Wilson and widow of Professor Ferrier, brought together social and philosophical coteries. Of streets of more modern date, Douglas Crescent can claim association with the last years of that "buoyant veteran of song and classical lore," John Stuart Blackie, and Chester Street with the genial Alexander Russel, prince of journalists.

The campanile of Free St George's Church in Shandwick Place is an excellent addition to the architectural features of this quarter of the city, although it rises from an incongruous base. But St Mary's Cathedral, "the most important ecclesiastical building raised in Scotland since the Reformation," is not likely to be disturbed from its place as the crown of the works of the West End.

The Cathedral is built on the lands of Coates, on ground and mainly from funds bequeathed by the late Misses Walker to the Episcopal Church of Scotland for the purpose. The architect was the late Sir Gilbert Scott, and it has been considered one of the finest of his works in church building. The style is Early Pointed, wrought out with great knowledge and elaboration in all the details of the building. It is 278 feet in length from the great western door in Palmerston Place to the fine triple lancet window at the east end commanding the perspective of Melville Street; and above the crossing of the transepts rises the central tower and spire to a height of 275 feet. Since the opening of the Cathedral in 1879 the chapter-house has been erected, through a bequest of the late Mr Hugh Rollo, the agent of the Walker Trust. The spires surmounting the two western towers have yet to be added to complete the edifice, the cost of which will thus be raised to over £130,000.

Near by, in the beautiful "Cathedral close" of turf and trees, and in strange conjunction with the Gothic church, the Song School, and spruce modern mansions surrounding the enclosure, is the manor-house of Easter Coates, left externally, as to its older part, in much the same condition as when it was erected in the early years of the seventeenth century by that "truly good and excellent citizen," Sir John Byres of Coates, whose initials and those of his wife Margaret Barclay, with the

St Mary's Cathedral

date 1615, are inscribed on one of the dormer windows. Lintels and other stones bearing figures, legends, and lettering, of still older date, are to be found built into the venerable mansion, and are believed to have been removed thither from the town residence of the family in Byres Close, High Street, and from the "French Ambassador's House," in the Cowgate. The heavily corbelled corner turrets, the crow-stepped gables, and tall dormers, with thistles and fleur-de-lys finials, of this typical Scottish country-house of three hundred years ago make it an object well worth the careful preservation it has obtained under the wing of the Cathedral, to which it renders lowly and grateful service by accommodating the driving machinery of the organ.

The Haymarket was long the Ultima Thule of Edinburgh's West End. Guide-books of the later 'forties inform us that "the open country" was then reached at "the Hay Weights." Streets and houses now extend for a mile or two beyond it, both by the Dalry Road and by the Corstorphine Road, which meet here at the point where the North British main line from Glasgow plunges into the tunnel to emerge in Princes Street Gardens. Dalry has, within a generation, been turned into a populous workmen's quarter, built upon lands which belonged of old to the passionate and ill-fated race of the Chiesleys of Dalry. Their mansion, containing a seventeenth-century moulded ceiling, is still to be seen in Orwell Place, and is occupied as an Episcopal Ladies' Training College. Tramway lines extend through and beyond Dalry to Gorgie, and the ground is set thick with tall tenements, churches, and cemeteries, and with distilleries and other public works.

The West End

The other highway, which, if it were pursued, would lead one past the "royal dwelling" of Linlithgow to Glasgow, preserves more of a suburban air. A few hundred yards west of the Haymarket the eye is arrested by Donaldson's Hospital, a building that has more the aspect of a palace than of a charitable institution for the housing and education of deaf and dumb and other poor children. The Hospital, designed by Playfair, stands on a terrace, well withdrawn from the street, in the midst of its own spacious grounds, which on the other side descend to the Water of Leith. It forms a great quadrangular mass, 270 feet on the side, regularly and ornately Elizabethan in style, with battlemented embrasures rising above the many mullioned windows, and surmounted at the corners and over the principal entrance by towers with groups of ogee-roofed pinnacles. Its founder, James Donaldson, who bequeathed a sum of £210,000 for its erection and maintenance, was a bookseller at the West Bow, and one of the pioneers of cheap literature.

Farther out, past the Murrayfield Station, on the Caledonian branch line to Leith, is Coltbridge and the crossing of the water already mentioned in connection with that ignoble incident in the annals of the King's Dragoons and of the '45, known as the "canter of Coltbrig." The lands of Murrayfield, beyond the stream, are being rapidly feued; the mansion-house is associated with the memory of the learned and accomplished Alexander Murray, Lord Henderland, the friend of Scott.

The wooded southern sides of Corstorphine Hill are sprinkled with villas and country residences, one of which, Beechwood, the home of the Dundases of

Murrayfield and Corstorphine

Dunira, is of age sufficient to have attracted the admiring notice of Cumberland as he marched past by this route on his way to Culloden. Below the firs of "Rest-and-be-thankful," by which goes a footpath over the hill, affording marvellously beautiful prospects of city and country, is spread the Murrayfield golf course. On the left-hand side of the high road are the level or hollow fields once filled by the lochs and marshes that at one time stretched for many miles westward to Gogar and beyond, and formed an important defence of Edinburgh on this side. Through the trees to the south, the glimmer of the white walls of the castellated old mansion of Saughton may be seen, and in the distance the range of Pentland makes a fine background.

Three miles from the Haymarket, the explorer is deposited, by train or motor-bus, at the growing and well-sheltered village of Corstorphine. Its church, an early fifteenth-century building, dedicated to St John the Baptist, is one of the sights of the neighbourhood. A lantern lighted above the porch guided the passenger who adventured after nightfall to make the passage of the bogs to southward. Within, under Gothic canopies, recline stone effigies of the Lords Forrester, aforetime lords of the manor, who endowed this collegiate charge. The traces of their castle have wholly disappeared from the Doocot Park, and the wraith of the wicked Lord Forrester has ceased to haunt the shadow of the great plane tree where he was slain by the woman whom he betrayed. But Corstorphine, although no longer famed for its cream and for the mineral spring that made it "a fashionable watering-place" a hundred years ago, is still much frequented, and is worthy of a visit by such as are in quest either of antiquities or of country air and scenery.

CHAPTER XXI

THE WATER OF LEITH

"I SUPPOSE you will tell me next," said Master George Heriot to the faithful but pragmatical servant of Nigel Oliphant, "you have at Edinburgh as fine a navigable river as the Thames, with all its shipping!" "The Thames!" retorted Richie Moniplies with ineffable contempt. "God bless your honour's judgment, we have at Edinburgh the Water of Leith and the Nor' Loch." Although the Water of Leith scarcely bears out the boasts of the future laird of Castle Collop—although it was not until the eighteenth century was well advanced that the city began to spread out its skirts to the banks of the stream—the little river that hurries down from the northern slopes of the Pentlands to the port and piers of Leith has exercised too important an influence on the history of Edinburgh, and is too interesting a feature in its topography, to be passed over lightly.

Twice, at least, we have crossed it in suburban excursions to the west and north. But it is worth while to glance rapidly down its valley from the source to the sea; for, whether the water brawls over its sandstone or whinstone ledges between high banks, or meanders lazily through fat meadows, it is, and has long been, in

From Source to Sea

close touch with the life and fortunes of the city. In former times the stream and gorge formed an important strategic defence of Edinburgh from enemies approaching from the west. In our happier days, when the Water, purified from pollutions and restocked with fish, has returned to its old golden amber colour, its valley has become one of the "beauty spots" of the capital. The Pentland Hills, from which it draws its life-blood, are brought so near at hand by the branch railway that follows all the windings of the water to Balerno, that they may be counted as one of the playgrounds of this most favoured town, and the breeziest and most romantic of them all. The last stage of its journey brings us to Leith—"to the place," as is written in "The Valley of the Water of Leith," "where French influences and manners stepped ashore on Scottish ground; the scene of so many struggles with our 'auld enemies' and 'auld allies'; whose pier has witnessed a long procession of kings and queens, warriors and churchmen, embarking or landing to make history; the busy modern port, which is still one of the chief links between Edinburgh and the great world without."

From time immemorial, the grain that fed the city has been ground by the Waterside; "its tail-races foamed, and the dusty sacks travelled by the Lanark Road before Magna Charta." As far as history or tradition carries us back, there has always been in the valley the hum of the wheel mingling with the sound of the water; every summer, in the words of R. L. Stevenson, that true lover of this much-abused, much-bepraised stream, it has "brimmed like a cup with sunshine and the song of birds." There are still large grain-milling establishments on or near its banks; but the water and

255

The Water of Leith

the water-power are in these modern times employed chiefly in the service of paper-making for Edinburgh's great printing and publishing industries, rather than in the grinding of oat and barley meal, or of snuff.

In the recesses of the Pentlands, where the Water of Leith has its taproots, one is far out of the ken of the town with its smoke and cares; on heathery hillsides or in mossy places, in which the hunted Covenanters once lurked while "men of Belial" were out in quest of them, and that sheltered the fanatic John Gibb and the "Sweet Singers of Bo'ness," what time they waited, in the fogs and swamps of the hills, to see Heaven's judgment descend on "the sinful, bloody city of Edinburgh." The Border raiders, also, were familiar with the passes into the valley, especially that by the Cauldstane-slap, between the East and West Cairn Hills, guarded by the now ruinous Cairns Castle. The Water Trust of the city has impounded the surplus water of the Pentlands for town supply or compensation purposes; and at Harperrig, Thriepmuir, and elsewhere, the hills are reflected in the spacious ponds formed at their feet, and coot and water-hen make their haunt on ground over which, if we may believe legend, partly supported by historical fact, Robert the Bruce was used to chase the buck from the royal hunting-lodge of Bavelaw, and Queen Mary to go ahawking from Lennox Tower.

This crumbling old keep by the waterside has traditional association also with George Heriot, and with the Great Montrose; and a little below it is the Brig of Currie, across which Dalyell rode with his troopers to intercept and scatter at Rullion Green the draggled and weary "Westland Whigs," who had halted for the night

The Pentlands

at Colinton. Half-way between Currie and Colinton is Juniper Green, which was already a favourite summer resort in Carlyle's time; and in quaint Baberton House, close by, Charles X. found quiet harbourage when revolutionary storms drove him across the Channel. Golf is usurping the place of literary and historical memories at Baberton; "the club-laden caddie may be seen faring afield by paths in which the author of 'Sartor Resartus' held Francis Jeffrey in discourse; and divots are turned and balls lost where the French King once promenaded in exile, and fed his thrushes and sparrows." Golf has also perched on the crown of Torphin Hill.

More famous as a retreat of lettered ease two or three generations ago was Colinton, which has been written of as the "Tusculum" of the neighbouring capital, where champions of the forum, the senate, and the academy came to wear their laurels or recruit for fresh conflict. Mackenzie, the "Man of Feeling," and Alison, the once admired but now neglected author of the "Essay on Taste," were among its literary law-givers. Cockburn's rural paradise, "bonnie Bonally," is scarce a mile away, in a "lirk," or fold of the Pentlands. But chiefly is Colinton made a place of pilgrimage as being the "Kirkton" of Stevenson's "Lowden Sabbath Morn"—the end of the "Kirkward mile" from Swanston.

> And aye an' while we nearer draw
> To whaur the Kirkton lies alaw,
> Mair neebours, comin' saft and slaw
>   Frae here and there,
> The thicker thrang the gait an' ca'
>   The stour in air.

The old brig and the kirk, the kirkyard and manse,

The Water of Leith

are in the jaws of Colinton dell, overhung by the cliffs of Colinton House and Hailes; and in the manse for many a year lived the Rev. Lewis Balfour, one of the best beloved and remembered of a line of distinguished parish ministers, and the maternal grandfather and namefather of "R. L. S.," who spent the holidays of his childhood in this secluded and rather ghostly spot, where "every sight and sound—the shadowing evergreens, the grey tombstones, the muffled roar of the water beneath, even the silence brooding in the churchyard above—conspire to feed a romantic imagination."

In the shadow of its ancient holly hedges is a fragment of Colinton Castle, the seat of the Fowlises of Colinton. It was besieged and taken by Cromwell, as was its neighbour, Redhall. Lower down the Water, Craiglockhart House, opposite Slateford, was the residence of three generations of the eminent dynasty of the Munroes, founders of the Edinburgh school of anatomy; while a little farther back from the stream is Redford, which has been acquired and is being laid out by the War Office as Cavalry Barracks. Slateford village itself, a squalid place enough, bestridden by the Union Canal aqueduct and the viaduct of the Caledonian Railway, remembers that Prince Charlie slept for a night in a cottage still standing at Gray's Mill, and that the magistrates of Edinburgh came to its brig-end to deliver up the city keys to the Young Chevalier. Close to its Station are the extensive new Abattoirs and Cattle Markets belonging to the Corporation.

Here the Water of Leith draws away from the neighbourhood of the hills and wanders for a space in flat and open country on the city margin. It is joined by the Murray burn, which has flowed under Dalmahoy

Colinton Dell

Crags, past Dalmahoy House, a seat of the Earl of Morton; past Hatton House, also, the fine old Scoto-French chateau, superinduced on a more ancient tower, where Bothwell halted on his ride to capture Mary Stewart, and where Jeffrey wrote his *Edinburgh Review* articles; past Warriston, Riccarton, and Hermiston, all of them names steeped in history or romance. On the banks of the Water itself, near where the Glasgow high road crosses at Gorgie, are the dilapidated old seventeenth-century mansion of Stenhousemills—which, like the neighbouring and contemporary Gorgie House, claims, on the slender ground of possessing a ceiling of his date, to have a chamber slept in by Charles II.—and the ivied walls and green meadows of Saughton Hall. This building and the adjoining grounds have been purchased by the City and incorporated in a new Public Park, which includes a golf course, and extends along the banks of the stream as far as Coltbridge. Near Coltbridge, screened by riverside willows, is a smaller and yet older manor-house, Roseburn, bearing curious sixteenth-century mural carvings and inscriptions, and possessing traditions of the Queen of Scots and of Protector Oliver, and more authentic records proving that it was built by Mungo Russell, City Treasurer, in 1583.

Below Coltbridge the stream again enters a deeply cut valley which becomes a rocky gorge. It hurries past the Doocot Park, rests for a little in the still, willow-shaded reach of the "Cauldron," and encloses the green island of the "Haugh," on which, it is said, the local sympathisers with the Pentland Rising secretly assembled and set up their standard by a thorn tree. Occupying the adjoining bank are the grounds of John

The Water of Leith

Watson's Hospital, an educational charity housed in a substantial building whose plain classic features are screened by its trees; more prominent are the white towers of its neighbour, the Orphan Hospital—successor to the institution that stood under the first North Bridge —which bears over its portico the Clock of the old Netherbow Port.

Bell's Mills and Sunbury, the new Bridge carrying the Old Queensferry Road across the stream, and the Dean Cemetery are the next landmarks by the waterside. The Cemetery, the New Town's "Père la Chaise," has taken up the beautiful and commanding site once held by Dean House and its grounds, the seat of the Nisbets, "Hereditary Poulterers to the King." Of their ancient castellated mansion all that remains are a few heraldic carvings and fragments of grotesque sculpture built into the terraced wall of the cemetery overlooking the stream. Their history, like that of the Easter Coates group, and of other sculptured stones in the neighbourhood of Edinburgh, is traced in articles contributed to the first volumes of the Book of the Old Edinburgh Club. In the Dean sleep a host of famous men of letters, of law, of art, and of science—John Wilson and his son-in-law, Aytoun; Jeffrey and Cockburn; Alexander Russel, and John Stuart Blackie; Paul Chalmers and Sam Bough; Edward Forbes, the naturalist (the last tenant of Dean House); Goodsir, the anatomist; Nasmyth, the inventor of the steam hammer; and General Sir Hector Macdonald, of Soudan fame. A goodly company in death!

Of the hamlet of Upper Dean the last traces have been removed. Its site is in part occupied by an extension of the Cemetery. But the lower village, known as

THE WATER OF LEITH VALLEY, FROM THE DEAN BRIDGE.

[*To face page* 260.

The Dean Cemetery

Water of Leith, holds its place sturdily in the deep hollow spanned by the Dean Bridge. Above the cauld and pool into which the radical weavers and gristers of the Dean flung their pikes and Lochaber axes when authority had got wind of the plottings of the " Friends of the People," there have arisen a new Board School and the picturesque group of the Wellcourt buildings, a successful experiment by the late Mr J. R. Findlay of Aberlour, showing how greatly the houses and surroundings of the poorer working classes can be improved without breaking with the spirit of the past and of the scene.

Of the Water of Leith dwellings as a whole, however, it can still be said that "they look as if they had been carted to the edge of the valley bank on either hand and emptied pell-mell into the hollow below," with the result that "every house acquired a quaint individuality of its own ; had its own level; its own angle to alley, terrace, or mill-lade ; its own style of outside stair and doorway." Over their neighbours continue to tower, as they have done for well-nigh three centuries, the tall gaunt walls, many-storeyed and many-windowed, and encrusted with the insignia of the milling and baking craft, of the mills and granaries of the ancient Baxters' Incorporation, for the most part turned in these days to purposes quite other than those for which they were originally designed.

A pleasant footpath follows the right-hand edge of the stream, under the arches of the Dean Bridge, and past St Bernard's Well. The mill-lade with its foul froth has been removed, and the little river again dimples in clear brown pools, and churns whitely over its ledges under the green slopes and screening foliage of the Moray

The Water of Leith

Place, Belgrave Crescent, and Ann Street Gardens. The spot, with its talking water and whispering trees, will "infinitely please" the visitor, as it did David Balfour, as he "took his way down the glen of the Leith river towards Stockbridge and Silvermills," to hold tryst with Alan Breck Stewart in "the scrog of wood besouth the mill-lade."

St Bernard's mineral spring, discovered about 1760, was at one time held in such high repute for its medicinal virtues, that the "nobility and gentry" took summer quarters in the valley to drink deep draughts of it and of the country air. Francis Garden, Lord Gardenstone, a judge of Session celebrated for his prodigious powers of snuff-taking and drinking, as well as for his learning and benevolence, raised the beautiful little Doric temple over the Well in 1789. In 1884 it was purchased and presented to his fellow-townsmen by the late Mr William Nelson, after it had been restored and redecorated by Mr Thomas Bonnar, a new statue of Hygeia, by D. W. Stevenson, placed under a canopy, and a charming pleasance formed around it. Under these new and attractive conditions St Bernard's Well has recovered something of its lost vogue.

Dean Terrace and Ann Street, which overlook the valley and Well, have associations with Christopher North and De Quincey, Sir Henry Raeburn and Sir James Young Simpson. The Scottish Reynolds was a "Stockbrig bairn," his father having been a poor yarn-boiler by the waterside, and he retained a kindly attachment to his place of birth. Afterwards, when he rose to fame, he became owner through his wife, of the lands of Deanhaugh, and traces of the footbridge by

St Bernard's Well

which he crossed the water from his house of St
Bernard's to his studio in York Place may still be seen
on the river bank opposite Dean Terrace. On the site
of the present Danube Street was the house of an
eccentric Writer to the Signet and antiquarian, Mr
Walter Ross, who built beside it a tower, known as
"Ross's Folly." In dread lest he should be interred
alive, he left directions that his body should be preserved
in the tower, and there accordingly it lay for many
years until it was buried in the West churchyard. Into
his "Folly" Mr Ross built all the carved stones of Old
Edinburgh on which he could lay hands; and some of
these, on its demolition, were removed to Abbotsford.
He also set up in his grounds, on the spot where Ann
Street overlooks the valley, a rough-hewn block,
intended by the city authorities of the day to be
chiselled into a statue of Cromwell, but which, after the
Protector's death, lay for a full century on Leith
Sands.

Stockbridge has many other notable memories.
James Hogg wrote "The Queen's Wake" in lodgings
in Deanhaugh Street; David Roberts was a native;
Sir John Watson Gordon, Horatio M'Culloch, and
David Scott were residents; Carlyle and his wife set
up house at Comely Bank, where Teufelsdröckh could
smoke his pipe in the front garden, "far from all the
uproars and putrescences, material and spiritual, of the
reeky town," seeing only "over the knowe the reflection
of its gaslights against the dusky sky." The town has
now swept down and seized upon Comely Bank; houses
partly enclose the ancient "Bowbutts," now the
Academy cricket park in Raeburn Place. But the
locality continues to preserve an air and character of

The Water of Leith

its own, inherited from the time when "Stockbrig" was
a rural village, with a wooden footbridge and ford across
the Water; and its inhabitants still continue to cherish
a special affection for it. To this crossing of the stream
formerly descended both the Kirk Loan and Gabriel's
Road. The latter has still a local habitation and a
name, and may be discovered by those who explore
Henderson Row, where behind their screen of trees
will be found the Deaf and Dumb Institution and the
Grecian front of that Edinburgh Academy of which
Cockburn, Leonard Horner, and Scott were among the
early patrons, and that has reared so many eminent
scholars and brave soldiers. In close proximity to the
water have risen two handsome structures in which the
working classes of the district have a special interest—
Public Baths and a Workmen's Institute, the latter
built, like similar institutions in other parts of the
town, from funds left by the late Mr Thomas Nelson.
Among other amenities of Stockbridge is the new
Northside Park, formerly Inverleith farm.

Immediately adjacent to this is a yet more attractive
pleasure ground, the Arboretum, now joined with the
Botanic Gardens. They form a shady and delightful
place of resort for citizens and visitors, especially on
fine Sundays in summer when the trees are in leaf, and
the shrubs and plants that adorn the walks, the Rock
Garden, and the greenhouses are in blossom; while
from the swelling hill on which Inverleith House is
built there is a magnificent view of Edinburgh from the
north. The house, now the official residence of the
Professor of Botany, is a later edifice, and stands
farther back from the margin of the Water than the
mansion of Inverleith, in which resided the proud

The Botanic Gardens

merchant families of the Touris and the Rochheids; but a relic of their time and of its artistic achievements may be seen in the grotesque stone animals—lions or leopards—that guard the entrance gateway from Stockbridge.

On the other side, the Botanic Gardens open into Inverleith Row, leading from Canonmills past Golden Acre to Trinity and Granton. Canonmills, we have already seen, was a village of ancient date, attached to the Barony of Broughton. The canons of Holyrood had their mills planted there in the twelfth century. Its Loch was a "fair-sized sheet of water," where angling and fowling were to be had before the town broke in upon the ground and drained it to form a site for workshops and a gymnasium, latterly a football ground. Milling, which had gone on for nearly eight hundred years at Canonmills, has ceased, and the granaries are tumbling down. The place is of note in the ecclesiastical annals of Scotland; for in the Tanfield Hall, now a bonded warehouse, adjoining the city gas stores, the Free Church of Scotland was instituted in 1843, and two or three years later the Secession and Relief Churches came together here to form the United Presbyterian Church. It is still remembered, also, that by this route from Granton, Queen Victoria and the Prince Consort made their first entry into Edinburgh, in the year before the "Disruption"; all was ready for the reception and welcome of the royal guests under an archway at Canonmills—all except the Lord Provost and Bailies, who had somehow mistaken the hour!

The neighbourhood, like others along the Water of Leith, is closely associated with R. L. Stevenson. He was born at No. 8 Howard Place; he went to his first

The Water of Leith

school in Inverleith Row; he was drilled in the Latin grammar at the Academy. The house of Warriston, whose trees overshadow his birthplace, was the scene of a memorable seventeenth-century murder, of which "Weir of Warriston" was the victim, and the wronged wife an actor in the crime; the name has an air of tragedy, and may have suggested "Weir of Hermiston." "Death's dark vale" was, to Stevenson's childish fancy, "a certain archway in the Warriston Cemetery—a forbidden, but beloved spot." In this beautiful and still secluded place, by the borders of the Water, rest many of the illustrious dead of the city, among them Sir James Young Simpson, and Alexander Smith, the poet and essayist.

Farther down the stream, beyond Powderhall and its race-track and the Destructor—erected by the Corporation for the disposal of the city refuse—is Bonnington. James the Fourth and his Court rode across its bridge in 1504, to be present at the launching of the "Great Michael," in the New Haven, which the king designed to be a great shipping and shipbuilding port that would cast Leith into the shade. Hertford's invading army crossed at Bonnington after their galleys had "laid their snouts to the craigs" at Granton, and the host which Cardinal Beaton had hastily assembled to oppose them had been scattered like chaff.

Bonnington was the cradle of woollen manufactures in Scotland; but of perhaps greater interest to the average visitor is the fine old mansion of Pilrig, which by the shield above a doorway and the date on a dormer window proclaims that it was built in 1638, by Gilbert Kirkwood and his spouse Margaret Foulis. Early in the eighteenth century it became the property of the

Bonnington and Pilrig

Leith merchant family of Balfour, with descendants of whom it still remains ; and it may be remembered how, on a certain occasion, David Balfour of Shaws paid it a visit, and had an interview with his far-away cousin, the Laird of Pilrig.

But at Pilrig and Bonnington we are already on or within the frontier of the separate burgh of Leith.

CHAPTER XXII

LEITH, PORT AND BURGH

THE Burgh of Leith lies outside the municipal bounds of Edinburgh, and the seaport town, which, with good historical cause, lays claim to being the "key of the capital and of the Kingdom," has successfully resisted attempts to amalgamate it with its bigger and more illustrious neighbour. But the story and the fortunes of the two places are so interwoven, they have grown so closely together, socially and topographically, that Leith and its 80,000 inhabitants may be considered part and parcel of the Greater Edinburgh.

Leith Walk has for generations been the main passage from the City on the hills to the Port on the shore. It is on the line of the earthen rampart behind which David Leslie baffled all the attempts of Cromwell to seize Edinburgh from this side; and along it Charles II., crowned King of Scots at Scone, rode from his lodgings in the Kirkgate into the capital. Down to the middle of the eighteenth century the Walk was a gravel path only twenty feet wide, and traffic followed more the older thoroughfare by Easter Road. But the opening of North Bridge, which had as one of its objects the improvement of the access to the port of Leith, made great changes.

Leith Walk

Between nursery gardens and open spaces—nearly all of them now built upon—there stretched, for more than a mile, one of the widest and airiest of thoroughfares. The shadow of the gallows was removed from the spot which had known for centuries the execution of criminals and the burning of witches, near the site of Leith Walk Station and not far from the modern common boundary of Edinburgh and Leith. The former rampart of defence became the favourite " walk " of citizens, old and young, on their way to enjoy the fresh salt breezes on Leith pier and to put an edge on appetites that could afterwards be blunted by feasting on the succulent " Pandore oysters," for which the Old Ship Inn and other taverns on the Shore were famed.

At the foot of the Walk we come to the historic limits of Leith, when it still dwelt within walls. The Kirkgate leads straight into the heart of the town—a narrow and crowded street that has not yet lost all traces of the antique and the picturesque. By the tramways—which in Leith are electric, while Edinburgh still hangs on to an antiquated cable system—one can pass along Junction Street, following roughly the direction of the old defences, and across Junction Bridge to North Leith and to Newhaven ; or proceed through Constitution Street to Bernard Street and the Albert, Edinburgh, and Imperial Docks ; or go eastward, along the margin of Leith Links, to Seafield.

Leith has had a stormy history. It has known much of siege and sortie. No place has been more battered by invasion and civil wars. And yet it has been disposed to set down as its greatest wrongs and injuries those which it suffered at the hands of its neighbour Edinburgh in times of peace. It has traditions of

Leith, Port and Burgh

Roman occupation. But its genuine annals do not go back beyond the date when a grant of its harbour was made by David the Saint to his monastery of Holyrood. A charter of Robert the Bruce, in 1329, confirmed a grant of the port and mills to the town of Edinburgh; and under the thrall of Edinburgh Leith remained until well into the nineteenth century. It had exacting Superiors in the restless, plotting race of the Logans of Restalrig, a fragment of whose fortalice forms part of the farmhouse of Lochend, poised over the waters of Lochend Loch. Edinburgh fell heir to these feudal rights also, and for many a day exercised a trade monoply and civil jurisdiction within the vassal burgh, which it treated as conquered territory.

But Leith has long been in the enjoyment of Home Rule, and the days of its bondage are only a memory, like the sackings and burnings which it endured from Hertford's troops; like its long siege by the English and the Lords of the Congregation, who fought desperately to take it from the hands of the French and the Queen Regent; and like its seizure by Oliver Cromwell, who built the Citadel to "bridle Scotland," and, far in advance of his day, started a newspaper to guide its perverse politics.

In and near the Kirkgate are some of the most noteworthy of the historic buildings and sites of the burgh. The old Balmerino mansion, the quarters of Charles II. while an unwilling guest of the Presbyterian party, has been turned into stores and small dwelling-houses. A house on the other side of the street, raised on low, pillared arches, is conjectured to have been "Cant's Ordinary," the hostelry where the Regent Morton and the lords who had thwarted his

The Kirkgate

plans "dined jovially" to celebrate their reconciliation. It has gone, and along with it has disappeared the reputed house of Mary of Guise, in Water Lane, and the battered form of the Council House in the Coal Hill, in which Mar, Lennox, Morton, Lethington, and other rulers of the kingdom plotted and debated. One or two fine old family mansions, with corbels, wheel stairs, and pious inscriptions may still be found about Quality Street. But the burgh improvers, in sweeping away the congeries of narrow, mean, and filthy streets and dilapidated houses that filled the space between the Kirkgate and the Shore, have made havoc with Leith's antiquities. The removal of the grim-featured old Tolbooth from Tolbooth Wynd is a story as old as Sir Walter Scott's day, and was done against his protest. St Anthony's Preceptory—the oldest of the Leith foundations—and King James's Hospital which succeeded it, have disappeared from the environs of St Mary's Church; and the Trinity House, standing opposite the church gate, preserves only a carved stone with the date 1555, of the original house built for the poor by the "Masters and Mariners" of the port.

St Mary's Church is a structure in which Leith takes just pride. It was built in 1483, and was handsomely restored about fifty years ago. In 1609 it became the parish church of South Leith in place of Restalrig, perhaps as a mark of royal favour to the first Protestant minister, "Davie Lindsay," who married James the Sixth to Anne of Denmark in Norway, and whom the grateful monarch afterwards made Bishop of Ross. A traveller who visited St Mary's about this period says that, like its neighbour of North Leith, it was "a fairer Church for inwork than

Leith, Port and Burgh

any he saw in London," and had "two seats-royal" in it. A later incumbent was the Rev. John Logan, reputed author of the "Ode to the Cuckoo," and of many of the "Paraphrases." He was ousted for what was then deemed the unclerical and irreligious exercise of writing dramas; and a similar fate, for a similar fault, overtook, it will be remembered, the author of "Douglas," the Rev. John Home, who was born in Quality Street, and is buried, with other men of distinction, in South Leith Churchyard.

The Churchyard opens on the east into Constitution Street, the most handsome of the Leith business thoroughfares. It contains the Post Office and the Corn Exchange, and in it and in Bernard Street which joins it, beside a monument to Robert Burns, are a number of the principal merchant and shipping houses and bank and insurance offices of the busy port. It leads to the Albert Dock, completed in 1869, when the centre of gravity of the trade of the harbour began to move back again from the left to the right bank of the river that divides North from South Leith. Opening from it is the newer and more commodious Edinburgh Dock; and the Imperial Dock, a third and yet more spacious receptacle, reclaimed from the foreshore for the accommodation of the growing shipping and commerce of the port, has since been added.

These three great works, stretching along what was once the sea-front of Leith Links, have cost not much short of a couple of millions sterling. They afford quay-room for large ocean-going steamers. For although a great part of the trade of Leith is still with the Baltic and the Low Countries, from which since time immemorial it has been a large importer of timber and

Leith Docks and Links

grain, the extension and deepening of its docks have enabled it to open up a profitable intercourse with the farthest ends of the earth.

As for the Links, they continue to be, as in the days when Charles II. and his brother the Duke of York golfed over them—the great playground of Leith. Like so many other sites in the burgh, this great, bare, open space has warlike memories. Duels have been fought upon it, and crowds have assembled here to see pirates and other malefactors strung up on the sands. "Giant's Brae" and "Lady Fife's Brae" mark spots whence the English troops and the Protestant party brought their batteries to bear on the walls defended by the Sieur d'Essé and the French garrison during the siege of 1560. On the Links Leslie held his leaguer, and the Presbyterian clergy purged the Scottish host of "Malignants" and "Engagers" previous to setting out for Dunbar. The spot has known also Borlum's Highlanders in the '15, and Prince Charlie's followers in the '45. It is skirted now by handsome houses; a cemetery and sea promenade are at its eastern extremity; Leith Academy and several of the churches of the burgh look out upon its turf and trees.

If Leith took its recreation on the Links, it resorted to the Shore for business. Nowadays, the Old Harbour above the lower drawbridge is neglected by trade, and only the smaller fry of shipping craft lie against the quay walls. The Shore has become a kind of backwater of commerce. There is a strong seafaring flavour about the groups that hang around the bridges and dock gates. In the range of tall houses that stretch from the Sheriff Brae and the Coal Hill to the Graving-docks there is still an antique and outlandish air—some-

Leith, Port and Burgh

thing reminiscent of the past and of Leith's long intercourse with Norway and Holland, Bremen and Dantzig. Some of the oldest and most picturesque of these houses have fallen. Among the newer buildings is a Sailors' Home. The dormer windows of the "New Ship," and the "Old Ship's" carven and gilded image of a well-manned vessel in full sail—the arms of Leith —look down upon wharf and pavement as in the brave days of old when Edinburgh society was more wont to come down to the neighbour burgh for fresh air and frolic.

The Shore and the wooden piers once attached to it have witnessed many historic landings and departures. "James I. of Scots stepped ashore here in 1423 with Joan Beaufort, the Queen he had won in exile. Here, also, landed Mary of Gueldres, wife of James II.; and Margaret of Denmark, the consort of James III. Another bride landed on Leith pier in 1537, and bending down as she put foot to shore, kissed the soil of the land of her adoption. This was Magdalen, the fragile Lily of France, first wife of James V.—'the Queen of twenty summer days.' Her successor, Mary of Guise, was of another strain; but she also brought sorrow for Leith and Scotland, and for herself." The next royal vision—"the loveliest and most fateful ever seen on Leith pier"—was that of Mary Stewart returning to her own stern land from the fair fields of France. If we may believe Knox, "never was seen so dolorous a face of heaven" as at her coming. There were later royal landings; for King James VI. handed ashore Anne of Denmark at Leith harbour after sore buffetings in the North Sea from storms which were believed to have been raised by the malignant Lothian witches;

and a tablet on the quay-wall points the spot where, to the ecstatic joy of Walter Scott and other loyal subjects, George IV. stepped to land, the first Hanoverian sovereign to put foot on Scottish earth.

At Brigend, the upper extremity of the Shore, Abbot Robert Ballantyne, of Holyrood, built in 1493 "three stonern arches" across the water, uniting South and North Leith. The piers were still standing when Sir John Gladstone, grandfather of the statesman, was born near the Brigend, where his father was a worthy flour and barley miller. Sir John's interest in his birthplace has substantial testimony in St Thomas's Church and almshouses, built and endowed by him in the neighbouring Sheriff Brae, in close vicinity to Leith Hospital.

Abbot Ballantyne's bridge was intended to be an access to the new Church of St Ninian's, which he erected on the Rude-side, as the North Leith lands belonging to the monastery were then called. It stood opposite to the Brigend; but there remain only an ancient steeple and the manse, on the lintel of which is inscribed the date 1600. The Parish Church has been removed some distance westward; and the old manse and steeple are now appropriated as warehouses and offices. In the churchyard behind, and extending along the waterside, are many weather-beaten tombs of Leith skippers and merchants; and here rests Robert Nichol, one of the sweetest of Scotland's minor poets.

The vicinity of the Sandport and Coburg Street contains some fragments of seventeenth-century Leith, although not to be compared in age and interest with those on the other side of the stream. Of Leith Citadel, to build which Cromwell demolished the venerable

Leith, Port and Burgh

chapel of St Nicholas-by-the-Sands, only an archway remains, and it will be found within a few yards of the North Leith Station of the North British Railway. The Citadel soon turned from its warlike purposes to trade and manufacture; but it mounted guns so late as 1779 to repel Paul Jones. Its successor is Leith Fort.

The main street of North Leith—Commercial Street—runs past the railway station and the Old Docks. The Custom-House stands upon it; and it is overshadowed by huge and dismal ranges of bonded warehouses. All the territory to seaward of it, covered by docks, wharves, shipbuilding yards, and esplanades, is "salvage from the Firth." The modern commercial progress of the port of Leith began in earnest on this ground with the opening of the nineteenth century. Work on the Old Docks was started in 1800; the Victoria Dock came fully fifty years later. The shipping traffic of Leith has grown until, compared with what it was a hundred years ago, it is "much what a first-class ocean liner is to an old Leith and London smack," of the type in which our great-grandfathers made the long voyage to the metropolis in the days of the Great War.

As the docks widened and the wharves filled with merchandise, the Piers of Leith pushed farther out to sea towards Inchkeith. The East Pier, the elder of the two, was long the favourite promenade with those who "flocked" on foot and in coaches to the Pier of Leith to divert themselves, to tussle with the strong sea-breezes, and drink in, along with health and strength, the views of Firth and shore, and of the rock-set city rising above the forest of shipping of its subject port. All that was learned and brilliant in the Edinburgh and Leith society of former days have paced here—Burns, and Scott, and

276

The West Pier

Carlyle among them; David Hume arm-in-arm with the author of "Douglas," on their way to end a friendly disputation over a bottle of port; Hugo Arnot, "riving at his speldrin," and looking, as the Parliament House wit said, "like his meat."

The West Pier has in these latter days become the familiar platform for bracing walks and for meetings and partings. From it sail the Forth passenger steamers, making for Aberdour Bay and the arches of the Forth Bridge; for all the windings of the Firth and the river to Alloa and Stirling; or eastward to where the breezes blow from the North Sea at Elie and Crail, or off the Bass and the May.

Newhaven harbour and fishing village are to the west of the piers and esplanade and within the municipal bounds of Leith. The place is worth a visit, if not for the fish dinners, now a little out of fashion, for what still remains after recent changes of the quaint aspect of the main street and closes, cumbered with forestairs and fishing gear, and the character, ways, and costumes of the seafaring folk that inhabit it. Steenie Mucklebackit may be seen leaning against the quay-wall; and Christie Johnston, in clean striped petticoat and white mutch, baits the lines on the doorstep, or carries her creel and basket afield on her stalwart shoulders. The old "Port of Grace" still gleans a considerable harvest from the salt water; although its oyster-scalps have been destroyed, the steam trawlers have thinned the nearer waters of their finny spoils, and the fishermen have to go further to sea in quest of daily bread. The community—an ancient and sturdy one—is conjectured by some to have in it admixtures of Dutch and Frisian blood, and rarely intermarries with stranger stock.

Leith, Port and Burgh

Beyond Newhaven is the pleasant sylvan suburb of Trinity, with its Baths and Public Gardens—a spot where one can enjoy shade and sun and wind.   Still further west is Wardie, and then Granton, the capacious harbour built and owned by the Dukes of Buccleuch.   Fleets of yachts, trawlers, and trading craft find shelter behind its piers ; and from Granton the ferry steamer makes regular passages to Burntisland, lying directly opposite.   Caroline Park, formerly Royston, a mansion of the period of Queen Anne, with richly-painted panels and ceilings, has been made into the offices of a printing-ink work. It belonged to the eminent Sir George Mackenzie, Viscount Tarbat, and first Earl of Cromarty, and was renamed by a later owner, the famous John, Duke of Argyle and Greenwich, after his daughter, who carried the property into the Buccleuch family.   The older Granton Castle is a ruin by the sea ; and both House and Castle are overshadowed and fumigated by the huge gasometer and works of the Gas Corporation.

To those who would prolong the walk by the shore westward, there can be promised many fine and changing views of the Firth and its islands.   The coast line is screened by the trees of Craigroyston and Cramond ; and at the sheltered and romantic inlet of Cramondmouth, famous in the annals of smuggling, one can be ferried across the Almond Water to the beautiful woods of Dalmeny and Barnbougle, which end only at the root of the piers of the Forth Bridge.

CHAPTER XXIII

PORTOBELLO

IN 1896 an Act was passed by which the burgh of Portobello was united to the city of Edinburgh. The process of municipal amalgamation was completed in 1900, and the new city Ward has derived from this change of municipal status many embellishments and additions to its amenities. Socially, the annexation of Portobello to Edinburgh is an old story; from its first beginnings it has been "Edinburgh-on-the-Sea." The nexus of union was, for a time, little more than the principal highway which joins the capital to the watering-place three miles distant.

This narrow bond is the London Road, followed by the tramway line, which at Jock's Lodge passes near the old village of Restalrig, with its church, once a collegiate foundation, dedicated to St Mary and the Holy Trinity, and served by a Dean and prebends. The present church is the pre-Reformation choir re-roofed. The interesting churchyard contains a more notable relic of the past in a crypt, with groined arches springing from a central shaft, which is supposed to have been the mausoleum of the Logans of Restalrig, but which, it has been conjectured, may have been in earlier use as the chapter-house of the Collegiate clergy.

Portobello

This interesting specimen of fifteenth-century architecture was restored by the late Earl of Moray, under the direction of Dr Thomas Ross ; and among other discoveries it was found that it had contained a decorated upper as well as under chamber, and that below it was a strong spring of water, suggesting that here is the veritable site of the Holy Well of St Triduana, Virgin and Martyr, which of old brought many pilgrims to Restalrig. Outside of the city limits, likewise, are the artillery, formerly the cavalry, barracks of Piershill ; the loch and mansion of Lochend, of whose owners mention has been made ; and yet another seemly relic of the past, Craigentinny House, an old mansion of the Nisbet family, now represented by Mrs Nisbet Hamilton Ogilvie. The Craigentinny sewage meadows are being feued and built upon. It is worth while turning aside from the road a few yards to view the sculptures that adorn the monument of the late Mr Christie Miller, behind Craigentinny farm.

Those who travel to Portobello, however, usually have their thoughts fixed upon the sea and the sands, the pier and the esplanade. It has brickwork and other manufactures ; but its fortune is its site on sandy and shallow water facing the breezes of the Firth. It may be said to be bounded on the west by the Figgate burn and on the east by the Brunstane burn, both of them now drumlie brooks ; and the ground on which it is built was, only a century and a half ago, part of those " Figgate Whins," in exceedingly ill repute as the haunt of footpads and highwaymen—a spot from whence a President of the Court of Session was once kidnapped and whipped off to a. Border keep by moss-trooping " Christie's Will."

Portobello Sands

The name dates the beginnings of Portobello as following upon Admiral Vernon's great naval victory in the Bay of Carthagena. Tradition connects it with a buccaneering veteran — another " Admiral Guinea "— who here brought himself to anchor after a wild career in the Caribbees. At the close of the eighteenth century Portobello could still be described as " a rising village of 300 inhabitants," [employed in the manufacture of brick and pottery. But when its reputation as a place of summer residence and sea-bathing began to grow, it spread amain along its sands; streets and villas covered the once waste places of the Figgate Whins, and lodging-house keeping competed with brickmaking as a source of profit to the population.

In 1833 Portobello was formed into a burgh. But before that date it had begun to attract a little literary coterie, and to attain some social consequence. George the Fourth had paid it a visit; Walter Scott often came to it, especially when his son-in-law, Lockhart, occupied a house in Melville Street; " Nairne Lodge," outside Portobello bounds, on the large new thoroughfare of Willowbrae Road, is a memento of the residence of the sweet singer of " The Land of the Leal"; in a later generation, Hugh Miller, David Laing, and Sir David Brewster were frequenters of Portobello.

The town has continued to spread and to prosper, not so rapidly indeed as the great watering-places of the South, but perhaps sufficiently to justify the claim it puts forward to be the "Brighton of Scotland." It has its full share of public institutions and recreations— its Town Hall and Municipal Buildings, its Baths and its Golf Course, churches galore, and, above all, its pier and sands. On Saturdays and trade holidays Edin-

Portobello

burgh empties itself on Portobello beach. Joppa, its western extremity, enjoys a greater measure of quiet and seclusion. Behind the town are historic sites and old mansions not a few, among them Brunstane House, the heritage successively of the Crichtons, the Lauderdale Maitlands, and the Argyle Campbells.

The coast road, which for seven miles carries an electric tramway, winds on past New Hailes and through Fisherrow, and crosses the Esk into the "honest toun" of Musselburgh. The famous Links come between it and the sea, and near at hand is "the battlefield of Eastern Scotland"—Pinkie Cleuch, and Carberry Hill, and, to the east of these, Prestonpans, where "Johnnie Cope" fled before the Highland claymores. Further on are delectable spots, sacred to golf, famous in story, and well winnowed by the east wind—Cockenzie and Gosford, Aberlady and Gullane, Dirleton and North Berwick; and on each and all of them Edinburgh has laid or is laying its grasp. In the summer season, at least, they are part of the Royal and Romantic City.

INDEX

ABBEY LAIRDS, 110
Abbey porch, 5, 110, 112
Abbey Strand, 110
Abercrombie, Sir Ralph, 151
Acheson, Sir Archibald, 103
Adam, Dr, Rector of High School, 138, 150, 152
Adam, Lord Chief Commissioner, house of, 233
Adam, Robert, architect, 144, 174, 217
Adam Square, 174
Adam, William, architect, 158
Advocates' Close, 56, 187
Advocates' Library, 52
Ainslie Place, 240, 242
Albany, Robert, Duke of, 32, 74
Alexander III., 73, 248
Alison, Rev. A., 257
Alison, Sir Archibald, 236
Alison Square, 133, 150
Allan, David, 91, 105
Allan, Sir William, 242
Almond Water, 248, 278
Alva, Lord Justice-Clerk, 23
Ambrose's tavern, 209
Anchor Close, 54
Anderson, Sir Rowand, architect, 153, 237

Anne of Denmark, 64, 166, 180, 271, 275
Ann Street and Gardens, 262
Arboretum, 263
Argyle Battery, 66, 80
Argyle, Earl of, 77, 101, 135
Argyle, Marquis of, tomb in St Giles, 32
  his house, 44
  in Argyle Tower, 80
  his execution, 101, 160
Argyle Square, 147, 149
Argyle Tower, 77, 80
Arnot, Hugo, 5, 149, 277
Arthur Seat, 9, 112, 124-7, 207
Assembly Hall and its spire, 61
Atholl Crescent, 249
Auchinleck, Lord, 47
Audubon, the naturalist, 236
Aytoun, W. E., 59, 242, 260

BABERTON, 257
Bagimont Roll, 117, 140
Baird, Sir David, 68
Bakehouse Close, 103
Balcarres, Countess of, 88
Balfour, Sir Andrew, 12
Balfour, Rev. Dr Lewis, 258
Balfours of Pilrig, 267

Index

Baliol, Edward, 117
Ballantyne, Abbot, 275
Ballantyne, James, 100
Balm Well at Liberton, 178, 184
Balmerino family, 221, 270
Bank of Scotland, 59
Bank Street, 59
Bannatyne, Lord, 105
Banqueting Hall (or Parliament Hall), at Castle, 83
Barclay United Free Church, 195
Barnton, 248
"Barras," the, 169
Bavelaw, 256
Baxter's Close, 62
Baxters' Incorporation, 245, 261
Bearford Parks, 208
Beaton, Archbishop, 90, 134, 140
Beaton, Cardinal, 27, 90, 266
Begbie's murder, 89
Begg, Rev. Dr, 176
Belhaven, Lord, 116
Bellenden family, 99, 106
Bellevue, 239
Bell's Mills, 260
Bell's Wynd, 46-48
Beth's Wynd, 57
Big Jack's Close, 100
Bishop's Close, 88, 92
Black, Adam, 18, 218
Black, Dr Joseph, 137, 173
Blackford Hill, 177, 182
Blackfriars Monastery, 89, 137, 140
Blackfriars Street or Wynd, 54, 89, 92, 134
Blackie, Prof., 144, 212, 249, 260
Blacklock, Dr, 150
"Black Saturday," 108
Black Turnpike, 46
Blackwood, John, 243
Blackwood, William, 178, 215, 222, 243

Blackwood's Magazine, see "Maga"
Blair, Dr Hugh, 47, 149, 161, 187
Blair, Provost Sir William Hunter, 45, 173
Blair, Robert, of Avontoun, 148
Blair Street, 45
Bonally Tower, 190, 257
Bonnington, 266
Bore Stone, the, 182, 189
Borlum and his Highlanders, 13, 273
Borthwick's Close, 46, 48
Boswell, James, 7, 47, 64, 97, 132, 137
Bothwell, Adam, Bishop of Orkney, 57, 116
Bothwell Brig, 159
Bothwell, Francis Stewart, Earl of, 58, 90, 108
Bothwell, James Hepburn, Earl of, marriage of, 57, 116
  the murder of Darnley, 90, 141
  associated with Holyrood, 121
  with the Calton Hill, 224
  with Hatton House, 259
Bothwell, Lady Anne, 57
Bough, Sam, 260
Bourgois's tavern, 22
Bow-foot, 169, 171
Bow Head, 60
Braid Burn, the, 182
Braid Hills, 177, 181, 190, 191
Brewster, Sir David, 145, 249, 281
Bridgend, 180
Bristo Port, 75, 149, 150, 167
Bristo Street, 150, 152
British Linen Company Bank, 89, 230
Brodie, Deacon, 19, 47, 65, 100, 150
Brougham, Henry, 51, 138, 152, 166, 186, 232
Broughton, 97, 209, 214

Index

Brown, Dr John, 222, 249
Brown, Rev. Dr John, senior, 241
Brown Square, 147, 172
Bruce, Robert, 118, 192, 256, 270
Bruce, Sir William, of Kinross, 119
Bruntsfield, 187-8, 192, 195
Brunstane, 282
Buccleuch, 5th Duke of, statue of, 57
Buccleuch Parish Church, 150
Buchan, 11th Earl of, 88, 232
Buchanan, George, 46, 161
Buckstane, the, 192
Burgh Loch, 2, 154, 172, 178, 185, 195
Burgh Muir, 4, 182, 183, 187, 189, 195
Burke and Hare murders, 57, 145, 168
Burnet's Close, 43, 46-7
Burns, Robert, 19, 28, 47, 58, 159, 277
  in Daunie Douglas's, 54
  relics in Municipal Museum, 55
  in Baxter's Close, 62
  Lodge Canongate Kilwinning, 101
  and Robert Fergusson, 106
  and Clarinda, 150, 211
  Scott's meeting with, 173
  his new town lodging, 211
  his monument on Calton Hill, 223
  in George Street, 233
  statue at Leith, 272
Burton, Dr John Hill, 54, 193
Butter Tron, the, 60
Byres' Close, 56, 250
Byres, Sir John, of Coates, 161, 250

Caird, Principal, 140

Cairns Castle, 256
Calton Burgh, 214, 221
Calton Churchyard, 221-2
Calton Hill, 2, 9, 12, 130, 211, 213, 220
Calton Jail, 220
Campbell's Close, 26
Campbell, Sir Ilay, 148, 150
Campbell, Thomas, 133
Canal and Basin, 197-8
Canal Street, 15
Candlemaker Row, 156, 160
Candlish, Dr, 199
Cannonball House, 67
Canongate, the, 2, 6, 85, 96-111
Canongate Burgh Cross, 104
Canongate Coachdrivers' Society, 105
Canongate Churchyard, 104-5
Canongate Parish Church, 104
Canongate Tolbooth, 97, 99, 103-4
Canonmills, 97, 209, 214, 265
"Canter of Coltbrig," the, 208, 252
Cap and Feather Close, 2, 18
Cape Club, 22, 54
Carlyle, Thomas, at Baberton, 257
  his description of Old High Street, 24
  on High Street pageants, 37, 78, 202
  as Lord Rector of University, 144
  in Simon Square, 175
  on Jeffrey and Cockburn, 235
  on the National Portrait Gallery, 238
  at Comely Bank, 263
Carnegie, Andrew, 59
Caroline Park, 278
Carrubber's Close, 90, 92
Carstares, Principal, 80, 161
Casket Letters, 149

285

Index

Castle Barns, 199
Castle Braes, 66
Castle Church, 81
"Castle of Clouts," the, 138
Castle, Edinburgh, 16, 71-84
Castle Hill, 41, 61, 65, 66
Castle Rock, 8, 65, 66, 79
Castle Street, 211, 216, 233, 236
Cat Nick, the, 129
Cattle Markets in Portsburgh, 168
  at Slateford, 258
Cauldstane-slap pass, 256
Causewayside, 177
Chalmers Close, 91
Chalmers, Dr, 92, 149, 187, 231
Chalmers, Paul, 260
Chalmers' Hospital, founder of, 105
Chambers, Robert, 15, 20, 192, 243
Chambers, the publishing house of, 56, 215
Chambers Street, 136, 143, 174
Chambers, William, 56, 146
Charles Edward, Prince, at Bow Head, 61
  at Holyrood, 106, 119, 122
  first entry into Edinburgh, 126
  at Duddingston, 128
  visit of, to Grange House, 186
  at Slateford, 258
  associations with Leith Links, 273
Charles I., 37, 79, 167
  at the Castle, 77
  and Moray House, 101
  at Holyrood, 114, 119, 122-3
Charles II., 50, 112, 122, 268, 270, 273
Charles X. of France, 119, 257
Charles Street, 152
Charlotte Square, 229, 231, 235, 236
Chepman, Walter, 32, 91

Chessels' Court, 100
Chiesleys of Dalry, 59, 161, 251
City fever hospital, 139, 192
"Clamshell Turnpike," 46
Clerihugh's tavern, 21, 25, 55
Clerk Street, 176
Clockmill House, 125
Clubs in Old Edinburgh, 19-22, 41
Cockburn Association, 91
Cockburn, Henry, Lord, 11, 15, 51, 128, 186, 234, 260
  on George Square, 151
  on Hope Park, 155
  on the South Bridge, 173
  at Bonally Tower, 190, 257
  on Calton, 221
  house of, in Charlotte Square, 234
  on Drumsheugh, 239
  Edinburgh Academy, 264
Cockburn, Mrs, 150
Cockburn Street, 18, 55
College Wynd, 136, 137
Colinton, 257-8
Comely Bank, 263
Comiston, 190
Constable, Archibald, 54, 215, 222
Corn Exchange, Grassmarket, 170
Corstorphine Hill, 10, 247, 252
Corstorphine Village and Church, 253
County Buildings, 57-8
Court of Justiciary, 50
Court of Session, 51
Covenant Close, 46-7
Cowgate, 53, 59, 134-136
Cowgatehead, 166
Cowgate Port, 75, 132, 134
Craig, James, 210
Craig, John, Knox's associate, 136
Craig House, 192, 258
Craig, Sir Thomas, 56
Craigcrook Castle, 248

Index

Craigentinny House, 280
Craiglockhart Castle, 192
Craiglockhart Hills, 190, 192
Craiglockhart House, 258
Craigmillar Castle, 128, 179
Craigroyston, 278
Craig's Close, 54
Cramond, 248, 278
Crawford, Abbot, 114
Creech, William, publisher, 19, 36, 48, 54, 161, 232
Creech's Land, 18, 36
Crichton, the Admirable, 47
Crichton, Chancellor, 75
Crichton, George, Bishop of Dunkeld, 46, 108
Crochallan Fencibles, 20, 54, 238
Croft-an-Righ House, 109
Cromwell, Oliver, 56-7, 61, 77, 86, 101, 119, 142, 167, 201, 258, 263, 268, 270
Crosbie, Andrew, 56
Cross, Mercat, 4, 27, 36-38, 40
Crow Hill, 126
Cullen, Lord, 148
Cumberland, Duke of, 119, 122, 253
Cunningham, Dr, 187

DALMENY, 248, 293
Dalry, 251
Dalrymples of Stair, 51
Dalyell of Binns, 100, 256
Darien House, 152
Darnley, Henry Stewart, 104
  associations with Edinburgh Castle, 82
  with Holyrood, 121-2
  with Craigmillar, 180
  burial-place of, 116
  murder of, 140-1
Dasses, the, 126

David L, 13, 73, 96, 112, 114, 270
David II., 74, 81, 116, 117
Davie Deans's Cottage, 129, 133
Dean Bridge, 245-7
Dean Cemetery, 260
Deanhaugh, 262
Dean House, 260
Dean Terrace, 262
Defoe, Daniel, 48
De Quincey, Thomas, 150, 203, 242, 262
De Witt, "portraits" at Holyrood, 123
Dick family, 128, 178, 186
Dick, Sir William, of Braid, 185
Dickens, Charles, 242
Dickson, Rev. Dr D., 202
Dickson's Close, 89, 91
Donaldson's Hospital, 252
Douglas Cause riots, 176
Douglas, Daunie's, tavern, 41, 54,
Douglas, Duke of, house of, 44, 140
Douglas, Gavin, 134
Douglas Wars, the, 75, 133
Douglas, William, miniature painter, 239
Douglas, Sir William, 74
Doune Terrace, 243
Drumdryan Street, 196
Drummond of Hawthornden, 137 143, 167
Drummond, George, provost, 17, 105, 139
Drummond Street, 140
Drummore, Lord, 44
Drumselch Forest, 73, 128, 180
Drumsheugh, 210, 230, 240
Duddingston Lodge, 128
Duddingston Village and Loch, 127-8
Duke's Walk, 125
Dumbiedykes, 98, 129, 133, 134

Index

Dunbar, battle of, 165
Dunbar, William, 4, 34, 42, 118
Dunbar's Close, 57
Duncan, Admiral Lord, 151
Dundas of Arniston, 51
Dundas, Henry, the first Lord Melville, 19, 88, 229, 230, 249
Dundas, Sir Laurence, 230
Dundee, John Graham, of Claverhouse, 66, 73, 208
Dunecht telescope, 182
Dunfermline, 72, 245
Dunlop, Miss Alison, 245
Dunsappie Crag and Loch, 127
Durie, Lord, 48, 280

Easter Coates manor-house, 210, 250
Easy Club, the, 20
Edinburgh Academy, 264
Edward I., 73, 117
Edward II., 114
Edward III., 117
Edward VI., 86
Edward VII., proposed memorial of, 110
Edwin, King of Northumbria, 29, 71
Eglinton, Countess of, 54
Eldin, Lord, 238
Elf Loch, the, 192
Elliot, Jean, 148
Elphinstone Court, 88
Ermengard, Queen, 73
Erskine, Dr John, 158
Erskine, Henry, 51, 88, 152
Erskine, Lord Chancellor, 88, 138
Erskine, of Grange, 89
Erskine, Ralph, 152
Eskgrove, Lord, 51
Esplanade, Castle, 65-6

Fairlie family, of Braid, 188
Fairmilehead, 190
Falcon Hall, 189
Falconer, author of the "Shipwreck," 91
Fergus I., 123
Fergus, Lord of Galloway, 114
Ferguson, Adam, 173
Fergusson, Robert, poet, birthplace of, 18, 54
  on Old Edinburgh life, 39-42
  tomb, 106
  death of, 153
  sits to Runciman, 176
Ferrier family, 233, 249
Fettes, Sir William, 105, 236, 247
Fettes College, 247
Figgate Whins, 4, 48, 280
Findlay, J. R., 237
Fire Station, 168
Fishmarket Close, 43, 46, 48
Fleshmarket Close, 8, 19
Flodden, 38, 182, 188
Flodden Wall, the, 75, 130 et seq., 165-6
Forbes, Edward, 260
Forbes, Lord President Duncan, 51, 161
Forbes, William, Provost of St Giles, 29
Forbes, Sir William, 159, 233
Forresters of Corstorphine, 253
Forrester's Wynd, 134
Forth Bridge, the, 248, 278
Fortune's Tavern, 53
Fountain Close, 86, 88, 91
Fountainbridge, 196-7
Foulis family, 161, 258
Fraser, Sir William, 143
Frederick Street, 216
Free Church, founding of, 212, 265

Index

Free Church Assembly Hall, 67
in Johnstone Terrace, 70
Free Library, 59, 135
Friars Wynd, *see* Blackfriars Street
Fullarton Wynd, 57
Fullerton, Bailie, his house, 86

GABRIEL'S ROAD, 209, 264
Gallachlaw, 191
Gallowlee, 97, 210
Gardenstone, Lord, 262
Gay, the poet, 106
Geddes, Alexander, 239
Geddes, Jenny, and her stool, 30, 33, 37, 238
Geddes, Professor, 64, 69
General Assembly, annual opening in St Giles, 33
meeting-place on Castle Hill, 69-70
George IV., 58, 221, 231
George IV. Bridge, 57, 135, 148, 225, 275
George V., 120
George Square, 148, 149, 151
George Street, 229-35
statues in, 231
Gib, "Pope," 152, 161
Gib, Rob, his ordinary, 40
Girth Cross, 108-9
Gladstone family and Leith, 275
Gladstone, W. E., 37, 212
Gladstone's Land, 62
Glammis, Lady, 66
Glenlee, Lord, 148
Goldsmith, Oliver, 48, 137
Goldsmiths' Hall, 174
Goodsir, John, 260
Goose Dub, 154
Gordon, Duke of, Governor of Castle, 68, 78
Gordon, Jane, Duchess of, 88

Gordon House, Castle Hill, 68
Gordon, Sir John Watson, 105, 263
Gorgie, 259
Gosford, Earls of, 103
Gourlay's House, 58
Gow, Neil, 23
Grange suburb, 177
Grange Cemetery, 187
Grange House, 184-6
Grange, Lady, 89
Grant, Mrs, of Laggan, 249
Grant, Sir Francis, 152
Grant, President, 175
Granton, 278
Grassmarket, 165, 169-71
Gray, Sir William, of Pittendrum, 62
Great King Street, 241-2
Great Stuart Street, 242
Green Market, 2
Greenhill, Livingstones of, 188
Greenside, 224, 226
Gregory, Dr James, 105
Gregory, Dr John, 100
Greyfriars Church, 156, 158
Greyfriars Churchyard, 157-62
Greyfriars Monastery, 156, 169
Guest, General, 78
Guthrie, Dr, 187, 218
Guthrie Street, 137
"Guttit Haddie," 126
Guy of Namur, 195

HADDINGTON, Earl of (Tam o' the Coogait), 135
Haddo's Hole, St Giles, 31
Haggis Knowe, 126
Hailes, Lord, 99
Halkerston's Wynd, 3, 13, 17
Hall, Captain Basil, 233
Hammermen, Incorporation of, 32, 136

Index

Hamilton, "Cocked Hat," 232
Hamilton, Sir William, 242, 249
Hamilton's Entry, 151
Hanna, Dean, 33
Hanover Street, 212, 216
Harrison, Sir George, 182
Hart, Andro, printer, 54
Hart's Close, 2
Hatton House, 259
Haugh, the, 259
Hawse, the, 126
Haymarket, the, 251
Heart of Midlothian, the, 34
"Heave Awa" House, 92
Henderson, Alexander, 161
Henley, W. E., 19
Henrietta Maria, Queen, 123
Henry IV., 74, 117
Henry VI., 169
Herd, David, 54, 150
Heriot, George, senior, 163
Heriot, George, junior, 36, 48
  his Hospital, 163-5
Heriot Row, 212, 237, 242, 250
Heriot-Watt College, 145, 164
Hermand, Lord, 20
Hermitage of Braid, 182
Hertford, Earl of (Duke of Somerset), 76, 114, 178
High Riggs, 165, 168, 196
High School, 64, 137-9, 223
High School Wynd, 136-8
High Street, the, its closes and associations, 24-33, 34-44
Hogg, James, the Ettrick Shepherd, 59, 191, 209, 233, 263
Holyrood Abbey, 96, 112-18, 270
  notabilities buried in, 115-16
Holyrood Palace, 2, 112-23
  State apartments, 120
  historical apartments, 121-2
  gardens, 123

Holyrood Palace, the Picture Gallery, 123
Holyroodhouse, Lord, 57
Home, Countess of, 101
Home, John, 6, 100, 187, 272
Honeyman, Bishop, 90
Hope, of Rankeillor, 154
Hope Park, 155
Hope, Sir Thomas, 59, 135
Hopetoun, John, Earl of, 23, 231
Horner, Francis, 138
Horner, Leonard, 164, 264
Horse Wynd, 105, 136
Howard Place, 265
Hume, David, in the New Town, 4, 211, 232
  and Advocates' Library, 25
  dwellings of, 63-4, 100
  mausoleum of, 222
  associated with Leith, 277
Hunter Square, 45
Hunter's Bog, 126
Hunter's Tryst, 191
Huntly, George, second Marquis of, 103, 108
Huntly, fourth Earl of, 103
Huntly House, 103
Hyndford Close, 87, 92

INCH, the, 179
Indian Peter, 40
Inverleith House, 264
Irving, Edward, 92, 241
Isle of Man tavern, 54

JACK'S LAND, 100
Jacob's Ladder, 223
James I., 74, 113, 118, 156, 274
James II., 75, 116, 118, 131, 169
James III., 118, 123
James IV., 79, 83, 118-19, 169, 188-9, 266

Index

James V., 51, 79, 90, 119, 133, 179, 180
  burial-place, 116
James VI., 38, 57, 58, 64, 102, 108, 111, 128, 180, 193, 271
  relations with George Heriot, 36
  birth in Edinburgh Castle, 77
  and Edinburgh University, 140, 142
  marriage of, 274
James VII. (James II. of England), 77, 104, 114, 115, 119
James's Court, 62-3
Jamieson, Dr John, 175
Jane, or Joan, Beaufort, Queen of James I. of Scots, 74, 118, 274
Jeffrey, Francis (Lord Jeffrey), 51, 257, 259
  office held by his father, 110
  at High School, 138
  birthplace of, 152
  dwelling of, in George Street, 234
  in Moray Place, 242
  burial-place of, 260
Jeffrey Street, 91, 131
Jock's Lodge, 279
John of Gaunt, 117, 140
John Watson's Hospital, 260
Johnnie Dowie's, 58
John's Coffee-house, 49
Johnson, James, 47
Johnson, Dr Samuel, 64, 97, 128, 132, 137
Johnston, of Warriston, 55
Johnston Terrace, 65
Johnstone, Chevalier, 210
Jones, Paul, at Leith, 276
Juniper Green, 257

KAMES, Lord Henry Home, 63, 100
Kay Stone, the, 191
Kay's "Portraits," 40, 49, 198

Keith, Bishop, 105
Keith, Mrs, of Ravelston, 248
Kemp, George Meikle, 197, 218
Kennedy's Close, 45
Kilwinning, Abbot of, 108
Kincaid, John, of Craig House, 193
King's Confession, the, 53
King's Park, 124-9
King's Stables Road, 65, 168, 199
Kirk of Field, 140
Kirk stile, the, 34
Kirkbraehead, 199, 244, 248
Kirkaldy of Grange, 58, 77, 93
Kirkgate, Leith, 269, 271
Kirk Loan, the, 199, 208, 264
Kittle Nine Steps, the, 65
Knox, John, 19, 29, 30, 140, 274
  grave of, 50
  house in Warriston's Close, 56
  house of, at Netherbow, 93-5
  at Holyrood, 121
Krames, the, 34

LADY LAWSON'S WYND, 168
Lady Stair's Close, 62
Lady Yester's Church, 139
Laigh Council-house, 35, 54
Laing, David, 174, 281
Lang Gait or Dykes, 9, 201, 208-9
Lauder brothers, painters, 242
Lauder, Sir Thomas Dick, 183, 187
Lauriston, 154, 159, 164
Lauriston Castle, 248
Law, John, the financier, 248
Lawnmarket, 60-5
Lee, Principal, 140
Leith, 268-78
  citadel of, 276
Leith Docks, 272
Leith Links, 273
Leith Shore, 273
Leith Walk, 210, 268

Index

Leith Wynd, 4, 97, 99, 130
Lennox Tower, 256
Leslie, Alexander, 77
Leslie, David, 191, 201, 208, 210, 268, 273
Leslie, Sir John, 148
Leven and Melville, Earl of, bequest, 31, 115
Leven Street, 196
Libberton's Wynd, 57
Liberton, 176, 177, 181
Lincoln, Abraham, 222
Lindsay, Lady Anne, house of, 88
Lindsay, Rev. David, 271
Lindsay, Sophia, of Balcarres, 77
Littles, the, of Craigmillar, 65, 143, 161, 179, 181
" Little France," 180
Livingstone, Dr David, 218
Lochend, 270
Lochiel, at Netherbow, 86
Lochrin, 154, 196
Lockhart, J. G., 59, 174, 211, 242, 249, 281
Lockhart, Lord President, 59, 89
Logans of Restalrig, 125, 270, 279
Logan, Rev. John, 272
Longmore Hospital for Incurables, 184
Lothian Hut, 105
Lothian Road, 198
Lothian Street, 150
Loughborough, Lord Chancellor, 88, 138
Lovat, Lord, 23, 89
Lovat's Land, 91
Lover's Loan, 187
Luckenbooths, the, 27, 34, 40
Luckie Middlemass's howff, 42
Luckie Wood's howff, 21
Lyceum Theatre, 200
Lyndsay, Sir David, 91, 224

M'Culloch, Horatio, 263
Macdonald, Sir Hector, 260
M'Ewan Hall, 153
MacGregor, Rev. Dr James, 203
Macgregor, James Mohr, 78
Macgregor, of Glenstrae, 38
Macintyre, Duncan Ban, 161
Mackenzie, Henry, 54, 148
  at High School, 138
  burial-place and birthplace, 161
  associations of, with Colinton, 257
Mackenzie, Sir George ("Bluidy Mackenzie"), 51-2, 88
  his tomb, 160-1
M'Laren, Duncan, M.P., 178
Maclehose, Mrs, 150, 211
M'Math, Janet, 186
MacMorran, Bailie, 64
MacQueen, Robert, Lord Braxfield, 48, 152
MacQueen, Michael, and his wife, 135
M'Vicar, Rev. Neil, 202
"Maga" (Blackwood's Magazine), 178, 211, 215, 234-5
Magdalen, Queen of James V., 116, 117, 274
Magdalene Chapel, 136
" Maiden," the, 38
Main Point, 167
Major Weir's Land, 166
Malcolm Canmore, 72
Mallet or Malloch, David, 138
Mansfield, Lord, 51
Mar, Earl, of the '15, 14, 211
Mar, Regent, 86
Margaret, Queen of Alexander III., 73
Margaret of Anjou at the Greyfriars, 169
Margaret of Denmark, 118, 274
Margaret Tudor, wife of James IV., 83, 118

Index

Marrowbones Club, 21

Martin, David, 239

Martyrs' monument, 160

Mary King's Close, 42, 55

Mary of Gueldres, Queen of James II., 11, 117, 123, 169, 274

Mary of Guise, Queen of James V., 67, 76, 166, 271

Mary, Queen of Scots, 46, 55, 60, 86, 90, 102, 107, 109, 140, 156, 186, 194, 224, 256, 259

  marriage with Bothwell, 57, 116

  with Darnley, 104

  associations with Castle, 76, 82

  with Holyrood, 119, 121

  with Craigmillar, 179

  her "Bath," 108

  at Leith, 274

Masterton, Allan, 58, 137

Meadows, the, 154, 176

Meggetland, 197

Melrose, Abbots of, 89, 93

Melville, Lord, see Dundas, Henry

Melville Column, the, 230

Melville Street, 249

Mercat Cross, see Cross

Merchant Maidens Hospital, 153

Merchants' House, 174

Merchiston Castle, 193-4

  suburb, 177

Merlin's Wynd, 45

Miller, Hugh, 179, 187, 281

Miller, Mr Robert, cited, 56, 93

Milton House, 106

Mint or Cunzie House, 135

"Mirror" Club, 48, 105

Mitchell, the Covenanter, 90

Monboddo, Lord, 101

Moncreiff, Rev. Sir Henry, 203

Monk, General, 150

Monro family, surgeons, 139, 258

Mons Meg, 77, 80-1

Montrose, James Graham, the Great Marquis, 32, 35, 102, 104, 107, 108, 159, 194, 256

Moray House, 101-2

Moray Place, 234, 242

Moray, Regent, 32, 109

  his lodging, 120

Morningside, 189

"Morocco Land," 99

Mortonhall, 191

Morton, Regent, 35, 58, 90, 149, 161

  his house, 90

Moryson, Fynes, 25

Mossman, James, 93, 163

Moubray House, 91

Moultrie Hill, 6, 209

Mound, the earthen, 8, 10, 15, 59

Moyes, Shadrach, 215

Municipal Buildings, 28, 55

Municipal School of Art, 168

Municipal Museum, 55, 160

Murray, Alexander, Lord Henderland, 137, 252

Murray, Miss Nicky, 48

Murray, Secretary, 101, 151

Murrayfield, 252

Museum, Royal Scottish, 146-7

Museum of Society of Antiquaries, 237

Mushat's Cairn, 125

Musselburgh, 282

Mylne family, 162

Mylne, John, master mason, 115, 162

Mylne, Robert, King's Mason, 119

Mylne's Square, 22

NAIRNE, Lady, 281

Napier family, of Wright's Houses, 194-5

Napier, of Merchiston, 33, 193-4

Napier, John, inventor of logarithms, 33, 194

Index

Nasmyth, Alexander, 238
Nasmyth, James, 49, 260
National Covenant and Magdalene Chapel, 136
  signed in Greyfriars Churchyard, 159
National Picture Gallery, 218-19
National Portrait Gallery, 237-8
Neaves, Lord, 237
Nelson & Sons, 61, 178
Nelson, Thomas, 264
Nelson, William, 80, 83, 262
Nelson's Column, Calton Hill, 224
Netherbow, the, 2-4, 27-8, 85-95
  clock at Orphan Hospital, 260
New Street, 26, 99
Newhaven, 266, 277
Newington, 176-7
Newington House, 178
Newton, Charles Hay, Lord, 20, 51, 238
Nicol, Robert, 275
Nicolson, Lady, 175
Nicolson Square, 175
Nicolson Street, 145, 173, 175
Nichol, William, 52, 222
Niddrie-Marischal, 179
Niddry's Wynd, 89
Nisbets of Dean, 203, 260, 280
North Bridge, Old and New, 1-23
North British Station and Hotel, 206, 217
North, Christopher (Professor John Wilson), 59, 200, 211, 218, 235, 242, 260, 262
North College Street, 137, 146
Nor' Loch, the, 2, 11, 23, 211
Nova Scotia Baronets, 67

Ogilvy, Lady, 78
Observatory, on Blackford Hill, 182
  on Calton Hill, 225

Old Assembly Close, 46, 48
Old Bank Close, 58-9
Old Playhouse Close, 100
Oldrieve, Mr, of Board of Works, 117
Old Stamp Office, 53
Oliver & Boyd's publishing premises, 89
Orphan Hospital, 6, 260
Outlook Tower, 69
Over Liberton House, 181

Palmer's Lane, 176
Palmerston, Lord, 105
Panmure Close, 105
Paoli, 64
Parliament Close, 34, 49
Parliament House, 51-2
Parliament Lobby, 50-1
Parliament Square, 49 et seq.
Paterson's Chophouse, 21-2
Paterson's Close, 62
Paul's Work, Hospital of, 131
Peffermill, 180
Penny Well, 184
Pentland Hills, 190, 255
Pentland Raid, 196, 259
Physic Gardens, 6, 12
Pillans, Dr, 138
Pilrig, 266
Piozzi, Mrs, 233
Pitcairn, Dr Archibald, 161
Pitt's statue, 231
Playfair, John, architect, 144, 225, 241, 252
Pleasance, the, 75, 98, 132
Poker Club, the, 22
Pont, Rev. Robert, 202
Porteous, Mob and Riots, 35, 129, 134, 161, 169
Portobello, 279-282
Post Office, General, 6, 48, 217

Index

Potterrow, 136, 150, 167
Potterrow Port, 75
Pow Burn, or Jordan, 183
Powderhall, 266
Presbytery Club, 22
President's Stairs, 49
Preston, General, 78
Prestons of Gorton and Craigmillar, 29, 55, 179
Prestonfield, 128
Prestonpans, 139
Prince Consort, the, 231, 265
Princes Street, 9, 204-19
  gardens, 15, 217-18
  monuments in, 218
Punch bowl, the, 126
" Purses," the, 34

QUADRANGLE, the College University, 141, 145
Quakers' meeting-place, in the Pleasance, 133
Queen Street, 213, 234, 235, 236-9, 240
Queen Street Ladies' College, 237
Queensberry Lodge, 106
Queensferry Road and Street, 209, 244, 246

RADICAL ROAD, 128
Raeburn, Sir Henry, 54, 203, 238, 262-3
Rae's Close, 99
Ramsay, Allan, 18, 20, 36, 54, 68, 90, 98, 106, 107, 161, 218
Ramsay, Dean, 203, 242
Ramsay Lane, 68
Ramsay Lodge, 68
Randolph Crescent, 210, 243
Ravelston House, 248
Redford Cavalry Barracks, 258
Redhall, 258

Regalia of Scotland, 79
Regent's Bridge, 213
Register House, 209, 217
Reid, Bishop Robert, 140
Restalrig, 270, 279
Rest-and-be-thankful, 245, 253
Richard I. of England, 117
Richard II., 114
Riddle's Court, 64
Rizzio, murder of, 46, 104, 108, 116, 121
Robert III., 29
Roberts, David, 242, 263
Robertson, Principal, 137, 140, 153, 186, 187
Robertson, Lord, 51
Robertson's Close, 135
Robertson Memorial Church, 187
Rood or Rude Well, 96
Rose Court, George Street, 214, 229
Rosebery, Lord, 62, 218
Roseburn, 259
Roslin, 190
Ross, Walter, 263
Rothesay, Duke of, 32, 74
Roxburgh Close, 56
Royal Bank, 230, 239
Royal Blind Asylum, 173
Royal College of Physicians, 237
Royal Exchange, 54
Royal Lunatic Asylum, 192
Royal High School, see High School
Royal Infirmary, old and new, 12, 89, 138, 139, 154
Royal Institution, 219
Royal Riding School, 175
Royal Scottish Geographical Society, 200
Royal Scottish Academy, 219
Royal Vault, Chapel Royal, 116-17
Ruddiman, Thomas, 137

Index

Rullion Green, 190, 256
Runciman, Alexander, 105, 176
Russel, Alexander, 54, 249, 260
Rutherford, Dr Daniel, 87
Rutland Street, 249
Rynd, Janet, 135

ST ANDREW'S CHURCH AND DIS-
RUPTION, 212
St Andrew Square, 211, 229, 230
St Anthony's Chapel, 125
Preceptory, 271
St Bernard's Well, 209, 261-2
St Catherine's Convent, 178
St Clairs of the Isles and of Roslin,
48, 90, 191
St Colme Street, 233, 236
St Cuthbert's Church, 134, 199,
200-3
St Cuthbert's Graveyard, 203
St Cuthbert's Loan, 198
St David Street, 232, 234
St Giles Church, 29-33, 56, 89
St Giles, Grange of, 184
St Giles, image of, 14
St Giles Street, 57
St George's Church, 208, 231
St James' Square, 209, 211
St John the Baptist's Chapel, 178
St John's Episcopal Church, 202
St John's Cross, 100
St John's Hill, 98, 132
St John's Street, 100
St Leonard's, 128-9, 132, 133
St Margaret, 72, 117, 244
St Margaret's Chapel, 80
St Margaret's Loch and Well,
125
St Margaret's Locomotive Works,
126
St Margaret's Spring, 13, 74
St Mary-in-the-Fields, 136, 140

St Mary of Placentia, Convent of,
132
St Mary's Cathedral, 250-1
St Mary's Church, Leith, 271
St Mary's Parish Church, 240
St Mary's Wynd or Street, 97, 132
St Ninian's Church, Leith, 275
St Ninian's Row, 9, 21, 130, 221
St Roque's Chapel, 184-5
St Stephen's Church, 240-1
St Thomas' Church, Leith, 275
St Thomas' Hospital, 108
St Triduana's Well, 126, 280
Salamander Land, 49
Salisbury Crags, 9, 124
"Samson's Ribs," 128
Sanctuary of Holyrood, 98, 109-111
Saughton House, 253
and Hall, 259
Sciennes, the, 134, 154, 178
Scotsman offices, 19, 54
Scott, David, 263
Scott, General, of Balcomie, 239
Scott, Sir Gilbert, 250
Scott, Sir Walter, 7, 36, 48, 57, 148,
165, 174, 177, 191, 215, 232,
235, 236, 248, 252, 281
and Princes Street Gardens, 15
associations with Parliament
Lobby, 51
with Bank Street, 59
with the Netherbow, 87
with St John Street, 100
with the Radical Road, 129
with Dumbiedykes, 133
with George Square, 151
with Greyfriars Church, 158
with Craigmillar, 180
with Blackford and Braid Hills,
181-3
with George Street, 233
with Ravelston, 248

Index

Scott, Sir Walter, associations with Edinburgh Academy, 264
. with Leith, 275-6
in the Advocates' Library, 53
and Regalia, 79
at Duddingston, 128
birthplace of, 137
at High School, 138
and Brown Square, 147
in Bristo and George Square, 150, 151
meeting with Burns, 173
at Grange House, 187
first love of, 159, 233
in North Castle Street, 233
Scott Monument, the, 217-18
Seafield, Lord Chancellor, 102
Seaforth Highlanders, 127
Semple family, 68
Seton, Lady Janet, 178
Seton, Mary, 186
Shakespeare Square, 6, 10
Shakespeare, William, 111
Shandwick Place, 248
Sharpe, Archbishop, 90, 92
Sheephead Inn, Duddingston, 128
Sheriff-Court Buildings, 59, 135
Sibbald, Sir Robert, 12
Signet Library, 52
Silvermills, 214, 242
Simon Square, 175
Simpson, Sir J. Y., 212, 218, 235, 262, 266
Sinclair, Catherine, 236
Sinclair, Sir John, of Ulbster, 236
Six-Foot Club, 21, 191
Skene of Rubislaw, 15, 233
Slateford village, 258
Smellie, William, 54
Smith, Adam, 63, 104, 173
Smith, Alexander, 266
Smith, Sydney, 152, 234

Smollett, Tobias, 36, 101
"Society," 147, 154, 172
Solemn League and Covenant, 38, 47-8, 53, 59, 159
Solicitors' Library, 52, 135
South Bridge, 45, 173-4
South Gray's or Mint Close, 88
Spence, Bishop, of Aberdeen, 131
Spence, "Lucky," 107
Spendthrift Club, 21
Spottiswood, Archbishop, 92
Stair, Countess-Dowager of, 62
Steell, Sir J., sculptor, 218, 231
Stenhousemill, 259
Stevenlaw's Close, 46 .
Stevenson, R. L., 150, 212, 222, 226
in Parliament Lobby, 50-1
at the University, 144
on Greyfriars Churchyard, 157
at Swanston, 190
on Princes Street, 207
in Heriot Row, 241
on Water of Leith, 255
on Colinton, 257-8
birthplace, 265
Stewart, Dugald, 225, 242
Stewart, of Goodtrees, 56
Stewart, Sir William, murder of, 90
Stewart's College, 247
Stewart's oyster shop, 42, 48
Stinking Stile, the, 34
Stockbridge, 263
"Stoppit Stravaig," the, 107
Strichen's Close, 88, 93
Stuart, Miss Belches, Scott's first love, 159, 233
Surgeons' Hall, 139, 145, 175
Swanston, 191
Sym, Robert (Timothy Tickler), 151, 209
Syme, James, the surgeon, 236

Index

Symson, Andro, 136
Synod Hall, 199

TAIT'S MAGAZINE, 215
Tanfield Hall, 212, 265
Tanner's Close, 168
Taylor, the Water Poet, 25
Templar Lands, 169
Tennis Court, the, at Holyrood, 110
Teviot Place, 153
Thackeray, 243, 249
Theatre Royal, Old, 7
Thistle Chapel, St Giles, 31, 34
  Holyrood, 115
Thomson, Dr Andrew, 249
Thomson, James, of Duddingston, 128
Thomson, James, the poet, 210
Thorneybauk, 196
Tinwald, Lord Justice-Clerk, 44
Tipperlin village, 189
Todrick's Close, 90
Tolbooth, 27, 28, 34, 58
Tolbooth, the New, 35
Tollcross, 196
Town Guards, 27, 38-39
Town Walls, *see* Flodden Wall
Town Wells, 27
Trades Maidens Hospital, 147
Training College for Teachers, (Moray House), 102
Treaty of Union, 23, 102
Trinity, 278
Trinity College Church, 6, 11, 91, 117, 123, 130-32
Tron, the, 38
Tron Corner, 45
Tron Kirk, 46
Trotter family, 161, 191
Trunk's Close, 91
Tweeddale Court, 89

Tytler, Patrick Fraser, 249

UNITED FREE CHURCH ASSEMBLY HALL, 69
University, the, 142-46
  new buildings of, 153, 154
Usher Hall, 200

VALLEYFIELD STREET, 196
Vennel, the, 165-6
Victoria, Queen, 116, 218, 265
Victoria Street, 62, 166

WALKER STREET, 249
Wallace, of Craigie, Lady, 88
Wallace, Sir William, 74
Warrender family, 187-8
Warriston Close, 55-6
Warriston House and Cemetery, 266
Warriston, Johnston of, 55
Wardie, 278
Water Gate or Yett, 3, 97, 99, 107, 109
Water House, 69
Water Lane, 214
Water of Leith, 208, 240, 245, 254-67
Water of Leith village, 213, 261
Waterloo Place, 216
Watson, George, painter, 238
Wauchope, General, 179
Waverley Station, 16, 204
Wellhouse Tower, 13, 66, 74, 75
Wellington's statue, 218
"Wells o' Wearie," 128
West Bow, 48, 60-2, 166
West Kirk, *see* St Cuthbert's
West Port, 166.7
West Princes Street Station and Hotel, 198
Wester Portsburgh, 167
White Hart Inn, 170
White Horse Close, 106-8

Index

White Horse Inn, 97, 132
Whitefield in Edinburgh, 6
Whitefoord House, 105
Whitehouse Loan, 187
Wild M'Craws, 127
Wilkie, Sir David, 176
William the Lion, 73
William of Orange, 161, 202
Williams, "Grecian;" 105
Williamson, Rev. Dr David (Dainty
    Davie), 202

Wilson, Sir Daniel, cited, 102, 188
Wilson, Professor John, *see* North,
    Christopher
Windy Gowl, 127
Wordsworths, the, in Edinburgh, 170
World's End Close, 91
Wright's Houses, 194-5

YORK, Cardinal, 79
York Place, 237
Younger's Brewery, 105

PRINTED BY
OLIVER AND BOYD
EDINBURGH

MAR 23 1939

JUN 4 1978

REC. CIR. 9 '78